Introduction

The cold war was a time of undeclared conflicts, proxy wars and rapid technological advancement for the US. In the wake of the Second World War, America became the global policeman – attempting to promote both peace and its own political and economic interests around the globe.

Pre-eminent air power was absolutely essential to this role, with US aircraft manufacturers regularly receiving contracts to develop state-of-the-art aircraft and weapons systems. The results were some of most powerful, most capable and perhaps most aggressively beautiful aircraft ever made.

Immediately after the Second World War, the US invested heavily in jet technology and the USAF, newly formed in 1947, was gradually reequipped with aircraft such as the Lockheed F-80 Shooting Star to replace its F-51, formerly P-51, Mustangs – although these and other piston-engined fighters would remain in service into the 1950s.

When the air war over Korea began in June 1950, aircraft such as the F-80 and the Republic F-84 Thunderjet (*P12*) ruled the skies, overmatching anything that the Chinese-backed North Korean forces were able to field. But by the end of the year the tables had been turned, with the introduction of Soviet MiG-15 fighters.

The appearance of these advanced swept-wing aircraft over the battlefield sounded the death knell for the surviving Second World War fighters and their derivatives. Even the first generation US jets were no match for a MiG-15 flown by an experienced pilot and so began a new aerial arms race that would continue throughout the cold war.

Another hangover from the previous war was the concept of the long range strategic bomber. Even as the conflict was drawing to a close, America had been progressing down the development path of ever larger and more powerful bombers. One expression of this was the immense Northrop B-35 flying wing (*P6*) – first flown as the XB-35 in June 1946. Substantial investment went into this awe-inspiring machine but it would ultimately be cancelled in favour of the more conventional Convair B-36.

Yet even the B-36 was an anachronism when it entered service in 1948 – using piston engines alongside turbojets in an age when pure turbojet propulsion was becoming the international standard for combat aircraft. Nevertheless, the huge B-36 could carry enormous loads and work was carried out to see whether its range and loiter time could be extended through the use of nuclear technology.

Today the idea of using a nuclear reactor to power an aircraft might seem far-fetched but such a machine was built and flown – the NB-36H (*P22*). The need to gather intelligence on America's cold war opponents would result in further far-fetched designs such as the extreme-altitude hydrogen-powered spyplane (*P46*) and Lockheed's plans for the Mach 2.5 capable CL-400 Suntan reconnaissance machine – neither of which would be built.

Back on the global front line, less ephemeral aircraft were needed to provide a nuclear deterrent and ward off the threat of Soviet expansionism. In 1954 the pilots of the 81st Fighter Interceptor Wing were less than delighted to be swapping their machine gun-armed North American F-86A Sabres for Republic F-84F Thunderstreaks (*P34*), particularly when the latter's attack involved performing a dangerous low-level loop in order to 'toss' its nuclear payload onto the target.

Relying on small aircraft to carry nuclear weapons was a hazardous business in more ways than one. It is a little known fact that carrier aircraft operating off the coast of Vietnam in the mid-1960s were regularly equipped with nuclear weapons in case the 'cold war' should suddenly become 'hot' and a retaliatory strike was necessary. In one tragic instance, this policy would result in a pilot, his aircraft and its nuclear payload being lost at sea (*P61*).

The Vietnam War was a watershed point in history for the US. The politics of the conflict, its physical location, the terrain, the enemy faced and the technology they employed relentlessly threw up fresh challenges that the Americans struggled to overcome. And while the war in Vietnam itself was being fought with increasing ferocity, a shadow conflict was escalating behind the scenes in neighbouring Laos.

America could not be seen interfering in Laotian affairs but neither could it stand by and see another country 'fall' to communism. It therefore acted through intermediaries – most notably the CIA's covert airline Air America (*P68*) and its equally covert 'rivals' Bird & Sons and Continental Air Services Inc. (CASI). These clandestine organisations delivered aid and arms, sometimes in equal measure, as well as providing emergency evacuation for downed USAF pilots and even occasionally fighting off hostile ground forces.

By the mid-to-late 1960s, the North Vietnamese were employing advanced Soviet weaponry including the MiG-21 Fishbed and the USAF was forced to adapt its tactics to bait, trap and destroy these difficult opponents using the agile McDonnell Douglas F-4 Phantom (*P96*). Providing overwhelming fire support for friendly ground forces were units such as HML-367 aka "The Scarface Klan" flying the fearsome new Bell HueyCobra gunship (*P110*).

Another aircraft developed to meet the requirements of the war in Vietnam was the incredible record-breaking SR-71 Blackbird (*P116*). Fired on by North Vietnamese surface-to-air missile batteries hundreds of times, it never once took a hit. And its post-war career would see it stationed on the front line... in the English countryside. SR-71s flew reconnaissance missions from RAF Mildenhall in Suffolk for more than a decade from 1974 right through the 1980s – almost to the very end of the cold war itself.

Finally, the Americans learned the hard way during the decades-long struggle against communism that there are always unintended casualties – such as the lone business jet carrying the President of Botswana that found itself on the receiving end of a MiG-23's air-to-air missiles (*P126*) during the Angolan civil war between the Soviet-backed MPLA and the US-backed UNITA.

Within this volume you will find a collection of articles concerning incidents, accidents, events, decisions, mistakes, oddities, arguments and above all incredible American aircraft from the cold war period. Each of the 15 pieces comes with a guarantee of painstaking research carried out by some of the finest aviation historians working around the world today. I hope you enjoy reading these 'cold war' stories as much as I have.

Dan Sharp

006 DETERMINATION & DIXIE CUPS
Northrop B-35
by Graham White

012 DISTANT THUNDER
The 27th Fighter Escort Wing in Korea *by Warren E. Thompson*

022 RADIANT SKIES
Nuclear Convair NB-36H
by Jakob Whitfield

031 FIT FOR A KING
Consolidated B-24 Liberator VIP transport *by Howard Carter*

034 DAYS OF THUNDER
Republic F-84F in Europe 1954-58
by Doug Gordon

046 AMERICA'S UNBUILT SPYPLANES: PART 1
Randolph Rae and the REX hydrogen-engine projects
by Dr David Baker

052 AMERICA'S UNBUILT SPYPLANES: PART 2
Lockheed CL-400 Suntan
by Dr David Baker

061 BROKEN ARROW
Douglas A-4E Skyhawk lost overboard
by Jim Winchester

068 AIR AMERICA IN LAOS: PART 1
The early years
by Jonathan Pote

080 AIR AMERICA IN LAOS: PART 2
The Tet Offensive and its aftermath
By Jonathan Pote

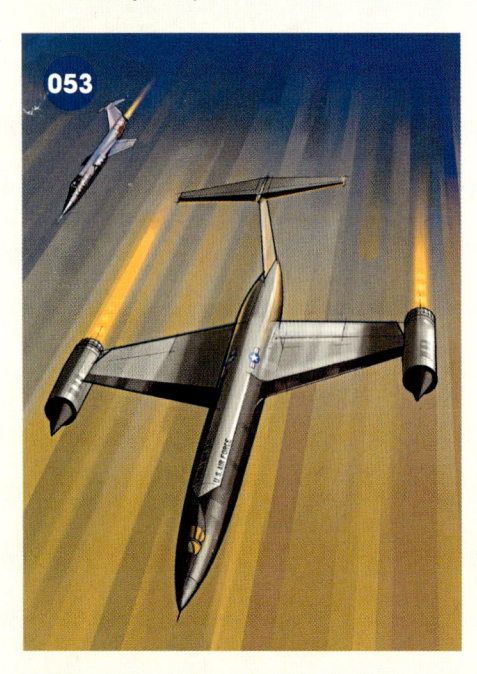

004 AVIATION CLASSICS: AMERICAN COLD WAR STORIES

Contents

116

090 AIR AMERICA IN LAOS: PART 3
New year on Skyline Ridge
by Jonathan Pote

096 OPERATION BOLO AND PROJECT SILVER DAWN
F-4 Phantoms vs. MiG-21s in Vietnam
by Albert Grandolini

110 THE SCARFACE KLAN
Bell HueyCobra in Vietnam
by Warren E. Thompson

116 GIANT REACH
Lockheed SR-71 Blackbird in East Anglia
by Bob Archer

126 BLAAAAM! SIX MINUTES OVER ANGOLA
MiG-23 vs. BAe 125
by Tom Cooper

FRONT COVER: Lockheed SR-71 Blackbird by John Fox.

EDITOR: Dan Sharp

Design: Sean Phillips – atg-media.com

Publisher: Steve O'Hara

Group advertising manager: Sue Keily
skeily@mortons.co.uk

Marketing manager: Charlotte Park

Commercial director: Nigel Hole

Thanks to: Mick Oakey and Nick Stroud

Published by:
Mortons Media Group Ltd,
Media Centre,
Morton Way, Horncastle,
Lincolnshire LN9 6JR
Tel: 01507 529529

Printed by: William Gibbons and Sons, Wolverhampton

ISBN: 978-1-911639-01-5

© 2019 Mortons Media Group Ltd. All rights reserved. No part of this publication may be reproduced or transmitted in any form or by any means, electronic or mechanical, including photocopying, recording, or any information storage retrieval system without prior permission in writing from the publisher.

MORTONS MEDIA GROUP LTD

Determination & Dixie Cups

Of the numerous technical challenges facing the team tasked with developing Northrop's extraordinary B-35 Flying Wing in the 1940s, perhaps the most daunting was the installation of the futuristic bomber's four pusher engines. GRAHAM WHITE describes how, through ingenuity and improvisation, the team overcame the odds and put the B-35 in the air

Although Northrop's hugely ambitious experimental XB-35 flying-wing bomber has often been justifiably criticised as a flawed and unsafe aircraft, the engineering concepts embodied within its design, particularly those applied to its powerplant installations, are indeed worthy of praise and a closer look.

Of the 15 airframes built, only the two prototype XB-35s and one of the 13 service trials YB-35s flew with piston power. In addition, two of the YB-35s were converted to jet power to become YB-49s. An incredible amount of time and energy was expended on the B-35 by engine maker Pratt & Whitney (P&W), and yet it is this company that has borne the brunt of unjustified criticism over the years. Despite the fact that so few examples ever made it into the air, in total five different engines were developed for this aircraft.

All things considered, the B-35 programme was a terrible waste of resources which accomplished nothing. Arguably it is probably a good thing that so few actually flew: this futuristic-but-flawed bomber was a deathtrap owing to its very limited centre of gravity (c.g.) range, marginal longitudinal stability and a host of other serious control problems. Powered by a similar configuration to that used by Convair's equally ambitious XB-36 – a fan-cooled pusher with dual turbosuperchargers for each engine – the B-35 posed daunting engineering challenges for Northrop. Eight turbo-superchargers, four massive air-to-air intercoolers as well as engine oil coolers, induction ram-air and a complex exhaust system had to be mounted in an efficient and lightweight manner.

DAUNTING CHALLENGES

As if this wasn't difficult enough, additional challenges facing Northrop engineers included the mounting of the extension shaft and propeller reduction gear with their attendant oil tanks and oil coolers etc. It would have been considerably easier simply to mount the propeller reduction gearing on the engine in a conventional fashion. The problem with that arrangement would have been an excessively heavy driveshaft owing to the torque multiplication (see panel on page 113). In addition, with more than 3,000 h.p. being transmitted through the reduction gearbox, a considerable amount of heat is generated. Even an efficiency of 95 per cent means that five per cent – or 150 h.p. – in heat needs to be rejected, the majority of this heat having to go into the gearbox oil cooler.

As an example of the desperation facing both Northrop and P&W engineers, the method of lubricating the shaft couplings could only be described as bizarre. A paper Dixie cup (the sort of thing one would drink water or coffee from), filled with 600W oil and loosely capped with a paper top, was inserted into the bearing cavity and the shaft was mechanically sealed. After the driveshaft was installed in the airframe the Dixie cup fell over, allowing the viscous oil to flow out slowly to the appropriate areas. Surviving

ABOVE: A test rig bearing one of the B-35's R-4360 engines with extension driveshaft connected to a pair of three-bladed contra-rotating propellers. As with Convair's B-36, the B-35's pusher-configuration engines had to be buried in the wing, this type of installation demanding a forced airflow over the engine to augment cooling, particularly on the ground. *Author's Collection*

> Eight **turbo-superchargers,** four massive **air-to-air intercoolers** as well as engine oil coolers, induction **ram-air** and a complex **exhaust system** had to be mounted in an efficient and **lightweight** manner.

LEFT: With eight contra-rotating propellers straining at the leash, powered by four 3,000 h.p. Pratt & Whitney R-4360 Wasp Major engines, the XB-35 undergoes a test flight in 1946. Note the prominent black exhaust stains on the underside of the wing.
Philip Jarrett Collection

P&W engineers still enjoy a chuckle over this somewhat primitive lubrication system.

Rarely do you see an accessory on a military aircraft driven by a rubber vee belt. And yet this is what Northrop engineers resorted to for the hydraulic pumps. Of course this may have been replaced by a more substantial gear drive for production aircraft – but maybe not.

COOL IT!
In a similar fashion to those fitted to the B-36, the P&W R-4360 engines buried within the wing of the B-35 required augmented cooling via a sophisticated variable-speed fan arrangement in order to keep engine temperatures under control. Ducts from the wing's leading edge fed air to the fan which then discharged over the engine. A sealed shroud encasing the engine ensured that all the output from the fan went to cooling the engine.

The hydraulically-driven engine fan was secured to the accessory drivecase at the engine's rear end. However, rear in the B-35 context meant the end facing the wing's leading edge. It was controlled ▶

BELOW: Engineers work on the XB-35 at the Northrop factory at Hawthorne, California. With the cancellation of its own proposed super-bomber, the XB-33, in 1942, Martin sent part of its workforce to work on Northrop's ambitious behemoth. *via Dick Curtis*

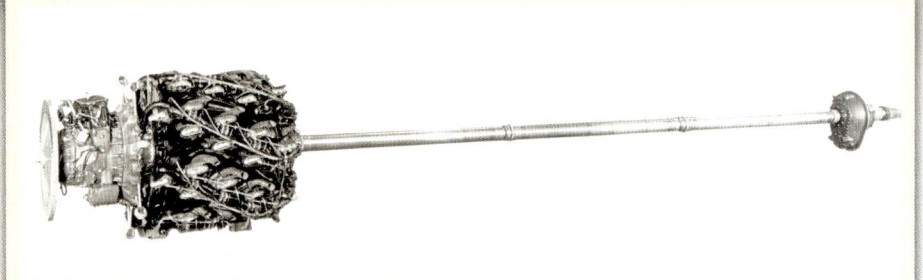

ABOVE: The Pratt & Whitney R-4360-11 four-row 28-cylinder piston engine was used on the XB-35 as the inboard-mounted powerplant, and was fitted with a driveshaft some 21ft long with the propeller reduction gearing mounted at its far end. *Author's Collection*

ABOVE: Examples of all three of Northrop's Flying Wings at Muroc (now Edwards AFB) in the California desert. Parked in the shade of the XB-35 is the flying wing proof-of-concept N-9M, with the jet-powered YB-49 making a pass overhead. *Alpha Archive*

manually by a selector valve (fan-speed control) in accordance with cooling demands by the flight engineer. The fan-drive low-ratio gear was bolted to the rear face of the fan-drive high-ratio gear and this assembly was splined on to the fan-drive shaft. The hub of the high-ratio gear sat against the inner race of the thrust-bearing and was retained in place with a spanner nut. The low-ratio gear meshed with the low-ratio hydraulic coupling fan intermediate drive pinion, and the high-ratio gear meshed with the two high-ratio coupling fan intermediate drive pinions. The cooling fan was bolted to the face of the flanged fan-drive shaft.

Engine fan speed was controlled by a hydraulic valve actuated by a 28v d.c. reversible motor. This was mounted on the right side of the accessory section of the engine, wired through the engine disconnect box to the flight engineer's junction panel located under the engineer's floor. The hydraulic valve controlled the fluid clutches in the engine. Fan speed control, located on the flight engineer's upper electrical control panel, was via a double-throw momentary toggle switch that was normally in the OFF position. Fan speed could be increased or decreased by the two ON positions designated WARMER and COOLER. When the switch was placed in either of these positions, the circuit to the motor was closed causing the motor to rotate in the appropriate direction to decrease or increase the fan speed respectively.

It should be realised that the cooling fan was capable of a prodigious output, resulting in a significant amount of parasitic power loss because the energy to run it had to come from somewhere – the engine itself. Leading-edge scoops supplied cooling air via ducts to the fan. These leading-edge scoops also provided cooling air for the oil coolers.

TURBOSUPERCHARGER INSTALLATION

Two General Electric CH-1 turbosuperchargers augmented each engine-driven single-stage single-speed supercharger. The two CH-1s operated in parallel. With this arrangement, one turbo could be shut down during cruise conditions. In this way, a single turbo would operate far more efficiently than a pair running in parallel. Part of the rationale for this was the fact that the waste gate would be almost, or completely, closed with a single turbo in operation; whereas, if both turbos were in operation, the exhaust waste gate would open, thus wasting some of the exhaust energy. At the critical altitude for single turbo operation, the other turbo would be brought online to offer greater high-altitude performance. This second turbo could also be brought online below the critical altitude in the event that emergency power was required. A simple butterfly valve closed off the engine's exhaust to one of the turbos when it was not needed.

As with any supercharging arrangement, considerable heat is imparted to the induction air which, of course, is anathema for detonation resistance – the combination of heat and pressure making the fuel/air mixture burn unpredictably and destructively. Excess heat is eliminated via air-to-air heat exchangers. Northrop engineers faced a huge challenge when trying to mount a pair of R-4360s and four massive turbosuperchargers in each wing. The solution was to mount four turbos between the engines on each wing. Each turbo was mounted at approximately 45° with the compressor facing forwards (towards the leading edge). It is worth noting that the B-36 shared a similar powerplant arrangement, but solutions to the engineering challenges made for an interesting contrast; not necessarily better but different.

Installing the CH-1 turbosuperchargers on the B-35 was quite a chore. Mechanics had to insert a crane into the leading-edge air intakes. If the aircraft had entered service, one could just imagine the hangar rash these critical air intakes would have suffered.

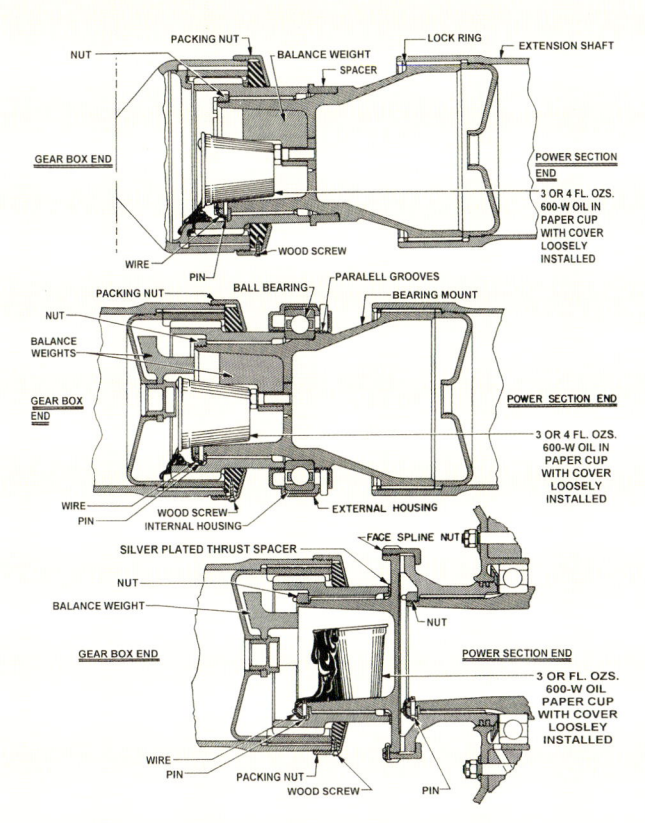

ABOVE: The Dixie cup solution — this diagram shows the shaft bearings for the B-35's R-4360 and the position of the cup in each. At top is the bearing at the engine end, the middle diagram shows the bearing midway along the shaft and the lower diagram the bearing at the prop end. *Author's Collection*

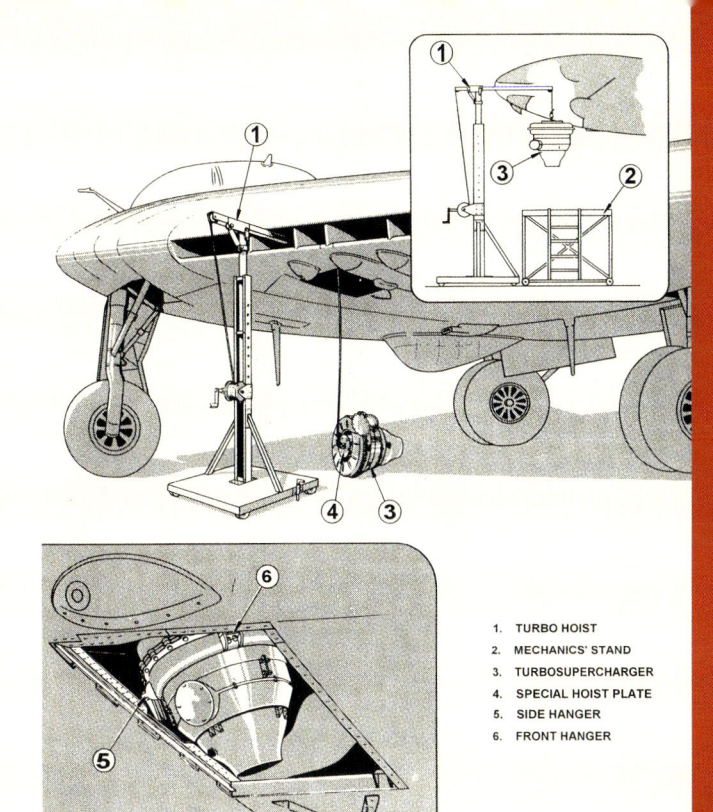

ABOVE: A diagram showing the installation of the B-35's CH-1 turbosuperchargers, which would have been a tricky and time-consuming task. *Author's Collection*

1. TURBO HOIST
2. MECHANICS' STAND
3. TURBOSUPERCHARGER
4. SPECIAL HOIST PLATE
5. SIDE HANGER
6. FRONT HANGER

REMOTE PROPELLER REDUCTION GEARBOXES

Mounted on the trailing edge of the wing, the heavy and bulky reduction gearboxes presented another significant design challenge to Northrop's engineers. Two styles were employed; single rotation and dual rotation. Internally, they were similar to the reduction gears employed on R-4360s with integral gearing, the primary difference being the requirement for additional pressure and scavenge pumps for the lubrication system. An oil tank, oil cooler plus ducting and an air scoop for the cooler were required. The dual-rotation gearbox used a pinion and reduction gear and then a Farman-type epicyclic gear to give opposite rotation of the additional propeller shaft. This resulted in the driveshaft being somewhat lower than the pair of co-axial propeller shafts, whereas with the single-rotation gearbox the driveshaft and propeller shaft were co-axial. Therefore it is possible that the single-rotation gearbox was mounted higher in order to maintain the same thrustline. This small and seemingly insignificant detail illustrates the engineering challenges facing Northrop when the decision was made to change from dual- to single-rotation propellers.

THE EXHAUST SYSTEM

In addition to conveying exhaust gases from the engine, the exhaust system was used to provide motive power for the turbosuperchargers, heat for outer wing anti-icing (outboard engines) and cabin heat (inboard engines). Exhaust gas from each engine was routed through a heat exchanger, diverted into a pair of turbosuperchargers, eventually escaping through an exhaust outlet (flight hood) or waste pipe. As described above, under certain conditions determined by the flight engineer, the exhaust gas could be directed through only one of the two turbosuperchargers.

The heat exchangers worked primarily to lower the temperature of the exhaust gas flowing into the turbosupercharger. At the time of the B-35 project, high-temperature alloys capable of handling the R-4360's stratospheric exhaust gas temperature had not yet been developed. Neither had an effective way to manufacture internally-cooled turbine buckets. Cool ram-air, after passing through and collecting heat from a heat exchanger, normally discharges into the slipstream through an overboard wastegate assembly; but it could be diverted for use in outer wing anti-icing or cabin heating.

The exhaust pipe coupling in the exhaust port of each cylinder was equipped with

BELOW: The XB-35 at Hawthorne, still in its original contra-prop configuration. The subsequent jet-powered YB-49 suffered from control problems, and although Jack Northrop's flying wing concept failed to gain traction with the military brass of the time, the idea would resurface some 30 years later. *via Dick Curtis*

The challenge of powering the B-35

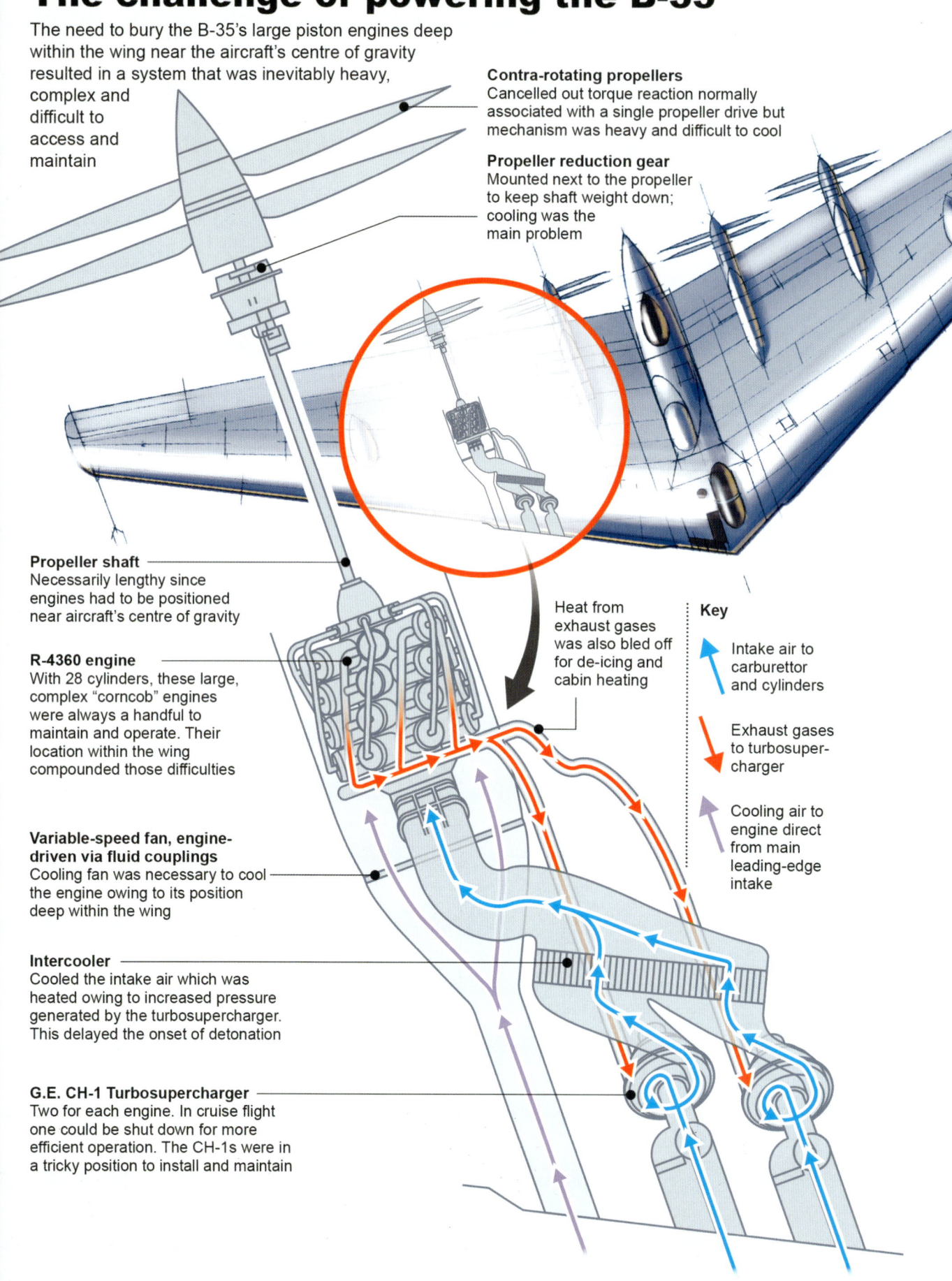

The need to bury the B-35's large piston engines deep within the wing near the aircraft's centre of gravity resulted in a system that was inevitably heavy, complex and difficult to access and maintain

Contra-rotating propellers
Cancelled out torque reaction normally associated with a single propeller drive but mechanism was heavy and difficult to cool

Propeller reduction gear
Mounted next to the propeller to keep shaft weight down; cooling was the main problem

Propeller shaft
Necessarily lengthy since engines had to be positioned near aircraft's centre of gravity

R-4360 engine
With 28 cylinders, these large, complex "corncob" engines were always a handful to maintain and operate. Their location within the wing compounded those difficulties

Variable-speed fan, engine-driven via fluid couplings
Cooling fan was necessary to cool the engine owing to its position deep within the wing

Intercooler
Cooled the intake air which was heated owing to increased pressure generated by the turbosupercharger. This delayed the onset of detonation

G.E. CH-1 Turbosupercharger
Two for each engine. In cruise flight one could be shut down for more efficient operation. The CH-1s were in a tricky position to install and maintain

Heat from exhaust gases was also bled off for de-icing and cabin heating

Key
- Intake air to carburettor and cylinders
- Exhaust gases to turbosupercharger
- Cooling air to engine direct from main leading-edge intake

Artwork by Ian Bott / www.ianbottillustration.co.uk

TORQUE MULTIPLICATION AND THE B-35

When an engine's output is passed through a reduction gearbox, it slows the rotational speed of the shaft but increases the torque or twisting force by the same proportion. This is called torque multiplication.

If the B-35's reduction gearboxes had been mounted on the engines instead of "remotely" at the propeller ends of the drive-shafts, the shafts would have had to be stiffer and therefore much heavier to cope with the increased torque resulting from their reduced rotational speed.

ABOVE: The first YB-35, 42-102366, fitted with single-rotation four-bladed propellers, over the distinctive backdrop of Muroc, where most of the Flying Wing test programme was undertaken. Note the main radar scanner blister atop the centre section and the gun blisters fitted to the outer wings. *Author's Collection*

a steel liner and four studs for securing to an appropriate exhaust pipe header. These headers were made from stainless steel and encased within removable individually formed cooling shrouds. They were installed somewhat differently on the inboard and outboard engines and, because of the close fitting tolerance necessary, were not ordinarily interchangeable – even from one cylinder configuration to another.

From the headers the exhaust gas was routed into a collector ring similarly encased within cooling shrouds. On the inboard engines the exhaust gases then passed through a transition chamber directly into the heat exchanger. On the outboard engines the exhaust gases were first routed through a tailpipe. The exhaust pipes aft of the heat exchangers and leading to the turbosuperchargers were also encased in cooling shrouds.

Exhaust gases were dumped overboard under the wing near the leading edge. Pictures from the time of the B-35's test flights show prominent black streaks under the wing owing to exhaust stains.

THE SPIRIT LIVES ON

In summary, the B-35 was a failure. After the expenditure of considerable funds and countless man-hours, the project was cancelled in 1948. Treading new territory is always fraught with difficulties, which in the case of the B-35 proved to be insurmountable with the technology available at the time. It was a brave attempt at something entirely new, and for that Northrop deserves credit.

Further exacerbating the XB-35's technological problems was the political intrigue surrounding it. The first Secretary of the Air Force, W. Stuart Symington, put his faith in the B-36, which sounded the death knell for the B-35. Symington ordered that all the Northrop flying-wings be scrapped, which must have been a painful task for Northrop employees who had poured their heart and soul into the project. The concept would ultimately see fruition several decades later; the B-35 was ahead of its time, but its spirit lives on in the eerie shape of the Northrop Grumman B-2 stealth bomber, which made its first flight in July 1989 and which is still in service today. ●

NORTHROP X/YB-35 DATA

Dimensions		
Span	172ft	(52·4m)
Sweepback	27°	
Length	53ft 1in	(16·2m)
Height	20ft ¼in	(6·1m)
Wing area	4,500ft²	(418m²)

Weights		
Empty (with turrets)	91,000lb	(41,277kg)
Gross (with turrets)	154,000lb	(69,853kg)

Performance		
Max speed (projected)	391 m.p.h.	629km/h
Cruise speed	240 m.p.h.	(386km/h)
Service ceiling original project	40,000ft	(12,200m)
actual	restricted to 20,000ft	(6,100m)
Range	7,500 miles	(12,000km)

Bomb load 16,000lb (7,257kg) with 7,500-mile (12,000km) range at 183 m.p.h. (295km/h) or 51,070lb with 720-mile (1,160km) range at 240 m.p.h. (386km/h)

BELOW: The dividend – the Northrop Grumman B-2 Spirit. Reportedly, Jack Northrop, a lifelong advocate of the flying-wing concept, was given clearance to see designs of the B-2 before his death in 1981. Very ill, he wrote on a piece of paper: "Now I know why God has kept me alive for the last 25 years..." *USAF*

Distant Thunder
The 27th Fighter Escort Wing in Korea

When North Korean forces rolled into South Korea in June 1950, it was imperative that Strategic Air Command's bombers be able to ply their trade without interference from the latest Soviet-built fighters. Enter the F-84E Thunderjets of the 27th Fighter Escort Wing. WARREN E. THOMPSON details the unit's brief but action-packed Korean adventure.

As the Cold War began to heat up between the USA and Soviet Russia, it was apparent that the former's Boeing B-29 and B-50 bombers would need plenty of protection should a major war start between the two. As the jet age was beginning to gain momentum, the Soviet Union's main focus was on defensive fighters in large numbers. Initially, the USAF's Strategic Air Command (SAC) fielded the piston-engined North American F-51D Mustang as its principal escort fighter, before introducing a development of the type, the F-82E Twin Mustang. By 1950 SAC had switched to jet power — albeit straight-winged — with Republic's F-84E Thunderjet.

When the forces of North Korea crossed the 38th Parallel on June 25, 1950, the curtain was raised on the jet warfare era. Although the Soviet MiG-15 didn't make an appearance in Korea until early November 1950, the USA already had front-line jets in the form of the USAF's Lockheed F-80s and the US Navy's carrier-based Grumman F9F Panthers.

Several B-29 bomb groups were brought in to destroy North Korea's ability to wage war, which they accomplished in a remarkably short time. It looked like the war would be over by Christmas, but in early November, the Chinese unleashed hundreds of thousands of troops against the United Nations (UN) forces in Korea.

As a result the USAF despatched the North American F-86A Sabres of the 4th Fighter Wing to counter the growing MiG threat. There were not enough F-86s in theatre to escort the bomber force fully, however, so SAC was ordered to send in the crack 27th Fighter Escort Wing (FEW), not only to fly escort missions in support of the bombers, but also to deliver bombs on targets along the Yalu River on the Korea/China border. The 27th FEW comprised the 522nd, 523rd and 524th Fighter Escort Squadrons (FES), and would be the first of many F-84 units to see combat during the three-year conflict.

The USS Bataan (CVL-29), an Independence-class light aircraft carrier, rushed all three squadrons to Japan, arriving on November 30, 1950. The forward echelon would settle in at Taegu Air Base (K-2) on December 5 and fly its first mission two days later. The rear echelon would set up shop at Itazuke Air Base on Fukuoka in Japan.

ABOVE: An F-84E of the 522nd Fighter Escort Squadron (FES) up over the Sea of Japan on a test flight after routine maintenance. *Jacob Kratt via author*

ABOVE: The badge of the 27th FEW (now 27th Special Operations Wing) incorporates a clenched fist and a magnolia, the state flower of Louisiana, where the original 27th BG was formed.

BELOW: Next stop Japan — Republic F-84E Thunderjets of the 27th Fighter Escort Wing (FEW) aboard the USS *Bataan* at San Diego, California, in late November 1950, before their sea journey to Yokosuka in support of operations in Korea. *Wilbur Segerson via author*

BELOW: The 27th FEW was initially drafted into action in Korea to protect Boeing B-29s from the defending North Korean fighters. This example, 44-87734 *Double Whammy*, was operated by the 19th Bomb Group, the first B-29 unit to see combat in Korea, and was lost as the result of a runaway prop shearing the fuselage in January 1952. *Robert Wollitz via author*

INTO COMBAT

Although photo-reconnaissance images showed that there were large numbers of MiG-15s based at Antung and Mukden in Manchuria, very few were venturing south of the river, so the 27th FEW's Thunderjets were initially tasked with bombing missions. Records show that the Wing logged 927 effective sorties in its first 38 days of operations. By this time, the North Korean People's Air Force had been completely put out of business and the rapid destruction of targets up in "MiG Alley", the north-western part of North Korea, could no longer be ignored by the Communists. The time had come for a face-off between the MiG-15 and the F-84E.

ABOVE: In early 1951 the 27th FEW's strategy was to send two squadrons of bomb-laden F-84s to attack the target, with the third squadron providing top cover. To get to the bombers the MiGs would have to fight through the defending squadron. This 522nd FES F-84E, fitted with long-range fuel tanks, is seen at a base in South Korea in early 1951. *Geroge Busher via author*

RIGHT: The view from the office — a group of 27th FEW Thunderjets patrol deep into North Korea while protecting a low-level strike force of North American F-51 Mustangs. The long-range fuel tanks attached to the inner wings were rather inelegant, but provided vital loiter time for extended missions in support of the "mud-movers" below. *William Slaughter via author*

ABOVE: A 522nd FES pilot poses beside his F-84E in the early summer of 1951. Each of the 27th's units had a signature colour; the 522nd's was red, the 523rd's was yellow and the 524th's was blue. *John Stroud/A Flying History Ltd*

Things did not initially go well for the Soviet-supplied MiGs, probably because the North Koreans had little information on the F-84 and how deadly it was at lower altitudes. In addition, most of the 27th FEW's pilots had flown as fighter pilots during the Second World War, so their experience level was high.

During January 21–29, 1951, four MiG-15s were shot down by the 27th's F-84Es. The first confrontation between the two occurred on January 21, when Lt-Col William E. Bertram was leading a flight up near the Yalu. His wingman, Lt Donald D. Watt, recalls the sortie: "Our mission was to take down a rail bridge in the vicinity of Pyongyang. En route we heard the radio chatter from one of our sister squadrons stating they had just encountered a bunch of MiGs and for us to keep our eyes wide open. Just as we were beginning our bomb-runs, the radio began heating up with MiG calls, and in a few seconds we were literally covered up. One of our pilots that got hit stated that they were so close, he could hear their cannon when they fired.

"As I broke off my second bomb-run, I saw Bertram climbing up into the sun, so I followed him, and out of the corner of my eye, I saw one of our jets on fire. It was about that time that Bertram pounced on one of the MiGs and shot him down in flames, which ended up being the first MiG-15 shot down by an F-84 in the Korean conflict.

> **Bertram pounced on one of the MiGs and *shot him down* in flames, which ended up being *the first* MiG-15 shot down by an *F-84* in the *Korean* conflict.**

The sky all around us seemed to be full of swept-wing fighters.

"I focused on a MiG that was in a gentle turn to port; I turned into him at full throttle, cutting inside of his turn and started firing, even though he was still well out of range. I was so intent on the kill that I failed to notice another MiG on my tail firing away in my direction. I was not aware of it at the time, but Lt [Jacob] Kratt was on that MiG's tail and couldn't fire because he had both of us in his sights. I broke hard left and hauled back on the stick; I suddenly felt a violent jar and found myself staring at the

ABOVE: Lieutenant Jacob Kratt Jr of the 523rd FES was awarded the Silver Star in June 1951 for his actions on January 23, 1950, during which he shot down two MiG-15s while providing top cover for low-level attacks on Sinuiju by the 522nd and 524th FESs. His Silver Star citation praises his "aggressiveness, determination and unswerving devotion to duty".

ABOVE: The opposition — the Mikoyan-Gurevich MiG-15 was a quantum leap from the World War Two-vintage prop-driven aircraft initially fielded by the North Koreans. This example, "Blue 823" (c/n 108023) of the 176th GIAP based at Antung, was damaged during a B-29 raid on bridges over the Yalu on April 12, 1951, in which F-84Es were used for close support.
Artwork by Juanita Franzi / Aero Illustrations © 2019 www.aeroillustrations.com

instrument panel with cold air rushing all around me. My plastic goggles were gone, but my helmet and oxygen mask were still in place. I dropped the nose and, at full throttle, headed down for the deck.

"As the howling of the wind increased, I looked down to check my airspeed and I was near the red line. I realised my canopy was missing. Dropping back on power, I stayed below the Mach level and hugged the ground so a MiG couldn't make a firing pass on me."

As Watt returned to Taegu, he reported his position every 5min to the others in his strike force, some of whom later remarked that, when they heard him, he sounded so cold they turned up the heat in their own cockpits! Watt approached friendly territory at 27,000ft (8,200m), with the temperature at -45°C.

Some 60 miles (100km) from the base, Watt was joined by another F-84 that helped him make a minor heading change and they landed without incident. It had been a tough day for the 27th; one of the pilots was hit and had to bale out. Official reports state that the pilot became a PoW but later died in captivity. Another F-84 was also badly mauled, the pilot limping back to Taegu trailing smoke all the way. Two days later the 27th FEW would exact revenge on the MiGs.

BACK ON TOP

The 27th's top scorer during this period was 1st Lt Jacob Kratt, with two kills on January 23rd. He later reflected on the events of the day: "Our assigned target was the enemy airfield at Sinuiju, which was just south of the Yalu and about 15 miles [24km] from the MiG base at Antung. Our mission leader was Col D.J.M. "Don" Blakeslee [a World War Two veteran with 12½ aerial victories to his credit]. Our strategy was to equip two squadrons with bombs, rockets and 0·5in-calibre ammunition, so they could take out any aircraft, hangars or bunkers they might encounter on that airfield. My squadron [the 523rd FES] was to fly top

> "Our assigned **target** was the enemy airfield at **Sinuiju**, which was just south of the Yalu and about **15 miles [24km]** from the MiG base at **Antung.**"

ABOVE: An F-84E of the 522nd FES departs Itazuke AB in Japan loaded with 1,000lb general-purpose bombs. It would complete its bombing mission over North Korea, land and refuel at a base in South Korea, complete a second mission and head back to Itazuke. *Richard Hellwege via author*

cover to protect the bombers in case any MiGs decided to interfere.

"As I scanned the sky for any sign of MiGs, I noticed the sun was positioned at our five o'clock position and about 40° above the horizon. Just as our two squadrons started their runs on the target, I saw dust plumes billowing from the airfield at Antung, which indicated that a bunch of MiGs were taking off. A minute later I saw a brilliant flash of light, the reflection of the sun off an object that was followed by several more flashes. The MiGs were already over the Yalu at about 3,000ft [900m], making a dash to the east and straight for the airfield at Sinuiju.

BELOW: Thunderjet 51-1083 of the 524th FES returns from a combat mission over North Korea in the early spring of 1951. This aircraft was one of many left behind when the 27th FEW left Korea in July 1951. On January 7, 1953, while serving with the 58th Fighter Bomber Group (FBG), it was hit by anti-aircraft fire and damaged beyond repair during a forced landing at K-14 Kimpo.
Richard Escola via author

ABOVE: Armourers work on servicing the 0·5in machine-guns of a 522nd FES Thunderjet at Taegu in February 1951. The F-84E could also carry 4,500lb (2,040kg) of bombs or 32 x 0·5in rocket projectiles. *Gerald Major via author*

"I radioed lead and told him. Time was critical; our guys below were on their bomb-runs and would easily be blindsided by the attacking MiGs. My element immediately began a dive towards the MiG formation from 14,000ft [4,300m] with speed brakes extended and red-line indicated airspeed. We were coming at them out of the sun and for a split second I thought about trying to distract them, but that wouldn't work."

Closing the gap quickly, the F-84s pulled in directly behind the MiGs at a distance of about 2,000ft [600m]. Kratt retracted his airbrakes and aligned himself perfectly with the tailpipe of the leading MiG. He pulled the trigger for two long bursts, with strikes on the MiG's tailpipe. Within seconds smoke started billowing from the Soviet fighter and the crippled MiG began a turn to port over the river and straight into the ground. The MiG's wingman had stayed in close with the stricken fighter and Kratt took the opportunity to get a few rounds off at him too.

"At this point our overtake speed was such that we were well within 1,000ft [300m] of the rest of the MiG formation, so I decided to pull up to starboard and see what additional opportunities might crop up. As we executed our pull-up, my wingman and I were suddenly put on the defensive as four

BELOW: Humid conditions during the Korean summer made it difficult for the Thunderjets to leave the ground with a heavy load. Here a pair of 522nd F-84s get off at K-2 Taegu with the help of jet-assisted take-off (JATO) rocket bottles in 1951. *Jacob Kratt via author*

MiG-15s, flying in elements of two, were firing their cannon at a great rate in our direction. We continued our climb and increased our turn-radius to a point at which they lost the advantage and disengaged.

"A short time later, I spotted another flight directly beneath us at much lower altitude. I began a spiral dive until I was in a good position to begin a healthy pull-out and was once again beautifully aligned at a range of about 2,000ft, at which point I fired several long bursts. This played out exactly like the first kill moments before; plenty of smoke ending in an exploding crash. Our cover unit had done its job as our two bomb-laden squadrons had hit their targets and done a lot of damage without having to worry about MiGs. All our jets returned to base safely."

Kratt's double kill had set a benchmark for other F-84 pilots that would be hard to beat.

THREE DOWN

On the same mission another 523rd FES pilot became entangled with an aggressive MiG that was determined to penetrate the top cover provided by the Thunderjets. Captain William W. Slaughter was a combat-experienced pilot in the 523rd and was credited with the squadron's third MiG-15 kill of the day. He remembers the experience well. "This mission was pretty messed up from the start. For some reason or another I was not scheduled to fly my assigned Thunderjet and instead had to take one that had been written up as firing 200ft [60m] low and to the far left. Our flight leaders on this mission had lots of combat experience from World War Two, and they knew how to extract the maximum from our F-84Es. I was one of the leaders on the day and our strategy was to arrive just ahead of the main bomber force and make a quick strafing pass on Sinuiju airfield to see if we could entice any of the MiGs to come across the Yalu from their base at Antung. We were itching for a fight with them.

"On my first strafing pass I tried to mark an 'X' on the windscreen with a grease pencil to show where my rounds hit, since I could not depend on the gunsight as being completely accurate. To make matters worse, some brain at the Pentagon decided we could not use tracer ammo because it was misleading, so we had no reference as to where our rounds were going. As we swooped down on the airfield, we could see numerous MiG-15s getting airborne from the runway at Antung. The first to take off were already mixing it up with the 523rd FES flight that was above us.

"As I glanced up I saw one of our '84s in a steep dive, trailing smoke, but I later found out that it was not smoke but fuel as he had taken a cannon round in one of his tiptanks. We were anxious to get into the fight. Our leader, Capt Alan McGuire, turned into them and took a long shot, my wingman and I covering for him. That didn't last long because a pair of MiGs were barrelling in on us from our four o'clock position. Those swept-wing fighters were so fast the only chance we had was to let them make a pass and then try to pick them up as they whizzed by."

STRENGTH AND INTELLIGENCE

The two MiGs that made the distant pass on Slaughter broke away some distance from the Thunderjets. This allowed Slaughter to get in a long-distance burst at the lead MiG. No hits were observed but some of the rounds must have hit or come close enough, as the MiG pilot popped his airbrakes out in an attempt to make the F-84s overshoot. Slaughter was able to slow down quickly, however, which enabled him to stay behind the attackers. His wingman told him to go ahead and close on the MiGs and he would protect his "six". Slaughter continues: "I fired several short bursts from very close range while trying to guess where my rounds were hitting. As I moved in closer I fired again and this time there was no doubt where my rounds were going; they appeared to be raking the MiG's cockpit area and starboard wing root. At almost point-blank range I fired a long burst and immediately the MiG started trailing smoke and dropped its nose into a shallow dive with no evasive action taken. Evidently, the pilot was either dead or severely wounded because I sat right on his tail so I could get a good picture when he crashed into the ground."

Both Slaughter and his wingman were so focused on the MiG that they didn't see another closing on them at high speed. Suddenly a string of big red "golf balls"

REPUBLIC F-84E DATA
Powerplant 1 x 5,000lb-static thrust Allison J35A-17 turbojet engine with 11-stage axial-flow compressor and single-stage turbine

Dimensions		
Span	36ft 5in	(11·09m)
Length	38ft 7in	(11·76m)
Height	12ft 10in	(3·91m)
Wing area	260ft²	(24·15m²)

Weights		
Empty	10,205lb	(4,629kg)
Combat weight	14,724lb	(6,679kg)

Performance		
Maximum speed at sea level	613 m.p.h.	(987km/h)
Cruise speed	481 m.p.h.	(774km/h)
Landing speed	142 m.p.h.	(229km/h)
Climb	6,060ft/min	(1,847m/min)
Service ceiling	43,220ft	(13,170m)
Normal range	1,485 miles	(2,390km)

ABOVE: As the conflict progressed, the quality of North Korea's defensive firepower increased dramatically, with sophisticated Chinese anti-aircraft artillery being drafted in. This 524th FES Thunderjet managed to make it back to Taegu with a sizeable part of the fin and rudder missing.
Charles Wills via author

ABOVE: The blue trim on this F-84E at Itazuke in early 1951 marks it out as belonging to the 524th FES. The markings were essentially the same for all 27th FEW F-84s, but in different colours. *Richard Escola via author*

ABOVE: The snug office of the F-84E. Although nicknamed the "Lead Sled" owing to its ground-gripping long take-off runs, the F-84E was nevertheless popular with its pilots, having the characteristic ruggedness of a Republic design. *Via author*

BELOW: Thunderjet 49-2420 at a base in South Korea while operating with the 524th FES. This F-84E went on to serve with the 136th FBW in Korea, and was lost with its pilot, Capt Herbert Ritter, when it was shot down by a MiG-15 on October 1, 1951. *Charles Wills via author*

> Suddenly a string of big red **"golf balls"** whizzed over Slaughter's right shoulder and passed **beneath the nose** of his F-84. The only thing he could do was **break hard to starboard** in an effort to evade the **MiG's cannon rounds.**

whizzed over Slaughter's right shoulder and passed beneath the nose of his F-84. The only thing he could do was break hard to starboard in an effort to evade the MiG's cannon rounds and maybe reverse the situation.

While trying to get a visual on his new attacker, Slaughter missed seeing the first MiG hit the ground and explode. He realised that his wingman, Capt Edens, was not behind him and radioed him to make sure he was not in trouble. The reply was instant; Edens told him he was far above him and had several MiGs "cornered"!

Slaughter pointed the nose of his fighter straight up and pushed the throttle all the way forward. Edens had eluded the MiG gaggle and joined up on Slaughter's wing. They both checked their fuel gauges and realised they had better head south immediately or risk not being able to make Taegu. It had been a very successful day for the 27th.

As the number of F-86 Sabres in Korea increased, the need for F-84s to fly escort missions dwindled other than in support of other Thunderjet fighter-bombers. The F-84s concentrated on precision bombing and strafing with great success. Captain Slaughter recalls that, after that one mission on January 23, he had very few opportunities to lay eyes on a MiG.

One such opportunity involved a mission in which 27th FEW F-84s were tasked with escorting a group of B-29 Superfortresses on a mission over MiG Alley. The F-84s were late for the rendezvous and, when they did join up, the bombers were already under attack by MiGs. Slaughter fired a burst at one that was bottoming out of his firing pass but did not observe any hits. The MiGs quickly broke off and crossed back over the Yalu.

HOMEWARD BOUND
The 27th FEW received the Distinguished Unit Citation for its actions in the Korean conflict, the citation covering the period from January 26 to April 21, 1951.

The Wing returned to Bergstrom AFB in Texas on July 31, 1951, after which it was re-equipped with new F-84Gs. The unit had left its war-weary E-model Thunderjets in Korea to continue the fight with other units. •

ABOVE: Tangling with MiG-15s proved dangerous at any altitude. This 522nd FES F-84 was on the receiving end of a MiG-15's 37mm cannon during a low-level chase, but managed to limp back to Taegu with a damaged tailpipe in May 1951. *Harold Saabye via author*

BELOW: Pilots of the 522nd FES pose beside F-84E serial 49-2404 *Gypsy From Po'Keepsie*, at Taegu in the spring of 1951. Kneeling third from right is Lt-Col John W. Lafko, the 522nd's Commanding Officer, who completed 134 combat missions over North Korea. The aircraft was lost on a strafing run in North Korea the following March.

Radiant skies

...or how America learned to stop worrying about nuclear power and love the Boeing B-52. Propulsion specialist JAKOB WHITFIELD details the history of the USA's troubled post-war attempts to power aircraft using atomic energy, including trials with a unique Convair B-36.

Even as the mushroom cloud faded over Hiroshima in 1945, scientists and engineers were looking for further ways in which atomic power might be harnessed and used. Nuclear fuel contained so much energy that it seemed to be an ideal power source for an aircraft. Might it be possible to build a bomber able to spend days, weeks, or even months at a time on station as an airborne deterrent?

In May 1946 the United States Army Air Forces (USAAF) initiated Project NEPA (Nuclear Energy for the Propulsion of Aircraft), conducting an initial study which concluded that there were three main

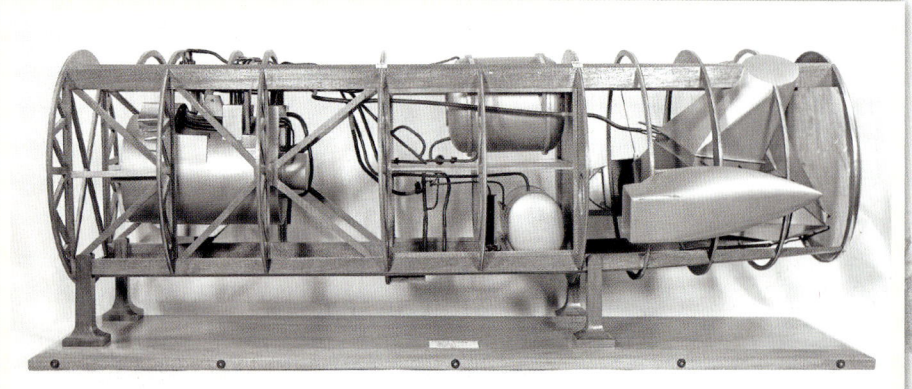

ABOVE: A model of the Aircraft Shield Test Reactor installation for the NB-36H. The unit, to be mounted in the massive bomber's capacious aft bomb-bay, was built by Convair and weighed some 35,000lb (15,900kg). It was configured to be removed from the bomb-bay after each test flight for further ground testing and examination. *Terry Panopalis Collection*

obstacles to a manned nuclear aircraft:

Materials needed to be developed capable of withstanding the reactor's intense radiation;

The radiation shielding required might be too heavy for a viable aircraft design;

The hazards to the public in everyday operation and in case of accidents might be unacceptable.

In 1948 the USA's Atomic Energy Commission (AEC), which had been formed in 1946, performed a similar study. This came to the same conclusions as the earlier report: nuclear-powered flight was possible but would be difficult and expensive to develop – rough time and cost estimates were 15 years and more than $1bn. The report did, however, consider nuclear aircraft propulsion more feasible than nuclear ramjets or nuclear rockets for missile and space propulsion. Encouraged by these recommendations, the AEC set up its own programme.

AIRCRAFT NUCLEAR PROPULSION

In 1950 the United States Air Force (USAF, as the USAAF had become in 1947) and the AEC decided to cancel their respective projects and start a joint programme called Aircraft Nuclear Propulsion (ANP). Its aims were to develop reactor materials, shielding, powerplant and aircraft design to the point where a nuclear aircraft could be built. As one wag put it at the time: "It will only have to land every couple of years for the crew to re-enlist!"

The following year it was decided that the programme would be expanded to include a flight test aircraft. Contracts were awarded to General Electric (GE), which would explore the direct-air cycle principle for a nuclear jet engine design, and Pratt & Whitney, which would develop the more complex indirect-air cycle concept. Contracts

TOP: Convair NB-36H 51-5712 was referred to as the Nuclear Test Aircraft (NTA) and made its first flight on July 20, 1955, at Carswell Air Force Base in Texas, in the hands of test pilot Beryl Erickson. The comparatively small nuclear reactor fitted within it was used only to test radioactive shielding and powered no part of the aircraft. Here it thunders into the air with the crew capsule hatch in the up-and-locked position. *Terry Panopalis Collection*

BELOW: The Aircraft Shield Test Reactor (ASTR) and crew capsule ranged in their approximate prospective positions within the NB-36H on test rigs before installation. Note the extensive security measures at bottom left... *Terry Panopalis Collection*

LEFT AND ABOVE: A pair of rare photographs of the interior of the NB-36H's capsule, including a view of the cockpit and the flight engineer's station. The capsule was so heavily insulated that the crew reported that the combined racket of six R-4360 piston engines plus four J47 jets at full pelt was barely audible during take-off.
via author

structure and roll along the ground. In doing so, the heavy shielding might compress the core to criticality, leading at best to meltdown and at worst to a low-yield nuclear explosion.

BUILDING A SHIELD
The shielding fitted to the NB-36H was of the divided-shadow type. Instead of

were also issued to Convair and Lockheed for the airframes. Convair planned to modify two of its massive B-36 intercontinental bombers as X-6 nuclear-powered aircraft. Another B-36H was to be modified as the NB-36H "Crusader"; conventionally powered but with a 1MW nuclear reactor in the bomb bay. This Aircraft Shield Test Reactor (ASTR) was intended to test crew shielding and radiation safety.

Of the many challenges facing the engineers, the toughest was the reactor and shielding design. Normal "slow" reactors were easy to design, but incorporated bulky materials to "moderate" or slow down the neutrons to create a sustainable chain reaction. All this bulk meant that a shielded reactor weighed about 200 tons – far too heavy for practical flight. A "fast" reactor used higher-speed neutrons and could be much smaller, weighing in at maybe 50 tons, but the temperatures inside were much higher, at over 1,000°C – so high that new materials would be needed if the reactor

were not simply to melt. In this respect the indirect-cycle design had an advantage, as the more efficient heat transfer allowed for a less powerful reactor, but the added weight of the heat exchanger and coolant piping negated some of the weight gains.

Given the weight limits on the reactor, there was no way to encase it to prevent loss of containment in a crash. The USAF had concluded that fallout would be relatively localised, with radioactivity being concentrated by the reactor itself and by any fuel rods that broke free. This overlooked the possibility of "roll-up", an effect identified in 1950. As the reactor was so heavy, in a crash it would almost certainly break free from the aircraft

> *As the **reactor** was so heavy, in **a crash** it would almost certainly **break free** from the aircraft structure and **roll along the ground.***

placing all the shielding around the reactor, it was divided between the reactor and the crew compartment. The reactor was placed at the rear of the fuselage, and the 11-ton lead-shielded crew compartment was located in the aircraft's nose. Where possible, equipment (which generally had higher radiation tolerances than the crew) was placed outside the shield, reducing the shield's size and weight, and producing a shielding effect of its own.

The bulk of the shielding was placed between the crew compartment and the reactor, putting the crew in the reactor core's radiation shadow, although scattering from the aircraft structure and the air meant that the crew compartment still needed some shielding. There was also a trade-off in crew location; moving them further away from the reactor reduced shielding requirements but increased structure weight, so at a certain point there was no benefit to moving them further away.

Safe radiation levels were disputed, especially as one of the easiest ways to increase performance was to reduce the amount of shielding. Some bizarre suggestions for increasing radiation tolerance were made, such as choosing crews from men who had already fathered families and had no desire for more offspring, or doing most of the training on simulators and limiting flight time to 2hr of familiarisation and one operational mission! Given that one of the attractions of the nuclear-powered aircraft was its long endurance – with the associated long radiation exposure – it is surprising that relatively little attention was devoted to this subject; then again, experimental radiation

BELOW: The fully pressurised lead-lined crew capsule for the NB-36H weighed some 11 tons. Note the panels installed on the side of the capsule with connection ports for the various control, electrical and hydraulic systems.
Terry Panopalis Collection

ABOVE: The unique role of the NB-36H called for unique ground support vehicles – the tracked vehicle on the left was a heavily shielded crane for the emergency removal of the reactor and the tug on the right was also shielded. *Terry Panopalis Collection*

tolerance testing could not ethically be performed on humans. The USAF did test other human factors, building a crew compartment simulator in which all the physical and psychological aspects of a five-day mission were evaluated, including calories consumed (from an all-American menu; chicken and gravy and peach pie) and number of bowel evacuations made.

In 1953 the new Eisenhower administration wanted to reduce the USA's defence budget, and the ANP was a prime target. Secretary of Defense Charles E. Wilson, who was under pressure to cancel the project for budgetary reasons, left commentators in no doubt as to how he felt about the NB-36H project, describing it as a "shitepoke… a great big bird that flies over the marshes, doesn't have much body or speed to it or anything," he chuckled, "but it can fly".

The planned X-6 was in no way a militarily useful aircraft, and was therefore cancelled. The NB-36H was far enough advanced that it was spared, however, and made 47 test flights between 1955 and 1957 before it was finally scrapped. On every flight it was accompanied by Boeing B-50 and Douglas C-47 chase aircraft loaded with paratroopers and parachute medics. In case of a crash these were to parachute down, secure the crash site, and render aid where possible. This knowledge was probably cold comfort to the NB-36H crew as they flew along, peering out of their 1ft-thick portholes.

A WHITE ELEPHANT?

Despite the cancellation, ANP was kept going, barely, with USAF funding. It concentrated on engine and reactor development, to which the AEC also contributed. In 1954, the USAF tried for an aircraft again, issuing a specification for a subsonic bomber with supersonic "dash" capability. In 1956 this programme was cancelled.

By now GE had run Heat Transfer Reactor Experiment No 1 (HTRE-1), which consisted of an air-cooled reactor, shielding, two X-39 engines (derivatives of GE's proven J47 jet engine) and associated ducting, controls, and instrumentation. The reactor core was designed to be upgraded as higher-performance versions were developed. The shielding for HTRE-1 was too heavy for it to have been flyable, but by 1957 the higher-performance and lighter HTRE-2 and 32MW HTRE-3 had been tested. The last-named was light enough and produced enough thrust to propel an aircraft, in theory, at 460 m.p.h. (740km/h) for 30,000 miles (48,300km). Although the range was impressive, the speed wasn't exactly sparkling, and there were problems with the release of radioactivity from the open-cycle design; indeed, in 1958 a momentary overload of the HTRE-3 reactor released enough radioactive material to contaminate 1,500 acres (6km^2).

The American government would probably have cancelled ANP but for the Soviet Union's Sputnik 1 launch in October 1957. As Congress and the Senate grasped at the straw of a nuclear aircraft that could take the Cold War to the Russians, it was decided to attempt a "Fly Early" project, which would aim for a flyable aircraft in just three years.

ABOVE: The NB-36H, with the distinctive radioactive warning symbol on the fin, during one of the 47 test flights it made during its successful test programme. The first of these with a fully functioning ASTR was made on September 17, 1955, and the last was completed in March 1957. *Author's Collection*

026 AVIATION CLASSICS: AMERICAN COLD WAR STORIES

Nuclear-powered flight: step 1, the NB-36H

A standard B-36H modified by Convair, the NB-36H flew 47 times. The working nuclear reactor on board did not power the aircraft, but was used to test contamination levels, shielding requirements and other practicalities of airborne nuclear power

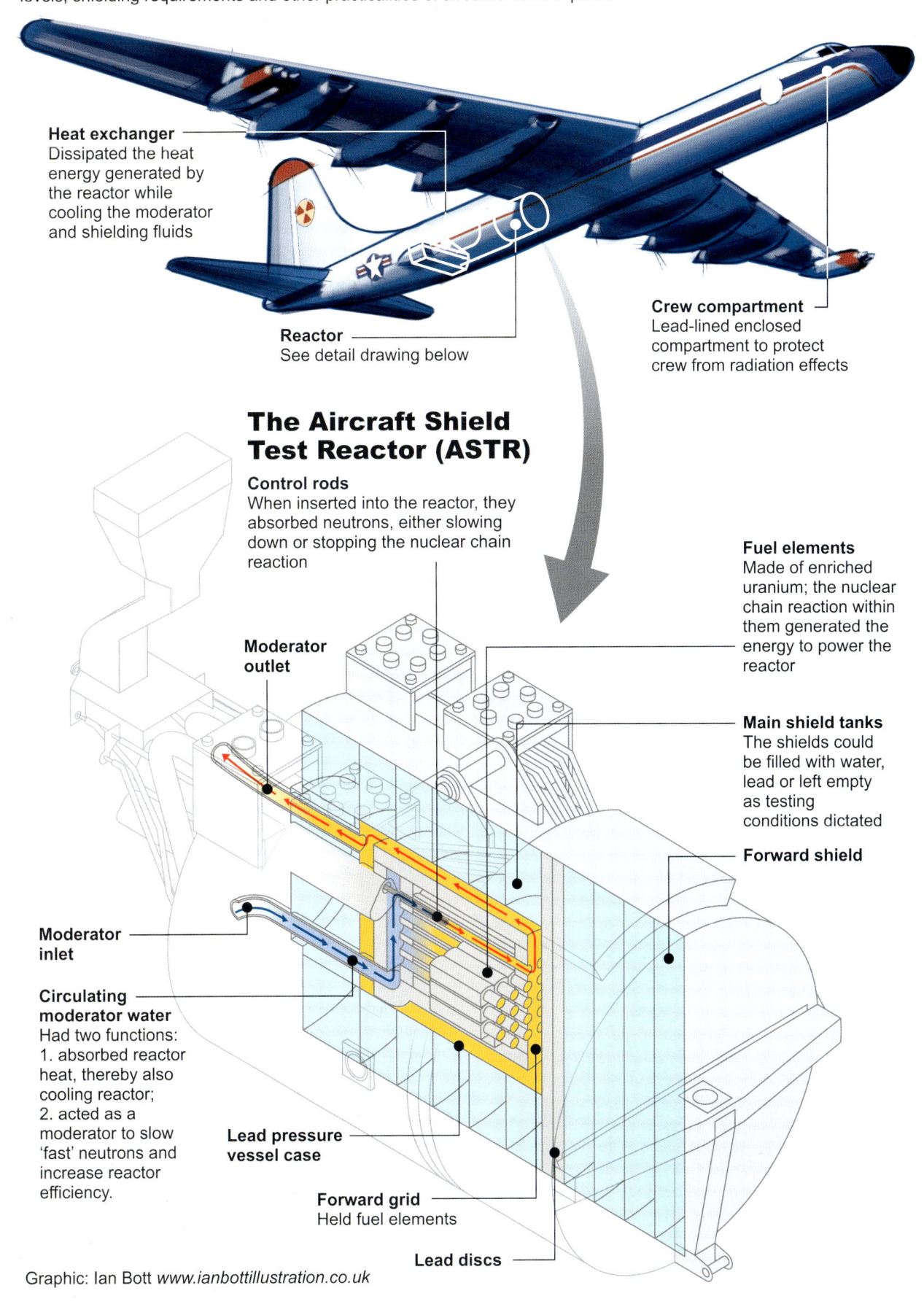

Heat exchanger
Dissipated the heat energy generated by the reactor while cooling the moderator and shielding fluids

Reactor
See detail drawing below

Crew compartment
Lead-lined enclosed compartment to protect crew from radiation effects

The Aircraft Shield Test Reactor (ASTR)

Control rods
When inserted into the reactor, they absorbed neutrons, either slowing down or stopping the nuclear chain reaction

Moderator outlet

Moderator inlet

Circulating moderator water
Had two functions:
1. absorbed reactor heat, thereby also cooling reactor;
2. acted as a moderator to slow 'fast' neutrons and increase reactor efficiency.

Lead pressure vessel case

Forward grid
Held fuel elements

Lead discs

Fuel elements
Made of enriched uranium; the nuclear chain reaction within them generated the energy to power the reactor

Main shield tanks
The shields could be filled with water, lead or left empty as testing conditions dictated

Forward shield

Graphic: Ian Bott www.ianbottillustration.co.uk

ABOVE: Convair constructed a large model of the proposed X-6 to demonstrate the various aspects of ground-handling that would be required. This front view of the model shows the bank of four J53 turbojets that would make up the P-1 powerplant, the reactor being given the designation R-1. Note the flattening of the fuselage as it fairs into the powerplant/reactor bay. *Author's Collection*

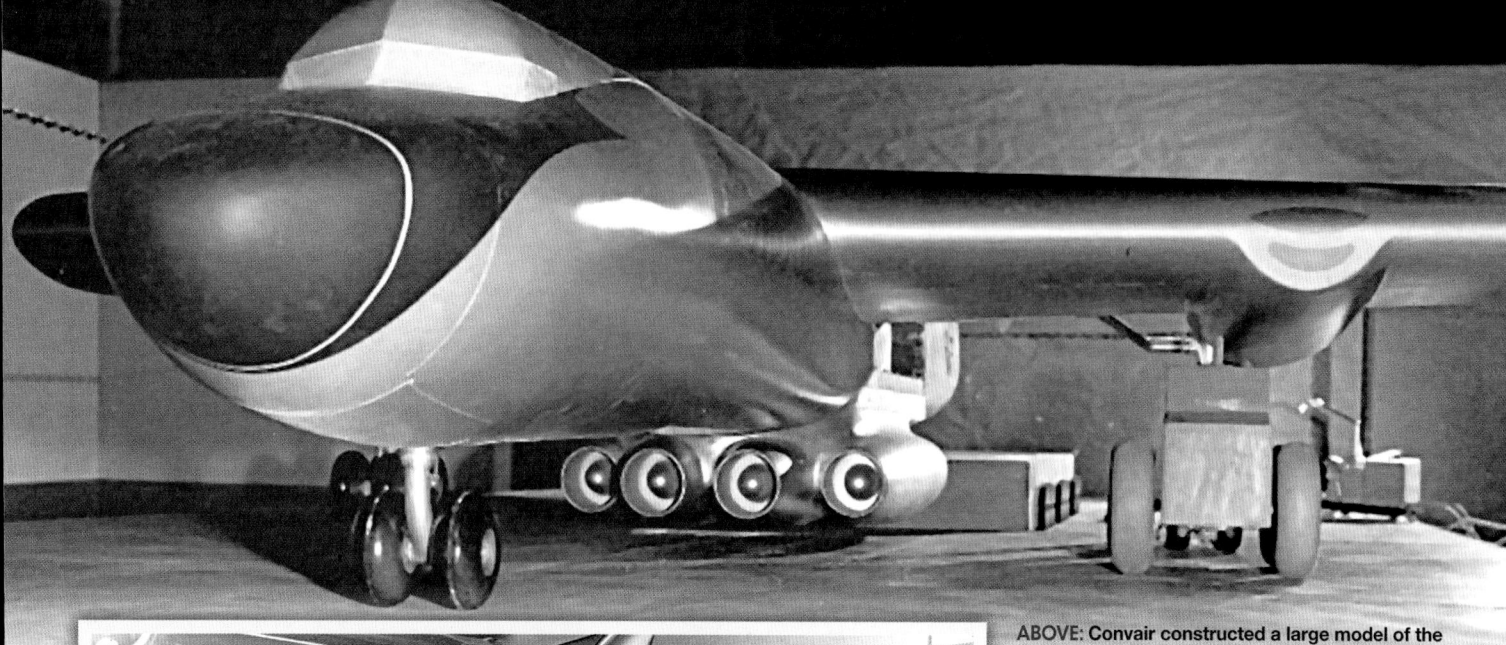

ABOVE: Another view of the model, looking forward from the rear fuselage. Note the staggered arrangement of the four J53s, in which the two inner engines are placed further forward than the outer pair. The X-6 would also have required a special pit to have been built for the installation and removal of the 14-ton P-1 nuclear powerplant. *Author's Collection*

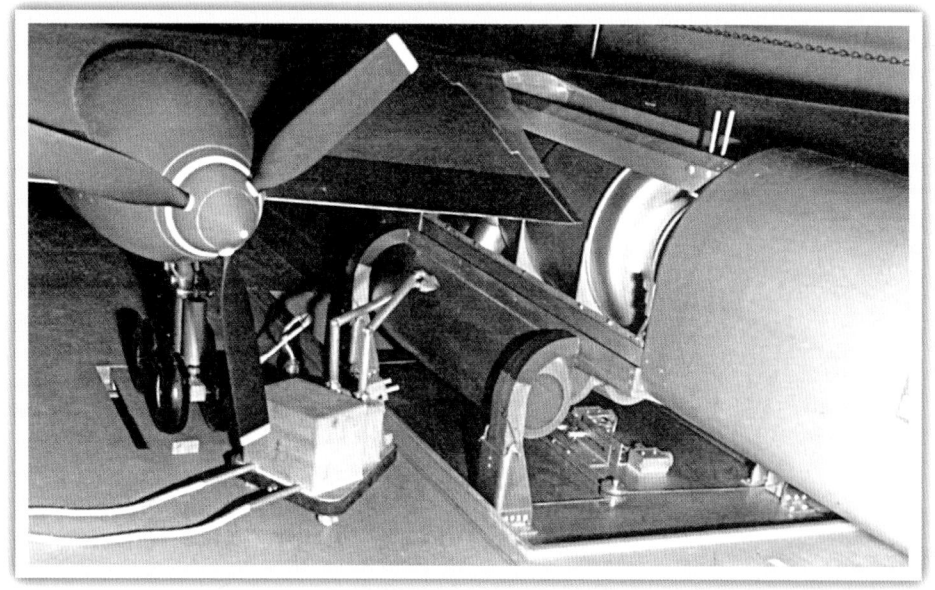

ABOVE: As this photograph of a specially-designed handling robot shows, it was intended that all ground-based activities involving the X-6 would be dealt with remotely, as the potential radiation hazards were deemed to be significant. A proposal to use the jet-powered Convair YB-60 was also mooted, but rejected. *Author's Collection*

DIRECT- OR INDIRECT-CYCLE?

The principles behind a nuclear jet engine are quite simple; instead of raising the temperature of the working fluid by burning fuel, the heat produced by a nuclear reactor is used instead. There are two ways of heating the air:

In an open or direct-cycle design, air from the compressor is ducted through the reactor core, cooling it, and is then passed to the turbine. This has the advantage of simplicity, although there are pressure losses in the reactor core and it has the unfortunate side-effect of expelling radioactive particles in the engine exhaust;

In a closed or indirect-cycle engine the reactor is not cooled by the engine airflow, but by a separate coolant with superior heat transfer characteristics. The engine flow is then heated by a heat exchanger on the reactor coolant loop. In many ways this is a more elegant solution than the direct-cycle; it is generally more efficient owing to better heat transfer. The engines may also be located further away from the core and it does not release radioactivity into the atmosphere. Conversely, with all the associated coolant piping, it is significantly more complex than the direct-cycle design.

In 1959, however, with the Fly Early concept no further advanced, the USAF proposed a more militarily useful aircraft – the CAMAL (Continuously Airborne Missile-Launcher And Low-level) weapons system. The idea was that a nuclear-powered aircraft could patrol outside an enemy's airspace for extended periods. In the event of an attack, it could launch stand-off missiles and follow up with low-level attacks on hardened targets. However, with the advent of in-flight refuelling, the then-recently introduced conventionally-powered Boeing B-52 Stratofortress was capable of reaching any target in the Soviet Union. For the cost of ANP to date the Pentagon could have

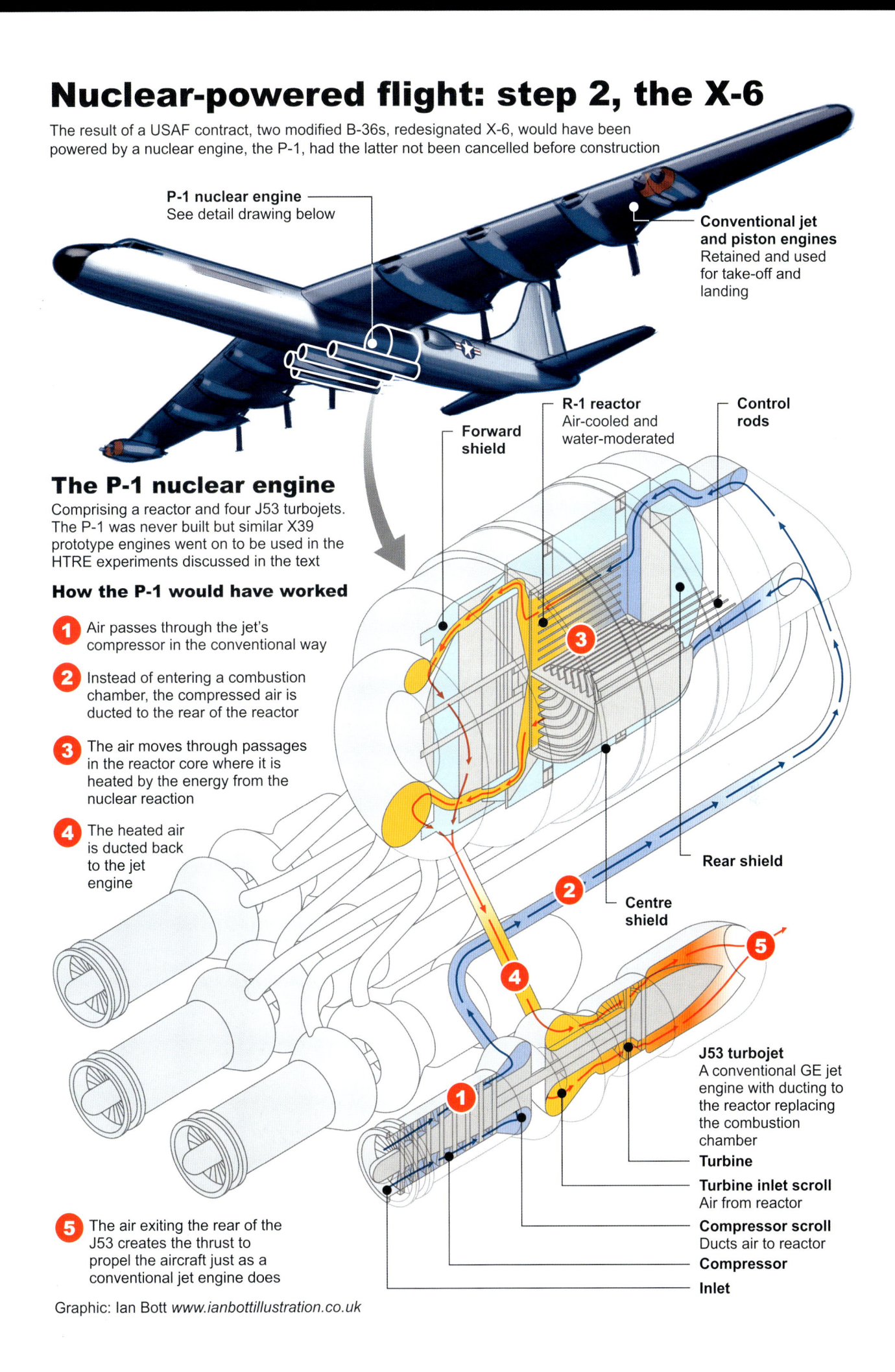

Nuclear-powered flight: step 2, the X-6

The result of a USAF contract, two modified B-36s, redesignated X-6, would have been powered by a nuclear engine, the P-1, had the latter not been cancelled before construction

P-1 nuclear engine
See detail drawing below

Conventional jet and piston engines
Retained and used for take-off and landing

The P-1 nuclear engine

Comprising a reactor and four J53 turbojets. The P-1 was never built but similar X39 prototype engines went on to be used in the HTRE experiments discussed in the text

How the P-1 would have worked

1 Air passes through the jet's compressor in the conventional way

2 Instead of entering a combustion chamber, the compressed air is ducted to the rear of the reactor

3 The air moves through passages in the reactor core where it is heated by the energy from the nuclear reaction

4 The heated air is ducted back to the jet engine

5 The air exiting the rear of the J53 creates the thrust to propel the aircraft just as a conventional jet engine does

Graphic: Ian Bott www.ianbottillustration.co.uk

Forward shield

R-1 reactor
Air-cooled and water-moderated

Control rods

Rear shield

Centre shield

J53 turbojet
A conventional GE jet engine with ducting to the reactor replacing the combustion chamber

Turbine

Turbine inlet scroll
Air from reactor

Compressor scroll
Ducts air to reactor

Compressor

Inlet

AVIATION CLASSICS: AMERICAN COLD WAR STORIES 029

bought some 1,200 B-52s. Furthermore, America's first generation of intercontinental ballistic missiles (ICBMs) were finally overcoming their development troubles and were about to enter service. The Pentagon's Director of Research & Engineering, Dr Herbert York, cancelled CAMAL, insisting that ANP concentrate on the fundamental research that was still needed, especially on reactor materials. In his view, the proposed projects would divert funds from much-needed basic research and would inevitably end in failure.

Such ill-will was in good supply by the end of 1958, the USA's Joint Congressional Committee on Atomic Energy running short on patience. "We find this an almost incredible situation," reported the Committee. "The program [sic] still has no firm set of objectives. No decision has been made regarding actual nuclear flight and no target dates have been set for such flight."

FINAL MELTDOWN

Following the November 1960 Presidential election Eisenhower decided to let the incoming Democratic administration decide the programme's future. His frustration with the continuing congressional and military support of what he saw as a white elephant contributed to his final presidential speech in January 1961, in which he famously referred to "the Military-Industrial Complex". On March 26, 1961, President John F. Kennedy finally pulled the plug on ANP, which was still no closer to a workable aircraft. The final project report stated that the three major obstacles to a practical nuclear aircraft still remained. Echoing the 1946 report, these were reactor materials, reactor shielding and crew and public safety.

In hindsight, what is surprising is that the programme survived as long as it did. It was ruinously expensive and never even came close to producing a test aircraft. Whether this was ever a viable goal is open to question. As the Project Director stated in 1954, "a manned nuclear aircraft poses the most difficult engineering job yet attempted within this century". The problems were never solved. On many occasions only the lobbying of its industrial, military and political supporters saved the programme.

Always responding to the latest idea or "red scare", the stop-start nature of ANP meant that little fundamental research was completed, although the programme did make advances in high-temperature reactor materials. As a result it produced remarkably little of enduring value for the 15 years and $1bn spent. Even its most fervent advocates were forced to admit the shortcomings of the project. Illinois Congressman Mel Price, an ardent and outspoken backer of the nuclear-powered aircraft concept, had to admit his disappointment in ANP in the wake of its demise: "The [ANP] records are filled with stories of divided authority, vacillating budgets, withheld funds, technical reviews, changed objectives, transferred personnel – the list goes on – it is a story of a good project being killed by indecision and bungling". ●

> "a manned **nuclear aircraft** poses the most **difficult** engineering job yet attempted within this **century**".

RIVALS: THE NUCLEAR NAVY

It must have been intensely frustrating for the ANP team to watch the building of the USA's "Nuclear Navy". *USS Nautilus*, America's first nuclear-powered submarine, was launched in January 1954 under the hard-driving and ruthless leadership of Captain (later Admiral) Hyman G. Rickover.

Compared to ANP, Rickover had both technical and organisational advantages; he was a master of bureaucratic in-fighting and had much tighter control over his project team. Technically, it was far easier to float shielding than to fly it. The *Nautilus* could use a "slow" pressurised water reactor that was safe and reliable; an aircraft reactor needed to be 1/20th the size and would run five times hotter.

Captain (later Admiral) Hyman G. Rickover.

BELOW: USS *Nautilus*, the world's first operational nuclear-powered submarine, with Manhattan as a backdrop. The *Nautilus* was launched on January 21, 1954 and went on to set numerous records for submarines.

Fit for the King

Following operations in war and peace with BOAC, Consolidated Liberator G-AHYB was sold to a new owner in French Indo-China to serve as a VIP transport for Vietnamese royalty. HOWARD CARTER traces the long history of a very unusual "Air Force One".

After World War Two, many European nations still had colonies scattered across the globe. Usually, some form of despot was installed by the governing nation in order to control the area's natural wealth and run the colony. Born Prince Nguyen Phúc Vĩnh Thuy on October 22, 1913, Bào Dai became the 13th emperor of the Nguyen dynasty, the last of Vietnam, then part of French-controlled Indo-China.

From 1926 to 1945 Bào Dai was the King of Annam, a protectorate within French Indo-China that covered some two-thirds of present-day Vietnam. Following the fall of France in June 1940, the area was controlled by the Vichy French government until the Japanese invasion of Indo-China that September. An accord between Vichy France and Japan was signed on September 22, 1940, which would see the Japanese directing policy through the French colonial administration, which in turn ruled the area through Bào Dai – his majesty apparently having little problem with switching sides.

In 1945, the French were ousted from Indo-China altogether by the Japanese and Bào Dai was encouraged to declare independence for the newly-minted Empire of Vietnam. Following the surrender of Japan to the Allies in August 1945, Bào Dai abdicated and handed power to Ho Chi Minh's Viet Minh the following month, taking the role of "supreme advisor". After a year Bào Dai left Vietnam to live in Hong Kong and China, just as the French retook its former colony in November 1946. Three years later he was back, having been persuaded by the French to return as the nominal head of state.

He spent much time in Europe and received criticism in Indo-China for his close French ties and for living the life of a playboy. Following the French defeat by the Viet Minh at Dien Bien Phu in 1954, Vietnam was partitioned into the communist North and pro-Western South, the latter retaining Bào Dai as a puppet leader, as a result of which he moved permanently to Paris and appointed Ngo Dinh Diem as his prime minister. Ousted by the latter in a blatantly fraudulent election in 1955, Bào Dai lived a life of exiled luxury in France and Monaco until his death in Paris in 1977.

A LUXURIOUS LIBERATOR

During his period as the French-controlled head of the Vietnamese state, Bào Dai largely did what his masters ordered, in return for which the French Government kept him in the elegant lifestyle to which he aspired. The French decided to supply their South-east Asian pawn with an "Air Force One", the aircraft selected being both unusual and interesting.

BELOW: Originally given the American military serial 40-2359 (c/n 11), Liberator AM920 was one of 20 bought for the RAF from the US Army Air Corps and delivered during April–August 1941. After a distinguished wartime career with BOAC as AM920, the inelegant but hardworking transport was given the civil registration G-AHYB in 1946. *Philip Jarrett Collectio*

ABOVE: The last word in Vietnamese luxury – this superb photograph of Consolidated Liberator F-VNNP, complete with whitewalled tyres, shows the much-travelled workhorse in its final colour scheme, while serving as a VIP transport for Bào Dai, the Vietnamese head of state during 1949–55. Following its long career with BOAC as AM920 and G-AHYB, it was one of five sold to French company STA Alpes Provence in April 1951, initially being registered as F-BEFR. It was overhauled, appointed to a luxury configuration and put on the French colonial register as F-VNNP. Little is known about its ultimate fate. *Via author*

BELOW: The first Liberators to arrive in the UK were six of the seven YB-24s built for US Army Air Corps service trials (serials 40-696 to 40-701), but which were delivered to the UK from March 1941 as LB-30As for transatlantic ferrying duties. This example is AM259, which was photographed with its civil registration, G-AGCD, in May 1941. *Philip Jarrett Collection*

When the US Army Air Corps ordered 36 Consolidated B-24As in August 1940, a decision was made to transfer 20 of these aircraft (serial numbers 40-2349 to 40-2368 inclusive) to the RAF as Liberator B Mk Is (serialled AM910 to AM929). However, it was soon determined that the type was not suited for operations over Europe as it lacked a number of essential combat features. Most of the aircraft were then converted by Scottish Aviation at Prestwick to Liberator GR Mk I general-reconnaissance standard (fitted with four forward-firing 20mm cannon and provision for rockets) and assigned to Coastal Command's No 120 Sqn at Nutts Corner, where they arrived in June 1941, and went on to give excellent service attacking enemy U-boats.

Three of the original group of 20 Liberators – AM915, AM918 and AM920 – were converted to C Mk I transports and put into the vital transatlantic role of flying ferry pilots back to the USA after they had delivered Lend-Lease aircraft. Liberator AM915 was operated by Ferry Command until it flew into a hill in Argyll in cloud in September 1941; AM918 was allocated to BOAC and given the civil registration G-AGDR, but was shot down by a Spitfire near the Eddystone Lighthouse on the Devon/Cornwall border in February 1942. Liberator AM920 was one of several opera-ted as part of the North Atlantic Return Ferry Service, having been allotted to BOAC in August 1942. These aircraft carried full camouflage for most of the war, but Theyre Lee-Elliott's distinctive "speedbird" insignia for BOAC was painted on the forward fuselage, along with a large Union flag, while the flight crews wore full BOAC uniforms in compliance with the Geneva Convention.

During January 1945 BOAC's surviving Liberators were returned to the RAF, but the demands of war had deprived the corporation of modern aircraft with which to re-enter the burgeoning international airline market. Desperate for long-range transports, BOAC worked out an arrangement whereby it could get a number of the Liberators back in order to undergo modification to a civilian standard, some 17 examples of the type being on strength with BOAC by the end of 1945. One of these was AM920, which was later given

> During January 1945 **BOAC's surviving Liberators** were returned to the **RAF,** but the demands of war had deprived the corporation of modern aircraft with which to **re-enter** the burgeoning **international airline market.**

032 AVIATION CLASSICS: AMERICAN COLD WAR STORIES

the civil registration G-AHYB. The Liberators were stripped of paint, completely overhauled and fitted with airline-standard seats, advanced avionics and other equipment. The aircraft were highly polished and wore the simple, austere BOAC markings of the immediate post-war period.

By 1947 the corporation was operating some 175 aircraft of 18 different types – a situation which made running a profitable airline extremely difficult. In addition the government was forcing BOAC to buy British at all costs, thus forcing the corporation to use a variety of obsolete types, including the Liberators. Ultimately, however, BOAC received government permission to buy a limited number of American-built airliners. The Liberators gave good service, and AM920 earned the distinction of making BOAC's 2,000th transatlantic crossing, on February 10, 1946. The Liberators were finally phased out of BOAC service in September 1949.

A NEW LEASE OF LIFE

The Liberators were sold off and G-AHYB found a new owner – STA Alpes Provence of France. Once again, the aircraft was overhauled, given a VIP interior, registered F-VNNP, and presented as a gift to Bào Dai.

Highly polished and sporting whitewall tyres, the Liberator served its new master well, delivering the former King of Annam and his sizeable entourage to gambling and holiday spots across Europe.

Little appears to be known of the ultimate fate of F-VNNP – it appears in the 1952 French Colonies aircraft register as operating with "Service Imperial Aer." at Da Lat, in the central highlands of South Vietnam, but is no longer listed in the same register for 1958. ●

ABOVE: Liberator II G-AHYF (formerly AL592) taxies out for another transatlantic flight for BOAC after receiving its civil registration in 1946, and is seen here in the corporation's restrained post-war polished bare-metal scheme. *Philip Jarrett Collection*

BELOW: At the end of December 1945 AM920 was listed as being part of the BOAC fleet and based in Montreal. On August 19, 1946, the Liberator was given its new civil identity, G-AHYB, after which it continued to serve the route between Montreal and Prestwick until the spring of 1950, when it was offered for sale to a new owner in France. *Philip Jarrett Collection*

AVIATION CLASSICS: AMERICAN COLD WAR STORIES 033

Days of thunder:
The Republic F-84Fs of the USAF's 81st Fighter Bomber Wing in Europe, 1954-58

In the summer of 1954 the Sabre jockeys of the UK-based 81st Fighter Interceptor Wing were disappointed to learn that they were to be retrained as tactical bomber drivers — and, to their even greater dismay, given a new aircraft: the troublesome Republic F-84F Thunderstreak. DOUG GORDON traces the mixed fortunes of the 81st Fighter Bomber Wing's F-84Fs in Europe and IAN BOTT illustrates their potential role in a nuclear war.

The 81st Fighter Interceptor Wing (FIW) had arrived in the UK in August 1951, equipped with the North American F-86A Sabre in the air defence role. Based at RAF stations Bentwaters and Shepherds Grove in Suffolk, the Wing, comprising the 78th, 91st and 92nd Fighter Interceptor Squadrons (FIS), had been responsible, with the RAF, for the air defence of the United Kingdom.

In August 1954 the 81st was redesignated as a Fighter Bomber Wing, and with this redesignation came a new role. The primary mission became "to destroy forces, resources and installations of the enemy". To accomplish this mission the 81st FBW was to fly the Republic F-84F Thunderstreak and deliver tactical atomic weapons.

Conversion began in October 1954, the first F-84 arriving by sea at Lisbon, Portugal, on October 4. Not all the pilots of the 81st were initially enamoured with the F-84F. Lieutenant Colonel Arlie Blood was CO of the 78th Fighter Bomber Squadron (FBS) based at Shepherds Grove: "They took our beautiful F-86s away from us and equipped us with the F-84F fighter-bomber. The F-84s were shipped to Lisbon, to a Republic crew that installed the wings, and were then test hopped by a Republic test pilot. I flew down there and set

ABOVE: Lieutenant Harry Eckes of the 91st Fighter Bomber Squadron (FBS) en route to Nouasseur, Morocco, in F-84F 52-6852. The flight to the North African base covered a distance of more than 1,200 miles (1,930km) and took about 2hr. Note the badge of the 81st FBW on the fuselage, and the individual squadron badge at the tip of the fin. *Don Mikler via author*

Juanita Franzi

up an 81st operation to 'buy' the airplanes after the test hop. I took off for England with our first F-84F. I was requested to do a flyby at Sculthorpe so all the generals could see this 'great' nuclear carrier. I did and they asked what I thought of the new fighter. I said, 'It's no F-86'."

TO NORTH AFRICA
Before the arrival of the F-84F and during transition, the 81st was obliged to accomplish much of its training for its new mission in the F-86. Indeed, the 78th FBS continued to receive F-86F-25s until October 1954. The unit deployed with F-86s to Nouasseur in Morocco during October and November 1954, specifically for practice in dive bombing and the Low Altitude Bombing System (LABS).

Nouasseur was chosen as the venue for the squadrons to make the transition to the F-84 as well as for training. Fair weather made for a high mission rate and efficient training. During 1954 a considerable number of pilots qualified on the F-84 at the Moroccan base. Sadly, these training operations took their toll on men and machines. Captain John T. Hale Jr of the 91st FBS and 1st Lt William Garney were both killed while transitioning in Morocco. Arlie Blood explains: "We lost a very skilled pilot at gunnery camp in Africa during a dive-bomb run. Being used to the manoeuvrability of the F-86 he did not pull out of his dive in time and mushed into the ground".

Not all pilots found the Thunderstreak as objectionable as Lt Col Blood. Major Bob Fredette was with the 78th FBS and described the transition from the F-86 to the F-84 as "like converting from a sports car to a dump truck". He did warm to the type, however.

"Before flying the F-84F I flew the F-86A and -F [models]. [The Sabre and the Thunderstreak] had different missions and could not be compared objectively. You are talking apples and oranges. Our aircraft had wing spoilers and a slab tailplane. Its overall performance was very good, had a

ABOVE: Lieutenant Joe Williams (left) poses with his crew chief at Shepherds Grove beside his Thunderstreak. "I was not overly fond of the F-84F or its mission. Going from fighter-interceptor to special missions was a big change for us all. But when you wear the uniform, you must go with the change." *Joe Williams via author*

AVIATION CLASSICS: AMERICAN COLD WAR STORIES 035

tremendous rate of turn, it was an honest aircraft. It had to overcome a bad reputation."

In March 1955 the 92nd FBS moved from Shepherds Grove to RAF Manston. In May of that year the last of the initial batch of F-84Fs arrived for the 81st FBW. All F-86As were returned to the USA, travelling by freighter from Belfast.

GOING NUCLEAR

The story of the service of the Thunderstreak with the 81st is characterised by both a catalogue of problems, modifications, replacements and frustrations on one hand and outstanding success in completing the assigned mission on the other. The

RIGHT: Lieutenant Don Mikler and F-84F at Nouasseur in December 1955. The USAF in Europe (USAFE) used Nouasseur in Morocco and Wheelus in Libya for fair-weather weapons practice for all of its units. *Don Mikler via author*

many snags associated with the aircraft's development inevitably followed it into service, and were compounded by new ones from time to time.

The primary offensive weapon of the F-84F was the Mk 7 atomic bomb, weighing approximately 2,000lb (900kg) and yielding in excess of a kiloton. For the carriage of this weapon the aircraft was fitted with a specially designed pylon to be carried under the port wing.

Special Weapons training, exercises and security occupied much of the Wing's time and energies. Training was hard and highly intensive. The bomb commanders, as the pilots were known, were used to much of

> The **primary** offensive **weapon** of the **F-84F** was the **Mk 7 atomic bomb**, weighing approximately 2,000lb (900kg) and yielding in excess of **a kiloton.**

the ethos that prevailed in an atomic strike unit, but it was a new experience for many of the pilots of the 81st, some of whom were new to the Wing as well as the mission. With the change in role of the Wing many of the experienced personnel had returned home, to be replaced by young pilots fresh from college.

Every bomb commander was obliged to attain a grade of at least 90 per cent every 90 days on knowledge of the weapon and the ramifications of its use. They would be monitored on a mock-up trainer and in flight; weapons loading and pre- and post-flight procedures were included.

Initial deliveries were of the F-84F-35 and F-84F-40 series, powered by the unmodified Wright J65 engine (a development of the British Armstrong Siddeley Sapphire), which brought its own problems. The new aircraft, despite being fitted with the Minneapolis Honeywell-Regulator Company's MA-1 bombing computer, was unsuited to LABS manœuvres. This was the same system that had been used in the Thunderstreak's predecessor, the F-84G Thunderjet, and was not entirely satisfactory. For this reason an alternative method of special weapons delivery (SWD) was devised. Lieutenant Joe Williams explains: "We used the 13,000ft [4,000m] release in a high-altitude dive-bomb run. We would go into the dive at 24,000ft [7,300m] and release at 13,000ft. One time during practice dive-bombing at the Dengie Flats [in Essex] in England, I forgot to pull the power off after climbing back up to the perch. On the next dive, after bomb release, the airspeed was 700kt [805 m.p.h – 1,300km/h]. Thank God for the 13,000ft release. For bombing practice we had a small rotating rack that held eight small 'Blue Boys' that were supposed to simulate the real thing, with a shotgun charge that went off when the bomb hit the ground to show where it hit in relation to the target, and this was used to score the hits. When we flew with the big bomb shape, the aircraft had a tendency to roll as your speed built up in the dive run. But this was easily countered with aileron. We had one fellow in our squadron that went in at the Dengie Flats range, flew the airplane right into the ground. You have very poor depth perception over water so it is best to watch your altimeter."

Later Block 45 and 50 F-84Fs had a spoiler to improve low-altitude bombing capability, as well as the MA-2 LABS computer, which was to become standard during most of the type's service life.

When LABS became the standard method of SWD, it was practised mainly at Nouasseur. Lieutenant Gil Leimbach recalls: "The 78th FBS went to Nouasseur to do LABS manœuvres on a Strategic Air Command [SAC] bomber range. LABS was an all-weather manœuvre. The aircraft would arrive over the target at 500ft [150m] at very high speed and pull up into a 4g loop manœuvre.

If it was cloudy, this would be on instruments. [The pilot would then] roll out at the top using the artificial horizon. The practice bomb would automatically release, go straight up, lose velocity and go straight down. This time allows the aircraft clearance to survive a nuclear explosion safely. Needless to say [it was] much better than high-altitude bombing."

ABOVE: Four 91st FBS pilots; from left to right: Lt Bob Stone; Lt Sterling Lee; Lt Bob Russ and Capt Dick Schoenemann. Stone was later shot down in Vietnam, Lee was killed after ejecting from an F-101; Russ and Schoenemann became high-ranking USAF Generals. *Don Mikler via author*

BELOW: This F-84F-45-RE, 52-6737, is seen in the distinctive yellow markings of the 92nd FBS, which was based at RAF Manston from March 1955 until the end of April 1958, at which time it joined the rest of the 81st FBW at RAF Bentwaters. *Mike Hooks*

AVIATION CLASSICS: AMERICAN COLD WAR STORIES

BELOW: Thunderstreaks of the Bentwaters-based 91st FBS peel off for a series of publicity photographs in 1956. Republic was keen to extol the type's virtues, the accompanying press release claiming that the F-84 "adds speed and atomic punch to the free world's air arsenal". *TAH Archive*

The change in the primary mission and aircraft of the 81st FBW necessitated a change in the role the Wing was called upon to play in the many exercises in which it took part.

GETTING PLENTY OF EXERCISE
Exercise *Carte Blanche,* one of the first significant ones in Cold War Europe, was undertaken on June 21–28, 1955. It encompassed all Nato countries and various tactical units and their aircraft. The scenario was the outbreak of an atomic war, and the exercise was designed to test all current plans in dispersal, tactical control and alert responses.

The 81st FBW was responsible for making simulated atomic bomb strikes on mainland Europe from dispersal points in the UK. The 91st FBS, part of the 81st, operated from Bentwaters in Suffolk and dispersed some aircraft to Manston in Kent. The exercise was a marked success and, certainly for the F-84F bomb commanders, it was a fitting reward for months of intensive training. The 91st FBS launched 26 strikes on targets in Europe and all were successful.

Leimbach was with the 78th FBS at Shepherds Grove; he flew to targets in France. He remembers: "I took off from Shepherds Grove and headed for a French aerodrome in the Lyons area. The weather was VFR [visual flight rules], a beautiful day. Low level all the way, 500ft [150m]. I contacted the airfield tower that I was coming. They acknowledged and I made a LABS manœuvre and headed back to the Grove. As far as I can remember all of my 'real war' targets were airfields in East Germany."

Exercise *Beware* in September 1955 dispersed squadrons of the 81st FBW to bases in Europe to launch strikes against the UK in a test of the latter's air defences. The F-84Fs were more than a match for the Gloster Meteors and de Havilland Venoms of RAF Fighter Command. The 92nd FBS was proud of its success in striking unhindered from its base in West Germany.

Success in penetration exercises such as *Carte Blanche*, *Beware* and *Fox Paw*, the latter taking place in November 1955, was achieved despite training facilities for the Thunderstreak Wings being far from adequate. One of the principal problems was the lack of suitable range facilities. In England the only option for bomb delivery was Dengie Flats. Effective use of this range was dependent on the weather, which put it out of use for several months in every year.

Operation *Long Stride* took the squadrons to North Africa for fair-weather training. Without such exercises there would have been little chance of the bomb commanders being proficient enough to do the job should "D-Day" ever happen.

In Exercise *Brown Cow* the 91st FBS bomb commanders' navigation skills were tested as well as their abilities in SWD. One 500lb (225kg) bomb was dropped by each of the bomb commanders on Dengie Flats. The delivery method was by high-angle dive-bombing. The 91st had only three F-84F-45 series aircraft at this time and only the pilots of these were allowed to use the "over-the-shoulder" LABS delivery technique, which achieved good results.

That the Thunderstreak was not very popular is probably due to the many problems associated with its development and early service career. It is a tribute to the pilots who flew it and the groundcrews who maintained it that they overcame many of the drawbacks and achieved a high degree of success in these exercises.

SIMPLY THE BEST
In July 1956 the 81st FBW flew down to Wheelus in Libya for an SWD meeting. Pilots from each of the squadrons represented their Wing in a competition to determine the

> The **scenario** was the outbreak of an **atomic war,** and the **exercise** was designed to test all current **plans** in **dispersal, tactical control** and **alert responses.**

038 AVIATION CLASSICS: AMERICAN COLD WAR STORIES

best SWD unit in USAFE (USAF Europe). The meeting did include other aspects of the mission assigned, but the atomic weapons delivery part was the most significant for the 81st. Pilots were selected for their skill and precision.

Other USAFE units at the meeting were flying different types, such as the F-86F Sabre. The fact that the 81st FBW and the 20th FBW, based at Wethersfield in Essex, were flying the F-84F made the competition keener, making the operators of both types all the more determined that their aircraft should prevail. The reputation of the F-84F had undoubtedly gone before it and this made victory or, at the very least, a respectable showing, imperative. Bob Fredette of the 78th FBS explains: "I have always been proud that the 81st won the USAFE bombing meet and, specifically, the 78th FBS, of which I was the CO at the time. The team representing

ABOVE: Wearing both the 81st FBW's badge on the fuselage and the lizard badge of the 78th FBS (nicknamed the "Bushmasters") on the fin, Thunderstreak 52-6749 was photographed at Bentwaters Armed Forces Day in 1958. The sunburst markings on the fin and the panel on the nose were dark red. *Robbie Robinson via author*

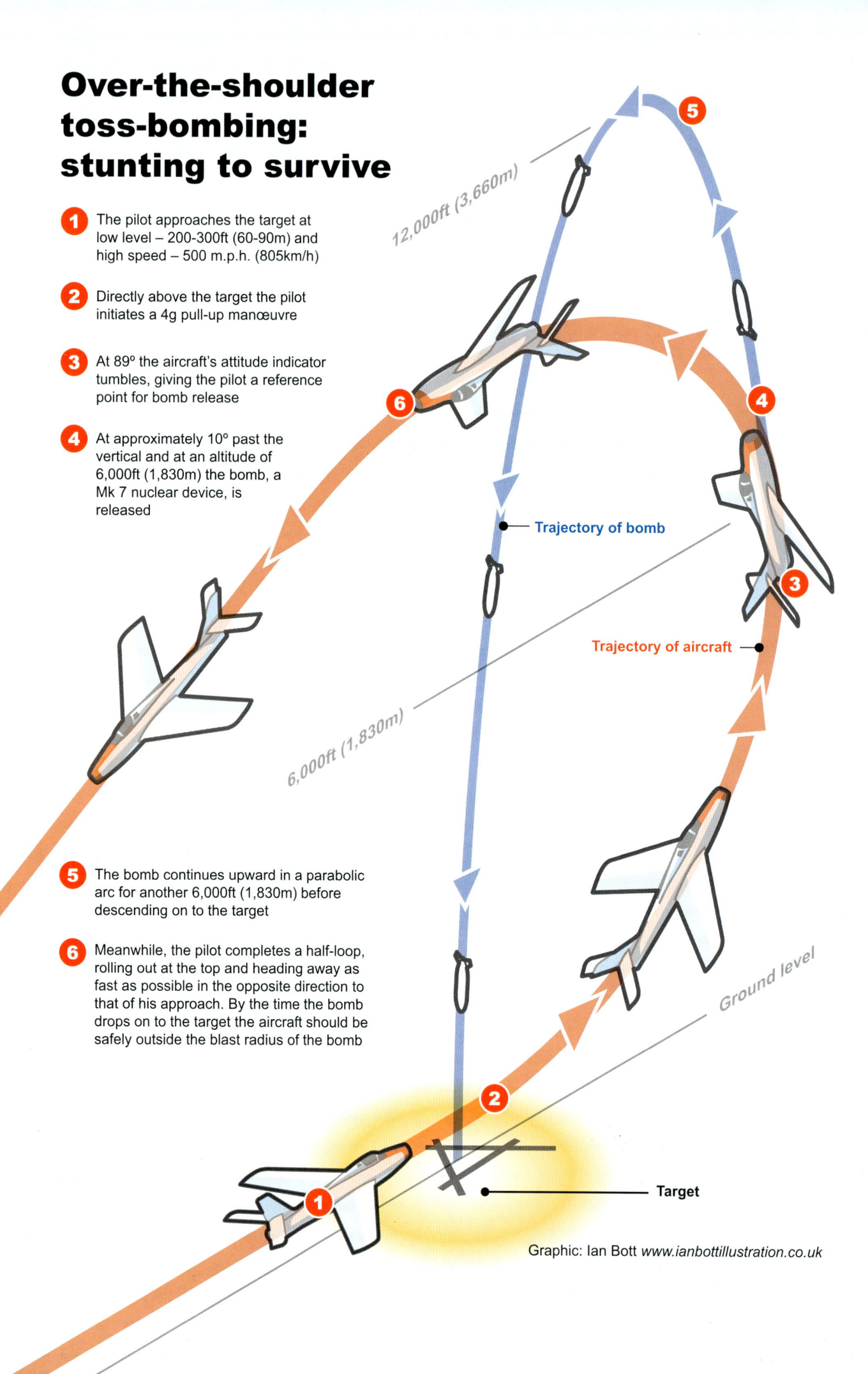

Over-the-shoulder toss-bombing: stunting to survive

1 The pilot approaches the target at low level – 200-300ft (60-90m) and high speed – 500 m.p.h. (805km/h)

2 Directly above the target the pilot initiates a 4g pull-up manœuvre

3 At 89° the aircraft's attitude indicator tumbles, giving the pilot a reference point for bomb release

4 At approximately 10° past the vertical and at an altitude of 6,000ft (1,830m) the bomb, a Mk 7 nuclear device, is released

5 The bomb continues upward in a parabolic arc for another 6,000ft (1,830m) before descending on to the target

6 Meanwhile, the pilot completes a half-loop, rolling out at the top and heading away as fast as possible in the opposite direction to that of his approach. By the time the bomb drops on to the target the aircraft should be safely outside the blast radius of the bomb

12,000ft (3,660m)

6,000ft (1,830m)

Trajectory of bomb

Trajectory of aircraft

Ground level

Target

Graphic: Ian Bott www.ianbottillustration.co.uk

ABOVE: "C" Flight of the 91st FBS flies a four-aircraft formation for a publicity shoot. Captain Jack Bowman leads the quartet, accompanied by Lieutenants Don Hanto, Jim Wilson and Harry Eckes. The blue lightning flashes on the fin were just one example of the variety of markings carried by the 91st FBS during the Thunderstreak period. *Don Mikler via author*

the Wing was composed of weapons-loading crews and a total of six pilots; two each from the 78th, 91st and 92nd. The materiel officer, Capt Barrantine, and the Fly Away Kit Section [parts and supplies] were all from the 78th.

"The meet was won by two 78th pilots – Captains Dee McCarter and Raymond Kingston. We became the USAFE Special Weapons Delivery Champions. They ran away with it! As a result, in October 1956 this team proceeded to Nellis AFB [Nevada, USA] for the USAF Bombing Meet.

"The team departed England, the pilots flying our aircraft to Nellis via Iceland and Goose Bay, Labrador. The maintenance team flew in a [Douglas] C-54 to Nellis. The entire team beat the favourites from the SAC team, and was totally independent. They did not rely on any other support except for fuel. Again, Kingston and McCarter won the meet on the final day by simply devastating the other teams on scoring. Upon return to England, the aircraft were painted with 'USAF CHAMPS' on the fuselage. As far as the meet was concerned, even in publicity terms, SAC was supposed to be the 'shoe-in'. Our team waxed them. Kingston celebrated by stopping in Las Vegas and was showered with affection by Miss Candy Barr, Las Vegas Entertainer."

It was fitting that the Thunderstreak was thrust into the limelight at such a time – it had been established at both competitions that here was an aircraft that could do the job for which it had been designed despite the numerous problems that had bedevilled it. By way of underlining this, the 81st FBW was awarded the USAFE Tactical Proficiency Trophy for the first half of 1956. The Operational Readiness Inspection (ORT) team had considered the Wing the best it had ever inspected.

RISING TENSIONS

The first-ever visit of the Soviet Union's Bolshoi Ballet to the UK in October 1956 should have been an occasion for cultural celebration, but, coming as it did at a time of crisis, a considerable amount of consternation ▶

BELOW: The Thunderstreaks of the 81st FBW were regular visitors to British airshows in the 1950s, 52-6718 of the 78th FBS being seen here alongside Boeing KB-29P 0-469716 of the 420th Air Refuelling Squadron — the 0-designation was added to operational USAF aircraft serials (in this case 44-69716) to indicate they were more than ten years old. *TAH Archive*

AVIATION CLASSICS: AMERICAN COLD WAR STORIES 041

and confusion was evident in military circles on the day of arrival, not least at RAF Manston where the 92nd FBS resided alongside the 406th FIW. No warning had been given of the imminent arrival of a Tupolev Tu-104 of Aeroflot which had diverted from Heathrow owing to fog. Hurried arrangements were made to cover up the sensitive special-weapon practice stores slung under the wings of the 92nd's F-84Fs.

That year also witnessed two major international events which underlined the necessity of maintaining a high degree of readiness in all Nato tactical strike units. The Suez Crisis of October–November 1956 saw no direct involvement from the USA. The USAF nevertheless placed its bases on high alert and was ready to react if any Soviet moves were made against its allies, Britain and France. Security of the bases was tightened considerably for the duration of the crisis. A 24hr alert condition was imposed, with weapons loaded and bomb commanders on standby. The plutonium cores of the special weapons were beside the aircraft in their cages, next to which was a guard and his German Shepherd dog.

Soviet aggression in Hungary, also in October and November, kept the tension, and thus the readiness of the F-84F strike units, at a high level. Wing Intelligence kept a watching brief on developments and a round-the-clock review of targets, charts and maps.

Tension eased towards the end of 1956, by which time the F-84F was receiving further modifications, including a selector switch to use with the MA-1 LABS computer. This enabled the pilot to select either a conventional or "over-the-shoulder" delivery. This was also used with the MA-2 system newly installed in some aircraft.

Although the F-84F had been in service for less than two years and was at the height of its mission success, moves were already afoot to replace it in the 81st. The aircraft to do this was the North American F-100 Super Sabre. Examples of this state-of-the-art fighter-bomber were already in service with USAFE with the 36th Fighter Day Wing and the 48th Fighter Bomber Wing, based in Germany and France respectively. The 81st FBW published its F-100D Conversion Plan 5-56 and was in regular contact with the 45th Fighter Day Squadron (FDS) based at Sidi Slimane in French Morocco. The 45th FDS was flying the F-100C and was tasked with converting USAFE pilots to the type. In the event, the 81st's conversion plan was unrealistically optimistic. The unit was destined never to fly the aircraft.

MORE EXERCISES – MORE FRUSTRATION

As the proficiency of the bomb commanders in SWD techniques increased, so did frustration with the F-84F and the nature of the exercises being undertaken. There was too great a restriction on low flying in the UK; 2,000ft (610m) was just too high for an authentic mission to be flown. Exercise *Vigilante,* undertaken in October 1956 against UK targets, led to an appeal from the pilots to be allowed to drop their fuel tanks on approach to the target just as they would in wartime.

The 81st pilots found that there was a dramatic increase in their target folders when the unit was forced to incorporate those assigned to other USAF units, while the latter converted to the F-100D. The 92nd FBS alone doubled its targets, many of which had been designed for the F-100D. The efficient attacking of these targets required the Super Sabre's advanced performance. The F-84Fs could reach the targets, but were limited by the necessity of being flown at optimum rather than maximum performance. In wartime this would mean an increase in the number of aircraft intercepted by the enemy. As 1957 progressed these frustrations became more profound. Exercise *Fog Cut,* undertaken in the latter part of the year, in which the 81st attacked targets in the UK, saw a number of F-84F intercepts – most of which, the pilots maintained, could have been avoided but for the restrictions placed upon the type.

The F-84F was, in any event, proving problematic in meeting the requirements of the ever- increasing developments in SWD. Several aircraft were destroyed while performing LABS delivery. Two aircraft hit the ground when they failed to recover from the manœuvre. The 91st FBS instituted an indoctrination programme on Instrument Flight Conditions (IFC) recovery from LABS manœuvres. There was a lack of confidence in the altitude gyro. It was made mandatory that each mission contemplating IFC LABS recoveries must first obtain permission of the commander or operations officer. There were other accidents. The undercarriage of Thunderstreak 52-6707 extended during a bombing run. Another aircraft aborted a take-off, crashed and caught fire, resulting in a pilot fatality; another crashed on approach owing to a hydraulic failure, also killing the pilot. A common accident was the loss of the drag 'chute in flight owing to excessive vibration causing the holding bolts to loosen. In November 1957 bomb commanders of the

ABOVE: The Thunderstreaks of the 81st FBW were occasionally fitted with jet-assisted take-off (JATO) rocket bottles to improve the type's take-off performance when heavily laden. In this photo of 78th FBS Thunderstreak 52-6780 the aft ends of the JATO bottles may just be seen behind the tail-end of the wing-mounted fuel tank. *via author*

92nd FBS attended an F-100D training course at RAF Wethersfield.

The dawning of 1958 saw a dramatic development. Moves were being made in the Pentagon to convert the 81st FBW, not to the F-100D as everyone had supposed, but to a type of which there was only one Wing operating in the entire USAF – the McDonnell F-101 Voodoo. Not only was the Voodoo at the end of its production run, but it had been designed as an escort fighter for SAC bombers, not as a tactical atomic strike aircraft. Having just one Wing of a particular aircraft type in the European theatre would seemingly pose considerable logistical problems. However, despite the protestations and indisputable logistical reasons not to convert to the F-101 put forward by the Commander of USAFE, General Frank Everest, the conversion was to go ahead at the end of 1958.

The 27th TFW was to move its entire inventory of Voodoos,

LEFT: Lieutenant Don Mikler heads out for the range on one of the 81st's many practice missions, in which the Wing's Thunderstreaks would rehearse the prescribed techniques for toss-bombing and the Low-Altitude Bombing System (LABS), either of which could be used to deliver a nuclear weapon should the need arise. *Don Mikler via author*

> *Moves were being made in the **Pentagon** to **convert** the **81st FBW**, not to the F-100D as everyone had supposed, but to **a type** of which there was only **one Wing** operating in the entire USAF – **the McDonnell F-101 Voodoo.***

ABOVE: The problem — Gil Leimbach's F-84F after having sailed through the arresting barrier at Shepherds Grove in March 1955. The barriers at Bentwaters and "The Grove" both proved inadequate, a situation that led to... *Gil Leimbach via author*

pilots and ground support to re-equip the 81st.

Before the arrival of the new aircraft there were other developments for the 81st. On May 8, 1958, the 92nd FBS moved to Bentwaters, heralding the unit's arrival with a 28-aircraft flypast. On July 8, 1958, the 81st was passed control of RAF Woodbridge in Suffolk from the 20th FBW. The previous day the 81st had been redesignated as the 81st Tactical Fighter Wing.

BELOW: In July 1958 the 81st FBW was redesignated the 81st Tactical Fighter Wing in preparation for deliveries of its new mount, the McDonnell F-101 Voodoo. This example, 56-0027 of the 81st TFW, was one of those that started replacing the F-84Fs in late 1958. *Alan Johnson via author*

By way of an introduction to the Voodoo, on July 28, 1958, Maj John "J.J." Burns led four F-101Cs of the 522nd Tactical Fighter Squadron (TFS) to Europe, calling at Liège in Belgium, Bentwaters, Soesterberg in The Netherlands and Nouasseur in Morocco.

Special weapons training remained relentless. Regular *Cold Wind* exercises were introduced to test the Wing's capabilities at performing atomic strikes. Missions were planned to hit friendly targets the same distance from base as those of the potential enemy. Detachments to North Africa continued. Lieutenant Charles Taylor was sent to Iran to train Iranian pilots on the Thunderstreak. First Lieutenants Thomas Adams and Paul Baker were detached to Pakistan as members of a special "aggressor" squadron for Pakistan Air Force exercises. The 78th FBS detached eight aircraft, accompanied by a Lockheed C-130, to Sola-Stavanger in Norway for Exercise *Full Play* in July 1958. In December the newly-redesignated 78th TFS moved in to Woodbridge.

THUNDERSTREAK TO VOODOO

In July 1958 the F-101 Mobile Training Detachment was established at Bentwaters, a simulator arriving from Bergstrom AFB, near Austin, Texas, home of the 27th Tactical Fighter Wing (TFW), at the same time. Pilots of the 81st TFW were detached regularly to the Texas base for training on the Voodoo during 1958. By December some 40 pilots had returned to the UK and the 81st had 48 F-101s on strength, as well as 25 F-84Fs. As the new aircraft arrived, so the Thunderstreaks were sent to Leeuwarden in Holland for subsequent use by the West German Air Force. The first to go were 52-6824 and 52-6792. Throughout the year more and more filtered away.

It required considerable skill and

> *Regular **Cold Wind** exercises were introduced to **test** the Wing's **capabilities** at performing **atomic strikes.***

dedication for the squadrons to remain combat-ready with the F-84F while simultaneously getting to grips with a new type. In July 1958 Operation *Blast Off* required a number of aircraft and crews to be maintained on alert around the clock, ready to take off at a moment's notice to strike key targets. During the 1958 Middle East crisis, centred on Lebanon the number of crews on *Blast Off* was increased.

It was during the latter part of 1958, when conversion to the Voodoo was well under way, that an F-84F of the 92nd TFS "inadvertently" violated East Germany's air defence zone. This navigational error resulted in an order going out from 81st headquarters that no aircraft must proceed across the West German border without first receiving positive radar identification. This ruling was rescinded at the end of the year as it proved a handicap to realism in operational flying training because of the necessity of turning round at the border.

By the end of 1958 all F-84Fs of the 81st TFW had departed for service with the air arms of Nato allies or the Air National Guard back home in the USA. The Thunderstreak had served for a comparatively short three years as a front-line fighter-bomber. Today, at a time when we measure the service life of combat aircraft in decades rather than years, it is easy to view the F-84F as a failure. It had a difficult gestation and initially an equally difficult Service career. It is highly probable that the pilots of the 81st TFW did not miss it one bit. Nevertheless, the memories of its successes, at Wheelus and Nellis in particular, have provided it with some degree of respectability as a competent strike aircraft. •

HEATH ROBINSON, SUPER HOGS & "THE THING"...

One of the "innovations" at both RAF Bentwaters and Shepherds Grove was the installation of an arresting barrier. The F-84F, often referred to as the "Super Hog", took up a lot of runway normally — but, in the event of an emergency occurring during landing, the type was guaranteed to run off the runway. In order to save lives and aeroplanes, arresting barriers were installed. Both were less than successful initially. On March 16, 1955, Gil Leimbach's F-84 suffered hydraulic failure at Shepherds Grove. He remembers: "On my second check flight I had hydraulic failure after take-off. I couldn't get my undercarriage up. I decided that I would stay in the pattern and shoot GCAs [ground-controlled approaches] until my fuel got burned down. As soon as I turned downwind, however, I had fluctuation in my controls and decided to land ASAP. We had a brand-new contraption called an arresting barrier. This consisted of anchor chains from a destroyer, which were hooked to a barrier that looked like a tennis-court net strung across the very end of the runway. The idea was to engage the webbing. This raised the 1in [2·5cm]-thick cable which flipped up and engaged the main undercarriage struts. Just before touching down I stopcocked the engine. I found that for a while I was the world's fastest tricycle. I hit the barrier in the middle as advertised but the cable hit the area 4ft [1·2m] in front of my undercarriage and bounced down. It did partly connect with my starboard strut and I thought I was going to flip over, at 100 m.p.h. [160km/h]. The aircraft found the ditch at the end and came to a halt. A rough ride but no bruises."

Gil's experience was published in the local Bury Free Press under the headline Heath-Robinson Rope Trick Saved Pilot's Life. It was evident that the barrier had malfunctioned, though, so steps were taken to find and rectify the problems. The 91st's Lt Don Mikler recalls: "We had had a few 'Hogs' with control problems going right through the barrier because it did not work properly. One day a second lieutenant from the civil engineering squadron [William H. Fleming] was waiting to cross the runway in his car. A red light held him for a while. He got bored and didn't wait for the green light and crossed the runway. Word got back to Colonel Ivan McElroy, the wing commander, and he invited the lieutenant to his office, and assigned him the onerous task of correcting the malfunctioning barrier.

"The lieutenant was a nice guy; we were drinking buddies. He rounded up an undercarriage off a wrecked Hog and attached it to a steel frame, so it was the same shape as a Hog. He then rigged it on the front of a Six-By truck. He put pierced-steel planking [PSP] in the truck bed for more weight. The truck performed poorly and he couldn't get it up to more than 60 m.p.h. [95 km/h] or so.

"I suggested he put some JATO [jet-assisted take-off] bottles on the Six-By. We also decided a few retro-bottles on the front might be appropriate. He got it all done as suggested. Nobody knew about it except a few of us second lieutenants. So he got it ready and one day drove out to the end of the runway. He had a jet helmet on and a flying suit. The convertible-like canvas top was down and the windshield was folded down and he was out in the breeze. He had installed a pitot tube on the rig and had an airspeed indicator on the hood in front of the steering wheel. It looked completely ridiculous. Somehow about 500 spectators had gathered around the field to observe a test of the truck and barrier. He had cameras set up and the whole shooting match was recorded on film. So at the appropriate time he took to the runway and headed for the barrier as fast as that Six-By would go; he then fired the JATO bottles and proceeded rapidly down the runway and through the barrier, at about 90–100kt. The barrier failed to engage the rig so he had to fire the retros and finally came to a stop in the over-run in a huge cloud of JATO smoke, with the crowd doubled over in laughter and applause."

Although this first firing of "The Thing", as it had been christened, was not a total success, three subsequent tests did ascertain where the problems lay. In the third test the lifter straps were raised by 39in (99cm). The Thing entered the barrier at about 85 m.p.h. (137km/h) and was stopped in approximately 140yd (128m) without the use of the retro-rockets. In the final test The Thing was loaded to 20,000lb (9,000kg) to simulate an F-84F with two 230 US gal (870lit) droptanks. It entered the barrier at 105 m.p.h. (169km/h) and was successfully brought to rest in 200yd (182m).

The final proof came when the pilot of F-84F 57-6716 called an emergency on approach to Bentwaters as he was low on fuel. He asked for the barrier to be deployed. The Hog, with a landing weight of 18,000lb (8,165kg), entered the barrier at a speed of 161 m.p.h. (260 km/h). The aircraft came to a stop 600ft (190m) down the runway. There was no fire and no injury. Subsequently there were several successful barrier engagements which saved lives and valuable aircraft.

ABOVE: ..."The Thing" — a Six-By truck fitted with a steel frame and an F-84F undercarriage to simulate the type's track. Six jet-assisted take-off (JATO) bottles were fitted to the contraption to give it the required grunt.
USAF via author

Plan H: America's Unbuilt Spyplanes

Part One: The British Connection; Randolph Rae and the REX hydrogen-engine projects

Kelly Johnson's famous U-2 and SR-71 spyplanes represented the apex of the USA's ability to spy on its Cold War enemies using aircraft that could operate well beyond the reach of Soviet defences. Dr DAVID BAKER introduces a series on America's unbuilt spyplane projects with the story of Randolph Rae, the British engineer whose ideas on hydrogen-powered aircraft were a major influence on the legendary Lockheed designer.

ABOVE: One of the most prolific and innovative aircraft designers in history, Clarence "Kelly" Johnson joined Lockheed in 1933 as a tool designer, and went on to design numerous aircraft for the company. *via author*

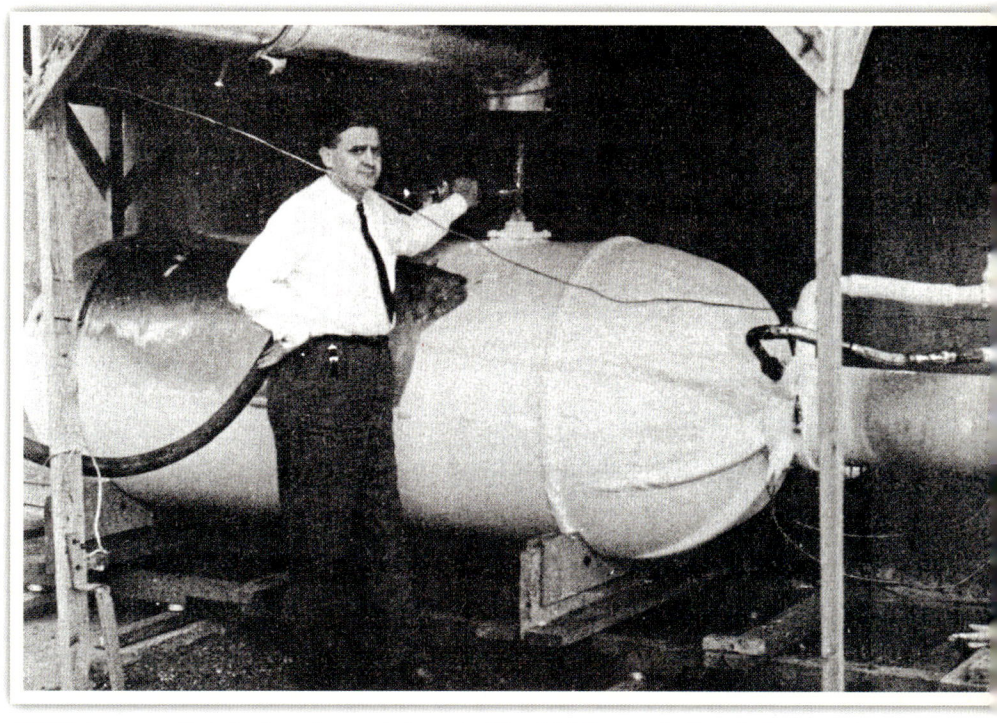

ABOVE: A poor-quality but extremely rare photograph of Randolph Rae conducting a hydrogen tank test in 1955. Although the theory of using hydrogen to power aircraft is sound, the relatively inefficient method of producing it with current technology has made it expensive in comparison to fossil fuels — a major obstacle to its adoption. *via author*

During the first half of the 1950s the American aircraft industry was tasked with a wide range of challenging possibilities. Many of these emerged from requirements predicated on the deepening Cold War with the Soviet Union; some because new information about high-speed flight and exotic chemistry promised unprecedented performance. It was to be a combination of both of these that gave rise to one of the more fantastic of these possibilities, when research began into a high-altitude supersonic reconnaissance aircraft propelled by hydrogen-fuelled engines.

The possibility of using hydrogen technology grew from an unsolicited proposal by famed aircraft designer Clarence "Kelly" Johnson early in January 1956. Johnson offered to build a successor to his subsonic Lockheed U-2 spyplane, development of which had begun almost three years earlier. It would be several years before the U-2 became operational but Johnson was already looking to the time when it would become prey to increasingly sophisticated Russian air defences.

Johnson had become familiar with hydrogen as a fuel when he was involved in developing design studies for another project a couple of years earlier; one which opened the possibility of a completely new way of powering high-speed, high-altitude aircraft. The idea had come from a very unlikely source.

THE BRITISH ARE COMING...

On March 24, 1954, British designer and engineer Randolph Samuel Rae turned up at the security office of the USAF's Wright Air Development Center (WADC) at Wright Field, Ohio, briefcase under arm, with an appointment to see key personnel in the Development Projects office. He had a proposal that had already garnered some attention from the USAF, and his visit to Wright Field was at the behest of Col Donald H. Heaton, who was certain that Rae had an ingenious solution to a persistent problem.

Born on Boxing Day, 1914, Rae was one of those very British boffins without a sense of importance for his own genius, but passionate about the possibilities of his inventions. Schooled in Switzerland, Rae had focused on marine science, working for four research

ABOVE: Harold Elstner Talbott served as the US Secretary of the Air Force from February 1953 until August 1955, and played an important role in expanding the mandate of the USAF during the Cold War. *via author*

LEFT: A classic Cold War image of American military planners devising ways of obtaining up-to-the-minute intelligence on Soviet strength. *via author's Collection*

and development groups at the Admiralty between 1939 and 1948, and then with the Applied Physics Laboratory of Johns Hopkins University in the USA.

It was at the last-named that he focused on aerodynamics and ramjet engines before taking on project development of a new guided-missile system. While wrestling with the knotty problems associated with gyroscopes and mechanical feedback systems, Rae started thinking about possible solutions to the missile's speed/altitude dilemma. The cruise-type missile was to be powered by a ramjet engine. The jet engine is efficient at relatively slow speeds but limited in altitude by reduced atmospheric pressure. Conventional rocket engines are very efficient at high-speed flight, but inefficient at slow speeds. In wrestling with these problems he was attracted to the idea of subsonic flight at very high altitude, and devised a way to get around the problem of reduced air density: provide very large propellers driven by a small rocket motor operating as a gas turbine. Rae calculated that by using hydrogen and oxygen as propellants for the turbine he could provide propulsion for an aircraft operating much higher than ever considered practical for an air-breathing engine, be it reciprocal or reaction-powered. Both fuel and oxidiser would be carried integral to the airframe, to eliminate the need for the aircraft to take in oxygen as it flew.

But this was not the kind of work encouraged at the Laboratory. Captivated by the possibilities, in the summer of 1953 Rae left Johns Hopkins to develop this idea, teaming up with his friend Thomas Summers of the Summers Gyroscope Company, a manufacturer of gyroscopes and guidance systems, which could provide financing and legitimacy. In mid-December Rae recruited Homer J. Wood, late of the Garrett Corporation, with which he had been working on gas turbines. ▶

By early March 1954 Rae had visited the USAF's Air Research & Development Command (ARDC) at its headquarters in Baltimore, Maryland, to explain his idea to Donald Heaton, chief of the aeronautics and propulsion division, and to Lt-Col Langdon F. Ayers, who ran the propulsion branch. Established in 1950, the ARDC was the USAF's centre for research and development, set up to balance short-term operational needs with long-term advanced weapons development. It was here that Rae's ideas found a receptive audience and from where he was directed to the WADC for the meeting on March 24, 1954.

Under normal peacetime conditions the procedures for getting new inventions reviewed would have been laborious and daunting. Money was always important for conducting preliminary tests, and a company to back the idea was vital. The government did not like lone inventors, who were unexposed to the discipline of corporate bureaucracy. Rae had the latter securely under his belt and could confidently market his idea, all credentials at hand. In ordinary times there would still have been resistance to boldly innovative or even radical new technologies. But these were not ordinary times. This was an age of unprecedented military expansion.

A CALL TO ARMS

In 1944 American military aircraft production peaked at 96,318 airframes, declining to 49,761 the following year. Post-war demobilisation had cut the annual production rate to 2,500 airframes by 1948, but increased international tension was responsible for raising that to 5,000 in 1951 and to almost 9,000 by 1953. A year later, in the month that Rae met with Col Heaton, Secretary of the Air Force Harold E. Talbott ordered full-scale development of America's first intercontinental ballistic missile (ICBM), the Convair SM-65 Atlas, and followed this with approval for its back-up, the Martin SM-68A Titan.

> *Rae met with Col Heaton, Secretary of the Air Force Harold E. Talbott **ordered full-scale development** of America's first **intercontinental ballistic missile (ICBM)**, the **Convair SM-65 Atlas.***

The American defence budget was increasing at an unprecedented rate, from just over 30 per cent of government spending in 1950 to nearly 70 per cent by 1954. The entire American economy was now based around the defence industry and there was money to spend on exotic and even highly improbable concepts. The root of this surge lay in global tensions between competing ideological systems – but the military was receptive to new technologies for a very surprising reason.

Although World War Two had clearly been won by overwhelming manpower and unprecedented levels of munitions production, the myth arose quickly in the USA that it would be quality of weapons that would decide the outcome of the next global conflict, despite the clear reasons why the Allies had defeated Nazi Germany and Imperial Japan. But the fact that this myth became entrenched opened doors ordinarily closed to new ideas and innovative technology; it had forged a unique alliance between scientists and the military, and it was to the former that the latter turned when pressure once again forced a new arms race, which is why Randolph Rae was able to obtain his ticket into the WADC.

The WADC had been set up by the ARDC in early 1951 as a facility where new weapon systems, airborne and ground elements and new materials could be developed. It was one of ten such facilities under the ægis of the ARDC, but it was exactly the place where Rae wanted to be to present his radical idea. On that cold March morning in 1954, he was but one of many who would be processed through the security gate to dozens of offices where USAF officials would sift the many ideas coming through. And the USAF had the money to follow through on them. The budget for USAF research and development had grown from $62·3m in 1950 to $460·5m in 1953.

Wright Field was vast and full of "No Entry" doors that required access keys. But for the 39-year-old British engineer it held no fears, only opportunities. Rae laid out a set of documents on a long table facing a group of specialists, all of whom received a brochure dated February 1954, each with the title *REX-I: A New Aircraft System* neatly typed on the cover above the name of its author, "R.S. Rae, Summers Gyroscopes".

AUDITIONING THE CONCEPT

The real innovation in Rae's proposal was for the hydrogen/oxygen gas-turbine engine which would drive a propeller-powered aircraft, but the brochure contained details not only of the unique method of propulsion but also of the airframe itself. Rae proposed a high-lift airframe with low wing loading, a maximum take-off weight of 72,000lb (32,660kg) and wing area of 4,671·5ft^2 (434m^2). Rae calculated that, powered by a 2,400 h.p. engine, the REX-I would have a range of 6,215 miles (10,000km) and a ceiling of 85,300ft (26,000m). At that altitude, cruising speed would be 400–500 m.p.h. (640–800km/hr).

LEFT: A massive escalation in American military spending in the mid-1950s heralded a new age of intercontinental ballistic missiles (ICBMs). The Atlas was the USA's first ICBM, and first flew in June 1957. *via author*

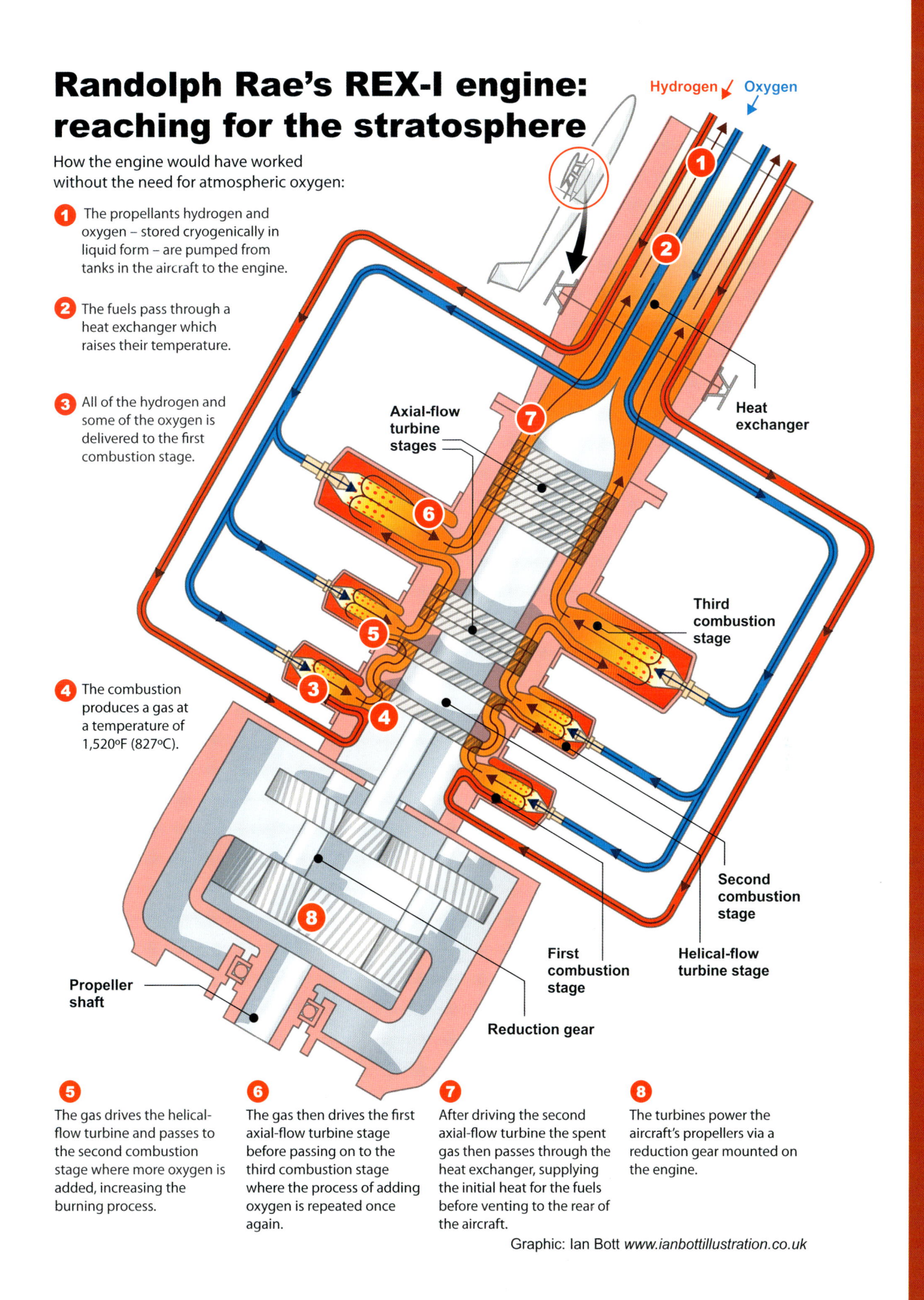

Randolph Rae's REX-I engine: reaching for the stratosphere

How the engine would have worked without the need for atmospheric oxygen:

1 The propellants hydrogen and oxygen – stored cryogenically in liquid form – are pumped from tanks in the aircraft to the engine.

2 The fuels pass through a heat exchanger which raises their temperature.

3 All of the hydrogen and some of the oxygen is delivered to the first combustion stage.

4 The combustion produces a gas at a temperature of 1,520°F (827°C).

Hydrogen   Oxygen

Axial-flow turbine stages

Heat exchanger

Third combustion stage

Second combustion stage

First combustion stage

Helical-flow turbine stage

Reduction gear

Propeller shaft

5 The gas drives the helical-flow turbine and passes to the second combustion stage where more oxygen is added, increasing the burning process.

6 The gas then drives the first axial-flow turbine stage before passing on to the third combustion stage where the process of adding oxygen is repeated once again.

7 After driving the second axial-flow turbine the spent gas then passes through the heat exchanger, supplying the initial heat for the fuels before venting to the rear of the aircraft.

8 The turbines power the aircraft's propellers via a reduction gear mounted on the engine.

Graphic: Ian Bott www.ianbottillustration.co.uk

AVIATION CLASSICS: AMERICAN COLD WAR STORIES   049

REX-I AIRFRAME DATA

The figures below are all speculative and are taken from the brochure REX-I: A New Aircraft System by Randolph S. Rae, Summers Gyroscope Co, February 1954

Dimensions		
Wing area	4,671ft²	(434m²)

Weights		
Empty	36,000lb	(16,330kg)
Max take-off	72,000lb	(32,660kg)

Performance		
Cruise speed	400–500 m.p.h.	(640–800km/h)
Take-off speed	70 m.p.h.	(113km/h)
Service ceiling	85,300ft	(26,000m)
Normal range	6,215 miles	(10,000km)*

* When empty the REX-I would be able to glide an additional 1,000km

Faced by a circumspect group of listeners, Rae solemnly and modestly went through what he considered a truly innovative way to achieve flight at very high altitude. A height so great that the amount of oxygen ingested by a conventional jet engine ran out of pressure before the high-lift wing ran out of molecular atmosphere within which to keep the aircraft stable. It was the engine that gripped the specialists at Wright Field and they listened as Rae described how it would work.

The compact engine itself was designed around a three-stage turbine on a common shaft, with a small combustion chamber attached ahead of each stage. Separate liquid-hydrogen and oxygen tanks provided pump-driven propellants, with all the hydrogen and some of the oxygen being delivered to the first-stage combustion chamber. This produced a gas with a temperature of 1,520°F (827°C), which was about the highest that could be tolerated by the turbine materials of the day. The gases were then passed to the second combustion chamber where additional oxygen was added, increasing the burning process with those products delivered to the second stage. The third and final stage was similarly re-heated with injected oxygen.

After emerging from the stage-three turbine the spent gas would pass to a heat exchanger with an initial pressure of 69·7 atm (1,024lb/in²) to heat the cryogenic propellants from the tanks for delivery to the first stage, the spent products then being vented overboard. Rae had selected hydrogen for its high specific heat, low combustion temperature and high energy efficiency. Calculating potential from a four-stage turbine, Rae believed this engine would deliver a propellant consumption of 1lb/h.p./hr (0·61kg/kW/hr) and it was this potential from a compact, simple design that interested the specialists at Wright Field.

The brighter scientists of the early 1950s already knew the advantages of hydrogen as a fuel. Boeing's J.M. Wickham calculated that the range of a hydrogen-fuelled aircraft would be 30 per cent greater than one powered by hydrocarbons. Others had designed hydrogen-powered turbo-rockets using principles acquired from German work on axial-flow compressors driven by decomposed hydrogen peroxide (producing steam). In 1946, William C. House described a turbo-rocket where bi-propellant rockets were placed aft of the compressor and upstream of the turbine for accelerated flow into the burning stage.

Rae's ideas were of moderate interest at Wright Field but of greater significance higher up the chain. In August 1954 Col Paul Nay at the ARDC evaluated the concept and found in it a means of satisfying the accelerating urgency for a very-high-altitude reconnaissance aircraft. Kelly Johnson had been touting his CL-282 spyplane concept around Washington DC, but had received little support from the USAF, if only because its proposed General Electric J73-GE-3 turbojet engine, untried and untested, was considered inadequate at high altitude.

Johnson had delivered a package of his CL-282 materials to John Seaberg, assistant chief of the New Developments Office at Wright Field, on May 18, 1954, but despite his stellar reputation built on his development of numerous innovative aircraft, the proposal was rejected. Looking elsewhere for a buyer, Johnson visited the Central Intelligence Agency (CIA) and Dr Joe Charyk, who was tasked by CIA Director Allen Dulles with finding an asset capable of conducting clandestine photo-reconnaissance of the Soviet Union to determine whether or not it was engaged in a major missile development, test and production programme.

The last few months of 1954 were to see rapid approval for the CIA to develop what was code-named *Aquatone*, headed by Richard Bissell and ultimately known as the Lockheed U-2. Johnson was told to redesign the CL-282 with the more promising Pratt & Whitney J57-P-37 engine, a project approved and funded by authorisation of President Eisenhower, to be operated by the CIA but with the USAF expected to acquire some examples in due course. A full cover story was set up assigning responsibility to the National Advisory Committee for Aeronautics (NACA), giving the project recognition as a "scientific tool for atmospheric research".

While the CIA was acquiring its very own spyplane, the USAF was busy planning for a much more ambitious system. On November 27, 1954, the ARDC capitalised on a three-year study from the RAND Corporation and approved the development of a military reconnaissance satellite, which it explained would be for "cold-war politico-psychological advantage". This would be developed as

> *Faced by a circumspect group of listeners, **Rae** solemnly and modestly went through what he **considered** a truly **innovative way** to achieve flight at very **high altitude.***

RAE'S PROPOSALS

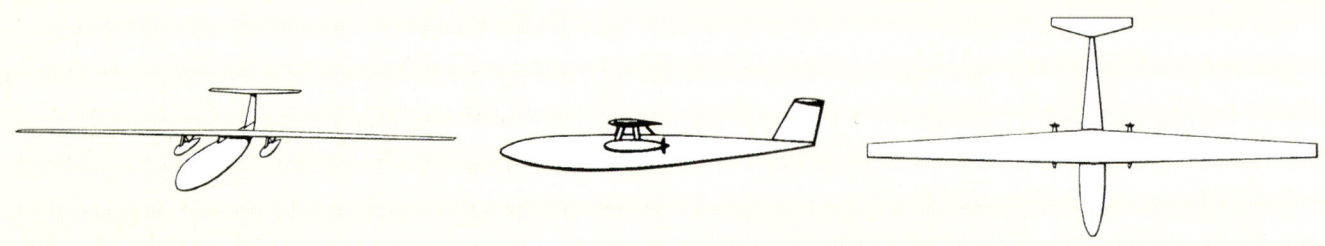

ABOVE: Rae's proposals included simplified drawings of the airframe into which he hoped to fit his hydrogen engine. The aircraft fed directly into the USAF's requirement for a very-high-altitude reconnaissance platform in the wake of the creation of the "bomber gap" myth, in which the Soviets skilfully misled American military intelligence analysts into wildly overestimating the number of nuclear bombers Russia had on strength. Hard facts were needed — and fast. *via author*

Weapon System WS-117L, codenamed *Corona* and publicly known as the *Discoverer* series of "scientific research" satellites when it emerged in 1959. But, after eight years of clandestine overflights of the Soviet Union using converted World War Two bombers, the USAF still sought its own dedicated spyplane. It was for this duty that Randolph Rae's REX-I showed promise, and the men in blue wanted to move in on the high-altitude reconnaissance game.

The sticking point was credibility; the USAF needed to know there was muscle behind the paperwork. Rae and Summers sounded out Garrett, which discreetly vouched for the REX-I team with the USAF before moving to acquire the engine, lending the project greater credibility.

A SIDEWAYS SHIFT

Part of the price Rae and Summers paid for selling out to Garrett was the marginalisation of the latter company by the ARDC, which thought it too inexperienced to integrate the many systems necessary to make the project work. Usual practice was for the USAF to let a prime contract for the airframe to an aircraft manufacturer and a separate contract for the engine. But Rae, Summers and Garrett wanted the whole package – and that had never been made to work.

Throughout 1955 negotiations and revised concepts staggered along, while the powerplant laboratory at Wright Field undertook tests on hydrogen and a wide range of other propellants. Colonel Norman P. Appold ran the engine laboratory at Wright Field and was well acquainted with Rae's REX-I concept. Kelly Johnson was having serious problems with the low-volatility brand of JP-4 fuel used to run the J57 in the U-2. At high altitude, elements of the fuel boiled away out of the vents, depleting the load and reducing range. Appold was appointed to solve the problem. During their close working relationship on the fuel boil-off problem, Appold told Johnson about REX-I. Lockheed had been contracted to perform airframe analysis for the turbo-rocket engine and was already familiar with its unique qualities.

The writing was on the wall. Frustrated at not being able to persuade the USAF to let him build the entire aircraft, Rae proposed REX-II, a variant in which the hydrogen gas from the turbines was burned in the air behind the efflux, and a REX-III which was completely different again. In this, heated hydrogen alone was used to power the turbines with the hydrogen burning with air to provide the power for the initial function.

By the end of 1955 the project was outgrowing the ideas of the unassuming Randolph Rae, who dreamed of revolutionising high-altitude flight. In addition, the requirement for a USAF successor to the CIA's U-2 had outgrown the capabilities of Rae's REX engines. Talk was turning to a supersonic spyplane with extraordinary capabilities; and it was with this idea that Kelly Johnson turned up in January 1956 with his unsolicited proposal for a hydrogen-burning aircraft, far beyond anything Rae could imagine – but inspired by the work of the quiet little Englishman. ●

THE EVOLUTION OF RANDOLPH RAE'S HYDROGEN-ENGINE PROJECTS

The original REX-I concept was for Rae's hydrogen expansion engine to drive a propeller shaft, but he quickly devised a modified system in which it was placed at the heart of a pure reaction powerplant. Atmospheric air would be admitted to the unit via an intake and compressed by a two-stage compressor, which was driven by a turbine within the hydrogen expansion engine. This would be developed even further with the addition of an afterburning system in the REX-II and REX-III variants.

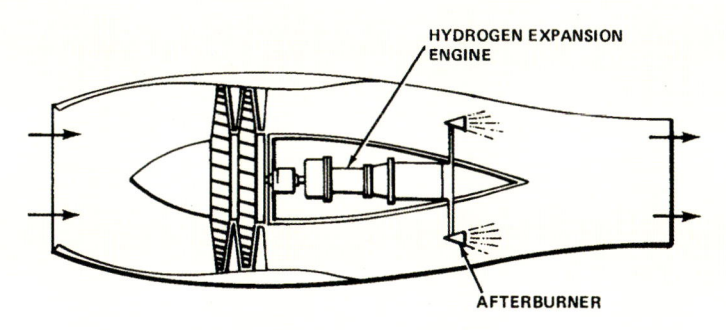

ABOVE: This is the revised REX-I adapted for jet propulsion rather than driving a large-diameter propeller. The system incorporates a two-stage compressor, with the compressed atmospheric air expanding via the exhaust nozzle to provide propulsive thrust.

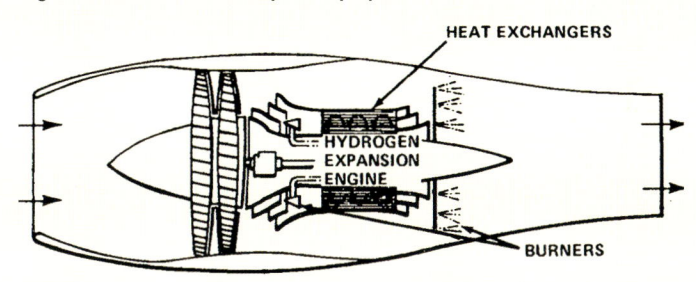

ABOVE: With additional fuel injected into the exhaust efflux, the REX-II system incorporated subtle modifications that leaned more towards already-extant research into afterburning on conventional jet engines.

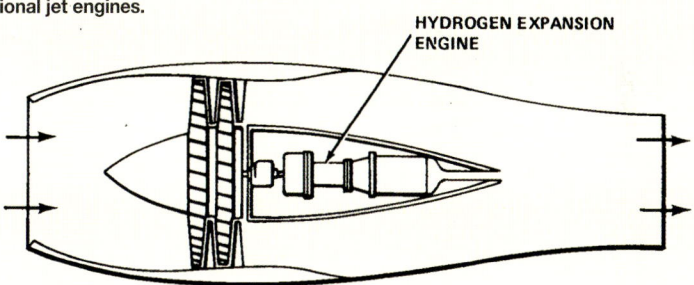

ABOVE: In Rae's REX-III system, the heat from hydrogen preheated from burning with air in the heat exchangers is transferred to hydrogen fed to the combustion chambers and drives turbines, the exhausted products of which are added to the jet flow to augment thrust.

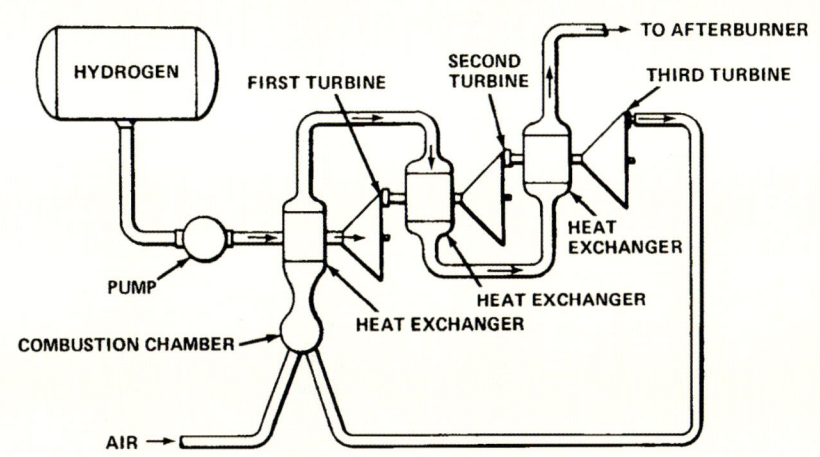

ABOVE: This diagram outlines the principles of operation of Rae's final iteration of the REX-III, which incorporated a much more sophisticated and more efficient arrangement than his earlier REX-I configuration. The revised REX-III system avoided the need for a dedicated oxygen supply and used only heated hydrogen to drive the turbines.

America's Unbuilt Spyplanes

Part Two: Fading Suntan – Kelly Johnson's ambitious CL-400 project

In the second part of his series on America's unbuilt Cold War spyplanes Dr DAVID BAKER tells the full story of the missing link between Kelly Johnson's innovative U-2 and the game-changing SR-71 Blackbird — the hydrogen-powered high-altitude Mach 2·5-capable CL-400 Suntan, a classic victim of vaulting ambition and wildly spiralling costs.

Early in January 1956 Clarence "Kelly" Johnson, Lockheed's chief design engineer turned up at the Pentagon with an extraordinary design proposal, one which he hoped would give the USAF a radical new way of obtaining strategic intelligence information. Johnson was there to see Richard E. Horner and Lt-Gen Donald L. Putt, Chief of Staff for Development. Johnson proposed to build a Mach 2·5-capable hydrogen-fuelled photo-reconnaissance aircraft able to fly at an altitude of 99,400ft (30,300m) and with a range of 2,530 miles (4,070km).

It was Johnson's second attempt to get the USAF interested in a dedicated spyplane. Only 18 months earlier he had proposed his high-flying sub-orbital CL-282. It had been rejected by the military but grabbed by the CIA. Under the codename *Aquatone* it would enter service in the first half of 1956 as the U-2. Designated CL-325, Johnson's supersonic hydrogen-fuelled reconnaissance concept was altogether different and within a completely new operational envelope.

The first iteration – the CL-325-1 – had a thin wing with a span of 80ft (24·35m) and a slender fuselage with a length of 153ft (46·7m). With a gross take-off weight of 45,712lb (20,731kg) carrying 14,450lb (6,553kg) of liquid hydrogen in a single fuel tank, it would be powered by two REX-III engines, each with a thrust of 4,500lb and cruise at Mach 2·25. The CL-325-2 differed in having two jettisonable wing-mounted auxiliary fuel tanks, which would reduce both the size and weight of the aircraft by 15 per cent.

A NEW DIRECTION
It was second time around for Johnson, who was determined to get the USAF to adopt his revolutionary new spyplane. His attention to hydrogen as a propellant had been directed by airframe studies on an unusual subsonic hydrogen-fuelled high-altitude aircraft proposed by British design engineer Randolph Rae. That project stalled in late 1955 when, unbeknown to Rae, the USAF had already made up its mind to probe further into hydrogen propulsion, but in a slightly different direction.

On October 21, 1955, the Fuel & Propulsion Panel of the USAF Scientific Advisory Board supported concerted efforts to study the advantages of hydrogen fuels, seeing no major obstacles to its use in aircraft. One decided advantage was its low mass per unit volume and the capacity for high-energy output compared to hydrocarbon fuels. Thus it was that in putting together the defence budget for fiscal year (FY) 1957, the year beginning on July 1, 1956, the USAF approved a request to increase the amount of research and development money for experiments with hydrogen propulsion from $1m to $4·5m.

In November 1955 Wright-Patterson Air Force Base in Ohio issued a requirement for nine hydrogen-fuelled engine systems which would be analysed by Robert P. Carmichael, the same man who had reviewed Randolph Rae's work in May 1954. These studies were sent to nine engine manufacturers and seven airframe builders, which prompted the Garrett Corporation, closely allied with Rae's work, to sue for damages on the grounds that its proprietary rights had been violated. It got nowhere, but stimulated further talk about the new possibilities for hydrogen-powered propulsion.

Kelly Johnson was already aware of Rae's work and quickly became a convert to the possibilities of taking this and its associated technology to a totally new level. Much of the design for his U-2 had been based on the CL-246, ultimately developed into Lockheed's comparatively simple F-104 Starfighter. The CL-325 would be completely different and posit a quantum step forward in aeronautical engineering and propulsion.

A DEDICATED SPYPLANE
Why was it so important to Johnson to push for a Mach 2·5 reconnaissance aircraft with such outstanding capabilities, especially when the USAF had already rejected the much less costly U-2? The answer to that lay in fast-changing philosophies at the Pentagon, driven by a severe bout of pragmatism in the White House and the

perception of a gathering threat from Russia.

Embedded within the sagely and respectable aura of Dwight D. Eisenhower, the presidential mantle hid a multitude of challenging conflicts within the American military. Still only a few years old, the independent USAF had an appetite for new capabilities and, during the second half of the 1950s, secured technological advances unprecedented in peacetime.

Following a period of major budget increases that had characterised the administration of his predecessor, Harry S. Truman, Eisenhower was determined to reduce expenditure, sharpen efficiency and procure a series of innovative breakthroughs that promised to achieve greater supremacy over Soviet threats.

Between 1947 and 1953 the American defence budget had increased from $52·4m to $442m, but under Eisenhower it would gradually reduce to stand at $344m in the final year before the inauguration of John F. Kennedy in January 1961. In those eight years of the Eisenhower administration were forged the war-fighting tools crafted by a new generation of scientists, engineers and managers, the architects of a wizard-war on conventional and traditional ways of managing new weapons systems.

It was into this environment that Kelly Johnson had introduced the U-2 spyplane to provide a major leap forward in intelligence-

ABOVE: Although a full-size airframe was never completed by Lockheed, the CL-400-10, codenamed *Suntan*, was clearly based on Clarence "Kelly" Johnson's F-104 Starfighter design for the same company. The hydrogen-powered Mach 2·5-capable CL-400-10 was more than three times the length of its stablemate, however, and was to be fitted with specially designed Pratt & Whitney Model 304 engines.
Illustration by IAN BOTT and NEIL FRASER

LEFT: At the end of his second term as President of the USA in 1961, Dwight D. Eisenhower warned against the dangers of massive military spending, which had bloomed in the previous decade.

BELOW: Although the Lockheed U-2, based on Kelly Johnson's CL-282 project, was a leap forward in high-altitude reconnaissance technology, initially it was flying at the limits of its performance during early CIA operations. The USAF wanted something with far superior performance — enter Johnson's hydrogen-powered supersonic CL-400. *TAH Archive*

> **Leghorn** pushed for an aircraft capable of flying at an altitude **greater** than **60,000ft (18,300m)**, above the perceived detection range of **Soviet radar defences.**

gathering, tied to new high-resolution camera systems from the Hycon Corporation. Approved in 1954, the U-2 project was part of a subtle transformation in monitoring Soviet activity that underpinned the Eisenhower administration's preference for a new form of clandestine surveillance. For, along with a new era in penetration and aerial reconnaissance, came approval the same year of a highly classified spy-satellite programme, a secret project kept far from the public eye and known only to a select few as *Corona*.

Concurrent with *Corona*, but formally approved only in March 1955, was the much-publicised scientific satellite Vanguard, planned for launch during the International Geophysical Year of 1957–58. *Corona* only emerged under the public name Discoverer after the first civilian satellites had been launched, setting a public precedent for secret military satellites. Before this, under the budget-busting chaos of the Truman years, strategic surveillance had been rather more fluid, with each service using existing assets to undertake clandestine photographic "raids" within Soviet airspace, wielding World War Two cameras aboard adapted wartime aircraft.

With new rocket technology capable of throwing lightweight nuclear weapons across whole continents, there was urgency too in obtaining highly accurate maps of military and industrial targets in Russia and China. Where atomic weapons had at first been regarded as "city-busters", fit only for destroying large urban centres housing an industrial workforce, the new generation of smaller and more powerful nuclear weapons were designed for a more selective range of targets. These included marshalling yards, ports, manufacturing plants, power stations, oil and coal production facilities and a wide range of specifically hardened military targets.

It was common knowledge that Soviet maps of Russia eliminated sensitive places altogether, or displaced them geographically to confuse the country's enemies. For a brief period after the Second World War, the best maps of Russia available to the USA and UK had been liberated from the German *Wehrmacht*, the most recent military force to occupy and produce its own highly accurate maps of that country.

Reliable maps were not only required for land and air operations but also for plotting targets for the new intercontinental ballistic missiles (ICBMs) approved in 1954, entering operational readiness by the end of the 1950s. There had never been a greater need for air intelligence and ground surveillance; and, while the CIA had the U-2, the USAF had an appetite for something much more capable.

THE RACE FOR HEIGHT

It was these imperatives that drove the need for a dedicated high-altitude reconnaissance aircraft. That search had already begun, when Lt-Col Richard S. Leghorn had taken over the Reconnaissance Systems Branch at the Wright Air Development Center in Dayton, Ohio, in April 1951. Leghorn pushed for an aircraft capable of flying at an altitude greater than 60,000ft (18,300m), above the perceived detection range of Soviet radar defences. In the immediate post-war period Soviet Russia had tolerated unannounced intrusions, but from 1950 it became increasingly aggressive, routinely shooting down unauthorised aircraft in Soviet airspace.

Leghorn pressed for engineers from British aircraft manufacturer English Electric to pay a visit to the Glenn L. Martin Company in Cleveland, Ohio, and work with their American counterparts on developing a very-high-altitude version of the Martin B-57, the American version of the British company's Canberra. Leghorn's calculations indicated the aircraft could achieve a maximum altitude of 67,000ft (20,400m) using two Rolls-Royce Avon 109 engines and new wings. However, Leghorn had proceeded without the authority of his boss, Lt-Col Joseph J. Pellegrini, head of Air Research & Development Command (ARDC). Pellegrini took the idea, however, and adapted the modifications to fit an operational version of the B-57, creating the RB-57D.

By stipulating that the RB-57D must satisfy military requirements – so that the aircraft could adopt a standard operational function in times of war rather than be exclusively a super-refined, dedicated photo-reconnaissance asset applicable only to this one role – Pellegrini limited the capabilities of the type. Good as it was, the RB-57D still left a gap for a USAF reconnaissance type of such outstanding performance that it would fly above the maximum capability of Soviet radar.

In reality Western intelligence had seriously underestimated just how far Soviet Russia had come technologically, the latter having already overtaken the USA in radar defence systems by the early 1950s. That the

Americans had fallen behind the Russians was not immediately apparent, but, in underestimating the technical and scientific capabilities of their potential adversary, they had seriously misjudged the operational requirements of a survivable high-altitude reconnaissance aircraft.

In effect, it was a race for height, with the Russians seeking to search out and destroy high-flying aircraft, and the Americans trying to outfly their adversary's air-defence systems. This was a situation only realised fully when Francis Gary Powers was shot down over Russia in a U-2 on May 1, 1960. Just six years earlier the search for a very-high-altitude spyplane had been driven by the need to map the Soviet Union accurately as well as monitor technical, industrial and operational developments across a broad front.

THE HYDROGEN AIRCRAFT

When Kelly Johnson gave his proposal for a Mach 2·5 spyplane to the Pentagon in January 1956, he saw not only a commercial opportunity for his company, but also a new and completely unprecedented means of blending the revitalised hunger for strategic intelligence with the new mood in the White House. With missile programmes and a new conventional Mach 2·2 bomber – the Convair B-58 Hustler – in full-scale development, Johnson's new CL-400 was a completely different solution to the requirement for urgent photographic evidence of Russia's expanding aerospace programme.

In seeking to give the USAF what it wanted, Johnson was aware that Gen Curtis LeMay had rejected the notion of a subsonic spyplane on the basis that it would have strategic rather than tactical value. The CL-400, however, would do both jobs admirably. Unconvinced that the impending availability of satellite photography would answer all requirements – as indeed it would not – Johnson promised to have two hydrogen-fuelled aircraft built and one flying within 18 months. It was optimism tainted with reckless exuberance.

The USAF wanted time to examine the plausibility of Johnson's design and Donald Putt, Chief of Staff for Development, insisted on six months to evaluate the technology. Project officer for this work was to be Col Ralph Nunziato, an experienced photo-reconnaissance specialist and former test pilot, with Norman C. Appold in charge of research at ARDC. Appold managed the Wright-Patterson propulsion laboratory and had run tests on Rae's REX-I engine. He knew about the possibilities of hydrogen as a fuel and approached powerplant manufacturers General Electric and Pratt & Whitney to produce possible engine designs.

Pratt & Whitney (P&W) was selected to produce a working engine and received a contract for this work in April 1956. The company was so confident of success that it opted for a fixed-fee contract rather than argue for a costs-plus arrangement. In the event P&W received $15·3m for the first phase of the work but spent $17·1m, losing money on the work. Lockheed was contracted to build the airframe but prudently opted to negotiate an interim contract that would be renegotiated and repriced at the end of the work. Lockheed designated the precise configuration of the design under contract as the CL-400-10.

Much other work was also needed, such as designing special tanks to hold the fuel, a task assigned to Lt-Col John D. Seaberg at the Wright Air Development Center (WADC), who was also to manage the development of the airframe and its incorporated systems. Seaberg had been assistant head of the Developments Office at Wright-Patterson and had been party to the rejection of Johnson's CL-282 proposal two years before.

Engine development was in the capable hands of Maj Alfred J. Gardner, a former combat pilot and an experienced engineer. The impressive Capt Jay R. Brill would manage the hydrogen supply and logistics side, initially working at Wright-Patterson before moving across to ARDC headquarters by the middle of the year.

FAST TRACK

Known only to a very few, the name *Suntan* was applied to what was, in 1956, one of the most closely held secrets in the Western aerospace world, receiving a classification grading above "Top Secret". Only around 25 people were aware of the full programme spectrum and great efforts were made to maintain secrecy. Through a series of designation and contract-number changes, tracing components and materials through to a single project became almost impossible, several different names and number sequences being used to hide the convergence of several subcontracts into the *Suntan* programme.

RIGHT: Chief of Staff for Development Lt-Gen Donald L. Putt was a major player in the Lockheed *Suntan* project.

BELOW: In total 20 Martin RB-57Ds were built, the first making the variant's maiden flight in November 1955. Incorporating extended and wider-chord wings of 106ft (32m) span and uprated Pratt & Whitney J57 engines of 11,000lb static thrust each, the type entered service in April 1956, but served with the USAF for only five years. *TAH Archive*

Speed of development and assembly was of the essence and, in order to bypass time-consuming bureaucracy, Col Lee W. Fulton was brought in to keep things moving and make the necessary approvals. As head of procurement at ARDC, Fulton was in the perfect position to make this happen, recruiting his deputy, Robert Miedel, to do the paperwork. High above both in the administrative hierarchy, Richard Horner, Assistant Secretary for Research & Development, provided a blanket bypass channel for awarding contracts and waiving the conventional and time-consuming procedures.

Johnson was attentive to the operational requirements of the CL-400-10 as well as the technical details of the aircraft's design. To be held in manageable tanks, the hydrogen would have to be transported and stored as a liquid (LH2). Liquid hydrogen boils at -253°C (-423°F) and has an improved volumetric capacity of 0·07kg/lit, as against 0·03kg/lit for high-pressure gaseous storage. Handbooks at the time asserted that LH2 was a laboratory curiosity with little or no practical application. To test this, Johnson tasked one of his assistants, Ben Rich, with studying the problems of working with liquid hydrogen and the feasibility of fulfilling daily production quotas of 99,000lb (45,000kg), 297,000lb (135,000kg) and 496,100lb (225,000kg).

Rich was a thermodynamics specialist and, with the signing of a contract with the J.H. Pomeroy company on March 16, 1956, set to work on exploring the possibility of achieving any one of these three production levels. Reporting back on October 1, Pomeroy defined a complete liquefaction production plant, with natural gas used for producing gaseous hydrogen and an underground storage facility for liquid hydrogen at cryogenic temperatures. It was on a scale never before envisaged, let alone studied, for any form of fuel. The conclusion reached was that the lowest quota level specified was about the limit for daily production.

There was an urgent need to get to grips with the handling of LH2 and the design criteria for the wide range of pipes, tubes, fittings and equipment needed to handle the cryogenic liquid. Johnson requisitioned an old World War Two bombproof revetment for this work. Known as "Fort Robinson", after the man who ran it during World War Two, it was used to set up a cryostat capable of producing 2·3 US gal (9lit) of liquid hydrogen per hour. For larger quantities the National Bureau of Standards' Cryogenic Laboratory at Boulder, Colorado, could provide up to 757 US gal (2,860lit) a day.

THE AIRFRAME

It is not difficult to look at the three-view drawings of the initial *Suntan* aircraft and see in its slender design the lines of the F-104 Starfighter. With the mid-placed wing showing a low aspect ratio of 2·5:1 (compared to 2·97:1 for the F-104) and T-tail configuration, its pedigree is evident, although with a length of 164ft 9½in (50·2m) and a span of 83ft 9in (25·5m) it was very much bigger.

> The **two** hydrogen-burning engines would be mounted at the **wingtips**, the **cryogenic liquid** fed by insulated delivery lines through the hot wing structure where **temperatures** would reach **163°C (325°F) at Mach 2·2.**

A retractable ventral fin provided stability at supersonic speeds. The CL-400-10 had a fuselage diameter of 10ft (3m), with a single fuselage tank capable of carrying 21,475lb (9,740kg) of LH2.

The two hydrogen-burning engines would be mounted at the wingtips, the cryogenic liquid fed by insulated delivery lines through the hot wing structure where temperatures would reach 163°C (325°F) at Mach 2·2. The engines were considered to be derivatives of existing gas-turbine engines, burning hydrogen rather than hydrocarbon fuels. The technology to do this was considered secondary to more pressing challenges such as handling the super-cold fuel and managing it within the aircraft's systems.

Confidence in Kelly Johnson's ability to meet these challenges was at a peak and his reputation was already legendary. Having responded to the call for an interceptor to outpace the Soviet Union's highly successful MiG-15, Johnson received a contract in early 1953 to produce what became the F-104. Powered by a licence-built version of the Armstrong Siddeley Sapphire axial-flow turbojet, it was the first combat aircraft capable of reaching Mach 2 and beyond. In 1954 Johnson secured the contract to produce the U-2. The close-knit team working on *Suntan* needed no persuading that the hydrogen-burning CL-400 could satisfy the need for a successor to the U-2.

The initial contract for Lockheed to build two prototypes was quickly followed by orders for a further four development aircraft. At inception, Lockheed worked in parallel with P&W, which regarded the project as an opportunity to develop its new J57 engine, which had emerged from the ashes of the XT45 turboprop engine initially proposed for Boeing's XB-52. As the big Boeing bomber's power requirements grew, the XT45 evolved into the J57, the USA's first homegrown 10,000lb-thrust axial-flow turbojet. ▶

BELOW: The epitome of America's bristling projection of global air power during the Cold War, Convair's delta-winged four-engined supersonic B-58 Hustler strategic bomber made its first flight in August 1960. Capable of carrying a nuclear weapon in the centreline pod, the type also saw service in the photo-recce role as the RB-58. *TAH Archive*

The CL-400's P&W Model 304 engine

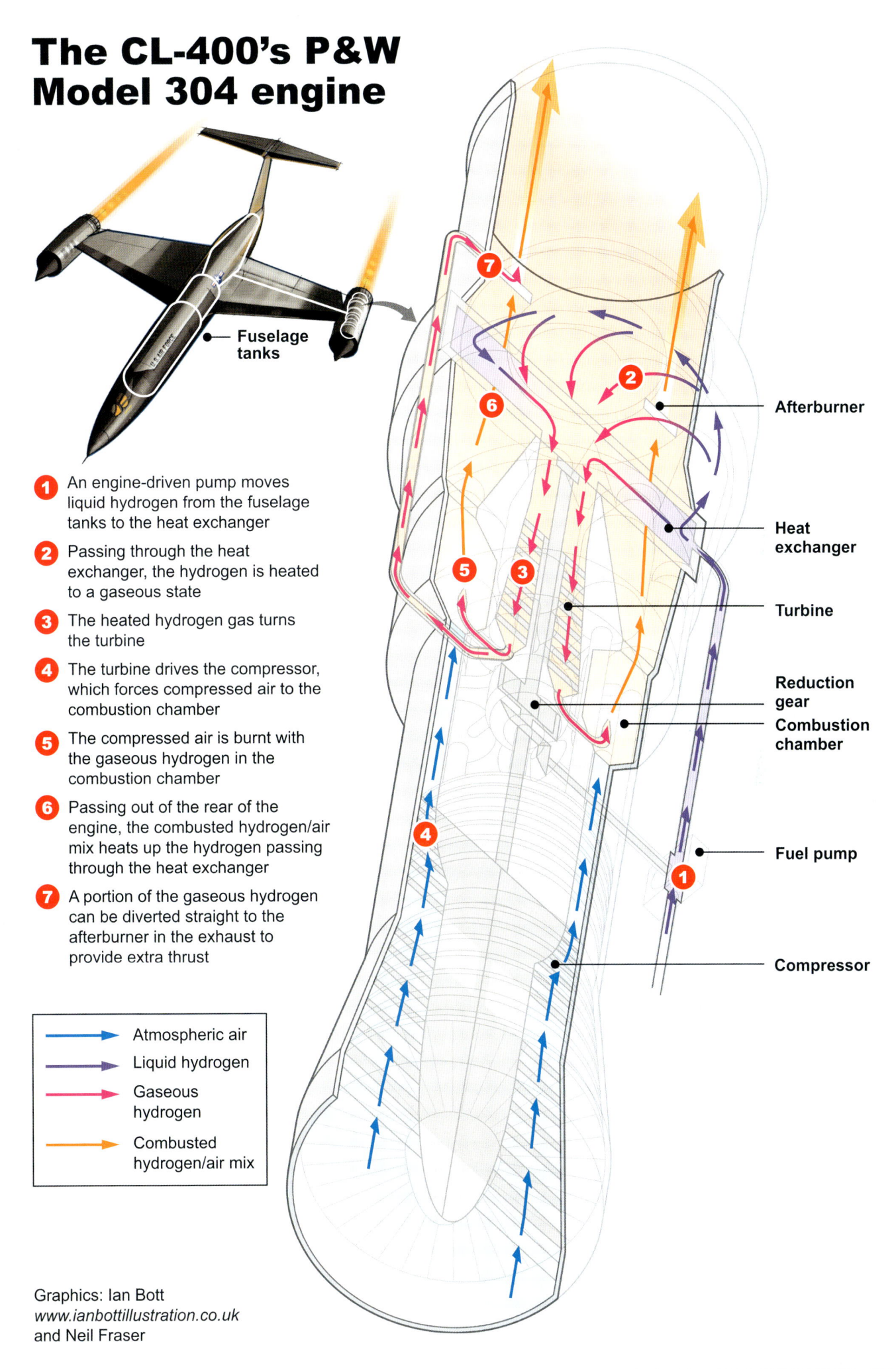

Fuselage tanks

1. An engine-driven pump moves liquid hydrogen from the fuselage tanks to the heat exchanger
2. Passing through the heat exchanger, the hydrogen is heated to a gaseous state
3. The heated hydrogen gas turns the turbine
4. The turbine drives the compressor, which forces compressed air to the combustion chamber
5. The compressed air is burnt with the gaseous hydrogen in the combustion chamber
6. Passing out of the rear of the engine, the combusted hydrogen/air mix heats up the hydrogen passing through the heat exchanger
7. A portion of the gaseous hydrogen can be diverted straight to the afterburner in the exhaust to provide extra thrust

- → Atmospheric air
- → Liquid hydrogen
- → Gaseous hydrogen
- → Combusted hydrogen/air mix

Graphics: Ian Bott
www.ianbottillustration.co.uk
and Neil Fraser

- Afterburner
- Heat exchanger
- Turbine
- Reduction gear
- Combustion chamber
- Fuel pump
- Compressor

AVIATION CLASSICS: AMERICAN COLD WAR STORIES 057

ABOVE: Now more than 65 years since the type's first flight in February 1954, and nearly 15 years after the very last examples were retired by the Italian Air Force, the F-104 still looks every inch the modern cutting-edge jet fighter. This view shows the mid-mounted trapezoidal wing and T-tail which was to be scaled up for the CL-400-10. *TAH Archive*

LEFT: Seen here placed on its back, the Model 304's heat exchanger turned liquid hydrogen into gas, which would be fed forward through the large circular aperture in the middle.

Under the codename *Shamrock*, P&W quickly adapted the J57 to burn hydrogen, the design being finalised in May 1956. With development and component testing proceeding in parallel, trials quickly confirmed the viability of the adaptation. Some changes would have to be made, however, such as a new heat exchanger using air from the compressor to warm the hydrogen to a gaseous state, and an oil-lubricated pump for the liquid hydrogen. Another part of the programme at P&W ensured the availability of a hydrogen liquefier, with equipment installed at its plant at East Hartford in Connecticut producing 500lb (227kg) per day.

A BESPOKE ENGINE

While the J57 ran on hydrogen as well as expected, a completely new purpose-built engine was necessary to maximise the efficiency and power of hydrogen as a fuel. Work on the detailed design of a derivative, the Model 304, began at P&W on April 16, 1956. While the adapted J57 proved that an engine could run on hydrogen, the 304, a designation extracted from a portion of the contract number, would show its full potential. By August the design was finished, based largely on the work of William Sens, a P&W engineer who had worked on the REX engines, and Wesley A. Kuhrt, a research engineer who had been playing around with hydrogen since the age of 13.

In the definitive design for the Model 304, liquid hydrogen was pumped at high pressure through a heat exchanger at the back of the engine to drive a multi-stage turbine, which in turn spun a compressor for the incoming air. A portion of the hydrogen from the turbine was directed to the airstream aft of the fan, the amount burned in this way limited by the need to restrict the temperature of the gases reaching the heat exchanger. The rest of the hydrogen was added to the afterburner behind the heat exchanger, adding to the thrust of the engine.

The development of new technology was vital to the effective operation of the Model 304. The hydrogen heat-exchanger comprised banks of 48mm stainless-steel tubing in an involute arrangement. Each of the 2,240 tube joints was furnace-brazed, about five miles (8km) of tubing being used. The rate of heating the hydrogen was enormous, going from -253°C (-423°F) to 1,226°C (2,240°F) at a transfer rate of 72 million Btu/hr. Nothing even remotely approaching this technology had been demonstrated before.

The turbine unit had 18 stages, the largest being 17·7in (45cm) in diameter, with an operating temperature of nearly 727°C (1,340°F) and a power output of 12,000 h.p. The high-pressure turbine expansion section had 12 stages. Overall, the engine was pioneering many of the engineering challenges which would be faced by those who moved on to develop hydrogen/oxygen rocket motors, and the technology studied in this period was crucial to accelerating that work.

Built at East Hartford, the first engine was completed by August 18, 1957, and was ready for testing to begin at a new facility at West Palm Beach, Florida. The United Aircraft Corporation, P&W's parent company, had been building the sprawling test centre for some time, aware of the need for a new location to test big and powerful jet engines and for dispersing facilities increasingly engaged on expanding defence work. Occupying ten square miles (27km^2), it was ideal for the highly classified *Suntan* engine programme.

Testing of the engine started on September 11, 1957, first with inert nitrogen to prevent damage to bearings, pumps and seals during evaluation, then with gaseous hydrogen and finally with liquid hydrogen. The tests continued for several months, accumulating data with periodic dismantling and reassembly for scrutiny and examination. A second engine, designated 304-2, was complete by late June 1958 and joined the first in tests at West Palm Beach. The second engine had a fifth compressor stage and a lower specific fuel consumption of 0·9kg/Nhr, as against 1·1kg/Nhr on the specification of the 304-1 and an achieved 1·2kg/Nhr on tests.

Meanwhile, a duplicate of the 304-1 was built and tested in runs that accumulated more than 6hr of bench time. In late July 1958 the second engine ran away and collapsed the turbine. Repaired and with a strengthened turbine section, it was returned to the test stand in September and continued to perform well, as another hydrogen engine neared completion. By this time, however, *Suntan* was no more and the engine testing ceased, after more than 25hr of operation and indications of a highly successful solution to a demanding challenge.

ENDGAME

Between early 1956 and mid-1958, the airframe for the CL-400 went through a series of growth spurts brought on by increasing dissatisfaction with the underwhelming

058 AVIATION CLASSICS: AMERICAN COLD WAR STORIES

performance of the paper aircraft. Within six months of starting his work on the airframe, Johnson had become acutely aware of its shortcomings. The calculated performance of the aircraft simply did not match expectations. Paradoxically, there were few technical barriers to achieving a Mach 2+ aircraft capable of flying at great altitude. Theoretically, it was possible to fly hydrogen-fuelled aircraft in the manner envisaged but, practically, it was essentially unworkable.

The USAF began to look hard at *Suntan* during the first half of 1956, with the only people really convinced of its possibilities being the technical teams at ARDC. Curtis LeMay, moving up to the Joint Chiefs board, remained hostile. With increasing pressure on USAF finances and a flatlining defence budget, everything had to count twice – there was simply no room for a speculative project with a single role. It is easy to underestimate the financial factor. In August 1957 Air Force Chief of Staff Gen Thomas D. White had to scale back the North American XB-70 Valkyrie programme for lack of money.

The single most critical aspect of *Suntan* was its limited range, the factor which turned Johnson against the project very soon after he started work on the airframe design. Its founding oracle, he was now its most staunch detractor. But the seeds had been sown and the technical possibilities gathered a momentum of their own. The team of engineers and scientists recruited for the *Suntan* project had fervent belief in the project, as did Seaberg, but when incoming Secretary of the Air Force James H. Douglas Jr visited Johnson in March 1957 he got short shrift. When asked about extending the extremely limited range of the aircraft he was told there was no more to be had. It was impossible to put fuel in the wings, and the fuselage already had the largest hydrogen tank possible.

This, it seemed, sealed the fate of *Suntan*. Johnson knew that he could get no more than a three per cent range extension at most and the Model 304 engine had limited potential for reduced specific fuel consumption – no more than six per cent at most. The CL-400-10 was cancelled; the Massachusetts Institute of Technology (MIT) lost its contract for development of the inertial guidance system, although Lockheed still continued fuel test work. In October 1957 funds fell dramatically, but advocates remained optimistic that by growing the airframe the aircraft could achieve the necessary range for the reconnaissance role. Seaberg managed to get contracts awarded to North American, Convair and Boeing for a fresh look at the concept.

It was during these additional studies that the CL-400 grew in size, with comparative analysis of hydrogen- versus hydrocarbon-fuelled aircraft. It came down to the same thing; hydrogen-fuelled aircraft weighed less on take-off but had shorter range. These additional studies were handed to the USAF Air Council on June 12, 1958, at a meeting chaired by LeMay, who, while deriding the concept, allowed full and frank debate. What the group reviewed was a plethora of increasingly large and more capable aircraft, beginning with the CL-400-11 with engines mounted under the wing at mid-span, through to the CL-400-12 with four engines similarly located but in pairs.

With a length of 296ft 6in (90·4m), the CL-400-13 may be considered the ultimate *Suntan* concept. The aircraft now carried its twin engines close in to the rear underfuselage section and consisted of a slender body with swept delta wings possessing a span of 84ft (25·6m) and an area of 6,500ft^2 (603m^2), mounted at the rear of the fuselage. With a gross take-off weight of 376,000lb (170,550kg) it was more than five times as massive as the original design and now carried a fuel load of 162,850lb (73,870kg). With foreplanes either side of the fuselage nose, it had the appearance of the Mach 3 XB-70 Valkyrie bomber, but it was more than 100ft (30m) longer and carried a bigger wing, albeit fixed and without downwardly-deflecting tips.

With its four engines, the CL-400-14 sought a compromise between size and deliverable engine power, the original diamond-shaped low-aspect-ratio wings giving greater span for the same area. The fuel load had increased to 180,000lb (81,650kg) for a marginally reduced take-off weight. The final option, designated CL-400-15JP, reverted to convention, replacing the Model 304 hydrogen-fuelled engines with P&W J58 engines burning JP fuel under a common enclosure beneath the rear fuselage with a single intake. This option was about two-thirds the size of the CL-400-10 but with more than twice the gross take-off weight.

SUNTAN'S LEGACY
The various options applied to the original concept had produced a range of different capabilities, with cruise speed up to Mach 4. Greater altitude was possible with hydrogen-fuelled aircraft, exceeding the height reached by conventional aircraft by up to 20,000ft (6,100m). One design from Boeing, which appeared optimum among all the possibilities, would have cruised at Mach 2·5 at a height of 100,000ft (30,000m) with a range of 2,500 miles (4,100km).

When the USAF Air Council reviewed the programme in June 1958, it had already been consigned to the scrapheap for two reasons. Although about $100m had been spent on *Suntan*, a further $150m was necessary for

> **Leghorn** pushed for an aircraft capable of flying at an altitude **greater** than **60,000ft (18,300m),** above the perceived detection range of **Soviet radar defences.**

ABOVE: The slender delta planform of the XB-70 Valkyrie, with large canards fitted to the forward fuselage, was similar to that of the CL-400-13. The unusual configuration utilised compression lift, in which the shock wave generated off the nose at supersonic speeds is used as a source of high-pressure air to generate additional lift. *TAH Archive*

the next phase. Above that, however, was another highly classified project that Kelly Johnson had begun work on within weeks of the issuing of the CL-400 contract back in April 1956. In late 1957 U-2 project manager Richard Bissell set up an advisory committee, chaired by Polaroid co-founder Edwin Land, to search for an optimum successor to the U-2.

Reminding the group that the U-2 would be obsolete within two years, Johnson recommended a major leap forward with a high-flying aircraft capable of Mach 3. "I want to come up with an airplane that can rule the skies for a decade or more", he said, and began designing such an aircraft. His rough draft, presented to the committee on July 23, 1958, was for the A-1, the first in a series of designs under the epithet *Archangel*, a follow-on from the first codename for the U-2, *Angel*. By mid-1959 it would mature into the A-12, precursor to the SR-71 Blackbird, and be absorbed into a major programme for the CIA under the codename *Oxcart*.

It was inevitable that with this second strand of activity under way, once again the USAF would be trounced in cutting-edge reconnaissance systems by the CIA, and there would be no purpose to the hydrogen-fuelled *Suntan*. Eventually, as with the U-2, the SR-71 would be operated by the USAF as well – not in the strategic role coveted by the CIA, but for tactical support in conventional conflicts. The work conducted on the *Suntan* programme was a good investment, however, and ultimately benefited the development of hydrogen engines in a very different sector.

On January 29, 1964, NASA launched its fifth *Saturn I* launch vehicle with a live second stage comprising six P&W RL-10 hydrogen-fuelled rocket motors. Less than five years after the issuing of the directive to produce a high-energy motor, the work on *Suntan* paid off, having greatly accelerated development of the RL-10. Had *Suntan* not stimulated a massive production effort increasing hydrogen production to 65,000lb (29,485kg) a day at liquefaction plants in Ohio, California and Florida, the *Saturn* upper stage would not have been possible – the large quantities of liquid hydrogen would not have been available when needed.

In June 1958, when *Suntan* was clearly heading for the dustbin of history, John Seaberg took the idea of hydrogen propulsion and forged a credible base for its most potent application. The same month, the Advanced Research Projects Agency (ARPA) ordered the development of a cryogenic liquid-hydrogen/liquid-oxygen upper stage for the Atlas missile called Centaur, improving its performance so that it could launch a heavy military communications satellite called Advent. The satellite was cancelled and while Centaur became temporarily bogged down in managerial problems, Wernher von Braun's Saturn rocket team applied it to its super-booster.

The RL-10 went on to become the mainstay of the Atlas launch vehicle. Its development stimulated the J-2 engine used in both second and third stages of the *Saturn V* rocket that propelled nine Apollo spacecraft to the vicinity of the Moon. Without these high-energy propellants, the lunar mission would have required much bigger rockets with challenging technology and great cost. Engineers at Pratt & Whitney who developed the Model 304 turbojet engine burning hydrogen applied that work to the RL-10, the elegance of the jet engine forming the fundamental design thesis for the rocket motor.

The turbopump designed for the Model 304 engine was imported to the RL-10 and when rocket engineers tried to adopt the standard practice of using a separate combustion chamber to start the turbopump, Perry Pratt lifted the expander cycle technology directly from the jet and applied it to the rocket. By mid-1959 P&W had performed 230 successful tests on the RL-10 at West Palm Beach, clearing the way for it to take its place as the most important contribution to the early rocket programmes, propelling the USA far ahead of its competitors.

From the outstanding work on hydrogen-fuelled jet engines, which began with a British engineer in the early 1950s, the USA built a lead over the rest of the world. And while *Suntan*, as originally conceived, died in 1958 with all concerned getting their wings burnt, the search for a truly outstanding jet-powered reconnaissance aircraft was to lead to one of the most bizarre concepts of all time – a wonder called *Fish*. •

ABOVE: Resembling a spaceship from the pages of the wildest contemporary science-fiction, the Lockheed A-12 high-speed high-altitude reconnaissance aircraft was developed from the *Archangel* series of designs, the first step on the road to the world-beating SR-71 Blackbird. *TAH Archive*

BELOW: What might have been — this impression by IAN BOTT and NEIL FRASER imagines USAF and Lockheed groundcrew taking advantage of the cool pre-dawn desert air to prepare the huge but sleek CL-400-10 for another test flight from Area 51 in the early 1960s. The aircraft was nearly 165ft (50m) long with a wingspan of 83ft 9in (25·5m). *Ian Bott and Neil Fraser*

Broken Arrow: Tico's south-east Asian secret

December 1965: the USS *Ticonderoga* steams away from the coast of Vietnam for Japan after a period of operations in support of the escalating conflict in South-east Asia. A routine arming exercise goes terribly wrong, leaving a pilot dead and an A-4E Skyhawk with a live thermonuclear weapon at the bottom of the Philippine Sea. JIM WINCHESTER investigates a trail of secrets and lies at sea.

During the height of the Cold War, when both American and Soviet forces were at states of constant high nuclear readiness, accidents involving atomic weapons were more common than generally supposed, most involving USAF Strategic Air Command's heavy bombers. The US Navy also suffered "Broken Arrows" – the code for accidental loss or destruction of a nuclear weapon – in the 1960s, but mostly in submarine accidents.

Only one incident involved the loss of a complete US Navy air-launched weapon. How it came about is a story involving secret international agreements, possible sabotage, cover-ups at many levels, outright lies and even the suggestion of murder.

In 1965 American involvement in Vietnam had not yet peaked. The modernised *Essex*-class attack carrier USS *Ticonderoga* (CVA-14) had launched the first strikes against North Vietnam in the Tonkin Gulf Incident of August 1964. Returning to Alameda, California, on December 15 the same year the *"Tico"* underwent a period of overhaul until June 1965 and conducted air wing exercises before departing San Diego for Pearl Harbor, Hawaii, on September 28. There the carrier passed its Operational Readiness Inspection (ORI), the final hurdle before venturing on a WestPac, or western Pacific cruise, which from 1964 to 1972 inevitably meant action over Vietnam. Embarked was Carrier Air Wing Five (CVW-5), officially tasked as an "Attack Carrier Air Wing for support of conventional and nuclear war in all weather conditions".

The *Ticonderoga* "in-chopped" to Dixie Station, the carrier-operating area off South Vietnam, on November 5. Fresh carriers were eased into combat by flying missions over South Vietnam, where the threat was largely small-arms fire and light anti-aircraft artillery (AAA), rather than the heavy guns and MiGs found over the north – plus, since July 1965, the new SA-2 *Guideline* surface-to-air missiles (SAMs).

THE CHAMPIONS

The most capable of the *Tico's* three light attack squadrons was VA-56 – "Champions" – flying the Douglas A-4E Skyhawk. The unit's own stated mission for the 1965–66 cruise was "to conduct offensive air-to-surface operations with conventional and nuclear weapons". So, despite a "hot" conventional war in Vietnam, the chance of a full-scale conflict with the Soviet Union or China was not far from the minds of the admirals in San Diego and Washington.

One of the newer VA-56 pilots was Lt (Junior Grade) Douglas Morey Webster of Warren, Ohio, who had received his Wings of Gold as a naval aviator under the Naval Aviation Cadet (NAVCAD) programme in 1964, and was quickly assigned to VA-56, destined for Vietnam. It appears that Webster ▶

BELOW: The USS *Ticonderoga* departs Hawaii for its WestPac on October 9, 1965. Ranged forward are Douglas Skyraiders, A-4 Skyhawks and Vought F-8 Crusaders, with Douglas A-3 Skywarriors and a sole Grumman E-1B Tracer of VAW-11 ranged aft. It was on this tour that Lt (jg) Doug Webster was lost along with Skyhawk "472". *via author*

ABOVE: Plane Captain George Floyd poses beside what is believed to be A-4E BuNo 151022, the aircraft in which Doug Webster was lost on December 5, 1965. Taken the year before the accident, this photograph shows the Skyhawk when it was numbered "406" and was the regular mount of VA-56 officer Lieutenant Job O. Belcher. *George Floyd via author*

ABOVE: Douglas Morey Webster was born on July 26, 1941, and is seen here receiving his pilot's wings on December 5, 1964. Webster was a new hand aboard the *Tico* for its 1965–66 tour and reportedly voiced misgivings about the purpose and prosecution of the conflict in Vietnam. Webster flew a total of 17 missions from the *Tico*. *via author*

soon became unhappy with the conduct of the war and with the Navy in general, and was saying as much in his letters home. He also wrote in his diary that the Vietnam situation was more serious and a far greater number of pilots were being lost than the American people were being told. Air Wing Five was spending more than half its flying exercises conducting nuclear war drills and it seemed as if the essential exercises for conventional missions were "...being conducted during the intervals", he wrote.

Described as "cheerful and likeable" by the sailors in the *Tico's* W Division, responsible for the ship's nuclear weapons, 24-year-old Webster was an accomplished high school and university gymnast. He had married his college sweetheart Marsha only shortly before the *Tico* sailed for Vietnam.

On November 21, 1965, the *Ticonderoga* moved north. Air Wing Five took part in raids on the Me Xa and Ha Chan bridges, the bridge complex at Hai Duong and on the Uong Bi thermal power station, Lt (jg) Doug Webster flying 17 operational missions. On December 2 the *Tico* pulled out of the line and headed for Yokosuka in Japan for a period of rest and replenishment. The transit to Japan itself was not a rest period for the crew, however, as nuclear war exercises continued.

At daybreak on Sunday, December 5, 1965, the *Ticonderoga* was steaming at 20kt on a heading of 049°, or roughly north-north-east, in company with four destroyers providing a circular screen. The weather that morning was rough, with water breaking over the bow, but by early afternoon was described as clear and sunny and the sea calm with occasional rolling waves.

As well as the conventional bombs, rockets and missiles employed against North Vietnam and the Viet Cong, CVW-5 carried a stockpile of much deadlier B43 thermonuclear weapons. The training version of the B43, used on shore-based exercises and in port, was not carried on cruise for space reasons, so on December 5, each aircraft participating in the day's exercise was to be fitted with a War Reserve, or live, weapon with an explosive yield of one megaton – about 67 times that of the Hiroshima bomb.

LIVE NUCLEAR WEAPONS

At 1300hr the codeword *Crewcut* was broadcast over the ship's loudspeakers, calling sailors to man their stations for a special (nuclear) weapons loading exercise. It was not on the posted Plan of the Day so for most of the crew it was a no-notice event, but W Division had been preparing for it since the

BELOW: Douglas A-4E Skyhawks of VA-56 — "The Champions". The unit, whose badge (as seen below) comprised a boomerang and black electron rings, received its A-4Es in June 1963 and converted to Vought A-7B Corsair IIs in January 1969. *via author*

Tico left Vietnamese waters. An electrical fire at 1335hr in an engineering space briefly delayed proceedings. The bridge was told the fire was out by 1341hr and all crew were at their stations by 1358hr.

The object of the exercise was to load all the aircraft in 30min and simulate their launch on a nuclear strike mission. The procedure was to arm the aircraft on the hangar deck, tow them to the No 2 elevator situated at the forward end of the angled deck, raise them, then tow them forward to the catapults. Instead of a catapult launch, they would sit there for a minute or so then go further forward to the No 1 elevator on the centre-line and down again to the hangar deck for de-arming. A pilot was not actually necessary for this evolution, so on many jets a sailor in the cockpit rode the brakes as the aircraft was moved, aided by others carrying chocks who would throw them in front of the wheels when needed.

SKYHAWK OVERBOARD!

The first aircraft in line, A-4E BuNo 151022, callsign "Champion 472", was pushed by blueshirts (regular sailors) from its spot in hangar bay No 2 to the weapons elevator with Plane Captain Bob Redding on the foot-operated brakes, although he later told his shipmates that "it had no brakes". All the other A-4s were towed across the hangar deck by tractors, but in this case the tractor was waiting above on the flight deck. The B43 was loaded on the A-4's centre-line pylon by armourer Paul Pizzarella of VA-56.

Just then, to the surprise of Bob Redding – who was now out of the jet and holding the boarding ladder – a fully kitted-out pilot appeared. Doug Webster had been ordered to man "472". He climbed aboard and strapped in. The armed A-4E was pushed backwards by many hands on to the elevator, followed by two sailors with U-shaped wooden chocks and at least three safety supervisors.

The sea was now (at 1450hr) a little rougher than before and at this moment some recall a loudspeaker announcement: "Standby for roll to port". The ship heeled and the A-4 began to roll back-wards. The safety director blew his whistle to tell the pilot to "hold brakes". Randy Wilson of VA-56, who was "hitching a lift" up on the elevator, saw that Webster's attention was focused in the cockpit, but could not tell if he was pumping the brakes. The two chock men threw the chocks behind the wheels, but the starboard chock landed just after the port and the A-4's starboard wheel slid. The port chock was knocked aside. The main-wheels reached the elevator edge and rolled over, damaging part of the safety net. As the Skyhawk tipped back on its stalky undercarriage, Webster appeared to try and stand up, but his harness held him back. He put his hands on the windscreen arch, but the canopy slammed down on his fingers. Witnesses recall a look of terror on his face as the aircraft continued its backflip and fell inverted into the water with a huge splash.

"It was so quick," says Wilson, "it happened in the blink of an eye". The A-4 went under before the fantail had passed it and began its long journey to the seabed, 2,700 fathoms (16,000ft – 4,900m) below.

A khaki-dressed officer or chief of W Division ran over to the edge. "Was there a weapon on that 'plane?" he asked Pizzarella, which seemed an odd question to ask, given his responsibilities. "There was a ****ing pilot on that 'plane!" retorted Pizzarella, and stormed off.

BY THE BOOK?

As the "man overboard" call repeated over the loudspeakers, W Division prepared a "Rainbow Message" – a pro-forma signal of the highest priority informing the White House, Pentagon and Seventh Fleet that a "Broken Arrow" had occurred. The *Tico's* commanding officer, Captain Robert N. Miller, a somewhat gung-ho type who was known to leave his executive officer in charge and fly missions over Vietnam in Douglas A-3 Skywarriors, looked at the message form and reportedly asked of nobody in particular: "Well, I guess we have to send this one?"

The carrier launched a helicopter and

ABOVE: The *Tico* in Hawaiian waters in 1965, before setting off on its WestPac tour of 1965–66. The *Ticonderoga* was one of 24 Essex-class aircraft carriers built for the US Navy during the Second World War and was launched on February 7, 1944. The *Tico* earned five battle stars in the Pacific theatre of operations during the war. *via author*

RIGHT: Commander William G. Nealon (furthest left) relieves Cdr Wesley L. McDonald (right) of the command of VA-56 in March 1965 as Cdr Macon S. Snowden, the commander of Carrier Air Wing 5, looks on. Allegations of tension between Webster and Nealon were made after the accident, although this remains pure speculation. *via author*

> At 1300hr the codeword **Crewcut** was broadcast over the ship's loudspeakers, calling sailors to **man their stations** for a special (nuclear) weapons loading **exercise.**

lifeboat and, together with the escorting destroyers, conducted a search for about two hours, but all that was recovered were parts of a droptank and the pilot's helmet. By 1603hr the *Tico* was "steaming as before" towards Japan. Two of the destroyers stayed until sunset, but to no avail.

Captain Miller ordered the crew to stay silent about the accident. Outgoing mail was blocked. The VA-56 pilots knew that Doug Webster's new bride was in a hotel somewhere in Yokosuka, but not which one. The carrier docked on the morning of December 7 and Randy Wilson was near the officer's brow (gangplank) when he saw a group of officers talking to Mrs Webster. He saw her slump down and start crying before being led away.

The *Tico* returned to action on December 17. After seven more periods on the line, during which five more aircraft, including two VA-56 Skyhawks and pilots were lost on operations, the carrier finally "out-chopped" from theatre and headed back to San Diego on April 20, 1966.

A DELIBERATE COVER-UP?

The events of December 5 were kept from the public and press from the start. Seventh Fleet's monthly summary of operations for December 1965 does not mention the loss of an aircraft, pilot or bomb, although it does list all other losses and significant events. The VA-56 and *Ticonderoga* Command Histories held by the Naval Historical Center say nothing about it.

Naturally, there were several investigations into the accident. A version of the US Navy Judge Advocate General (JAG) inquiry has only recently been released, although it omits mention of the nuclear weapon. Doug Webster's personnel record remains sealed. A two-paragraph summary of an initial investigation, eventually released under the Freedom of Information Act, reported that the accident was caused either by Lt (jg) Webster's failure to respond to the director's signal to apply brakes or that the aircraft suffered complete failure of the braking system. No evidence of malfeasance or gross negligence on the part of the handling crew or other naval personnel was found.

Ticonderoga sailor James Weber, who has done a great deal to uncover much of the source material for this article, believes that sabotage may have been involved. There were numerous fires and incidents on the cruise and two sailors later convicted of sabotaging aircraft were sent to Leavenworth military prison. On the morning of November 22 Weber saw a damaged B43 on a bomb elevator on one of the mess decks. Damaging a nuclear weapon, even accidentally, would be a career-threatening event for anyone even remotely involved, including the captain. Weber was subsequently twice ordered to the sick bay and asked about what he saw and how he was feeling. Although he believes that the bomb he saw is the one that went overboard, he has been unable to prove or disprove his suspicions.

Tensions between VA-56's CO, who was a Naval Academy graduate, and NAVCAD Doug Webster have been alleged. It seems highly unlikely, however, that a conspiracy to "dispose" of a problematic weapon and pilot took place.

The secret was kept until 1981, when the accident appeared as the shortest entry in an official Department of Defense list of nuclear weapons accidents released under a Freedom of Information Act request. The full text read: "December 5, 1965/A-4/at sea/Pacific. An A-4 aircraft with one nuclear weapon rolled off the elevator of a US aircraft carrier and fell into the sea. The pilot, aircraft and weapon were lost. The incident occurred more than 500 miles from land."

Most observers understood the last part to mean 500 miles from mainland China, but in reality it was a mere 89 miles from the populated Japanese island of Kikaishima in the northern Ryuku Islands, and only 239 miles from the southern tip of Kyushu, Japan's southernmost home island.

In May 1989 Greenpeace revealed details of the *Tico's* deck log, causing outrage in Japan and a severe embarrassment for the American government.

The text of the log read: "1450 [hr]. While being rolled from No 2 Hangar Bay to No 2 Elevator, A-4E aircraft BuNo 151022 of VA-56, with pilot LTJG D.M. Webster USN 666086 aboard, rolled off the elevator and sank in 2,700 fathoms of water at 27° 35.2'N, 131° 19.3'E".

THE FATE OF THE BOMB

The Japanese constitution prohibits the "introduction" of nuclear weapons into its territory, but a secret understanding agreed during negotiations for the signing of the Treaty of Mutual Cooperation between the USA and Japan in January 1960 exempted American military vessels from inspection. Following public protests, Japan demanded extra information but dropped the demand after meetings in December 1989 on the grounds that further discussion might

ABOVE: Pilots of VA-56 pose beside a Skyhawk during a weapons training exercise at NAS Fallon, Nevada, just before the unit's deployment aboard the USS *Ticonderoga* in 1965. Webster is not among the group. *via author*

> Damaging a **nuclear weapon**, even accidentally, would be a **career-threatening event** for **anyone** even remotely involved, including the captain.

BELOW: Skyhawk "402" of VA-56 catches the wire on the *Tico* in February 1964, just before the carrier departed for its 1964 WestPac tour and the Champions' first Vietnam combat cruise. The unit wore NF tailcodes from June 1956 until July 1966, when the unit joined Carrier Air Wing 9 and changed to NG tailcodes. *US Navy via Skyhawk Association/www.a4skyhawk.org*

Tragedy aboard the *Tico*

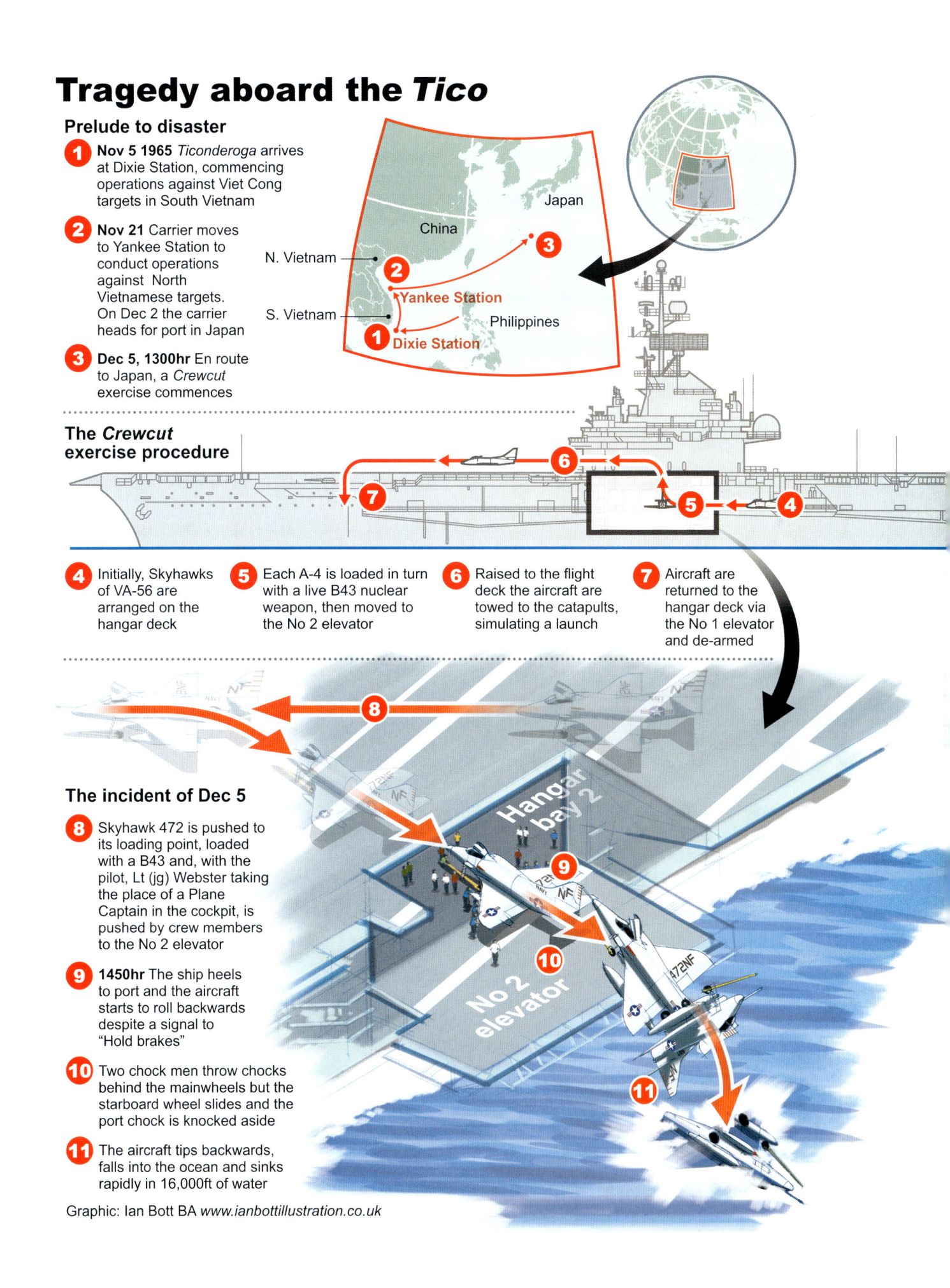

Prelude to disaster

1 **Nov 5 1965** *Ticonderoga* arrives at Dixie Station, commencing operations against Viet Cong targets in South Vietnam

2 **Nov 21** Carrier moves to Yankee Station to conduct operations against North Vietnamese targets. On Dec 2 the carrier heads for port in Japan

3 **Dec 5, 1300hr** En route to Japan, a *Crewcut* exercise commences

The *Crewcut* exercise procedure

4 Initially, Skyhawks of VA-56 are arranged on the hangar deck

5 Each A-4 is loaded in turn with a live B43 nuclear weapon, then moved to the No 2 elevator

6 Raised to the flight deck the aircraft are towed to the catapults, simulating a launch

7 Aircraft are returned to the hangar deck via the No 1 elevator and de-armed

The incident of Dec 5

8 Skyhawk 472 is pushed to its loading point, loaded with a B43 and, with the pilot, Lt (jg) Webster taking the place of a Plane Captain in the cockpit, is pushed by crew members to the No 2 elevator

9 **1450hr** The ship heels to port and the aircraft starts to roll backwards despite a signal to "Hold brakes"

10 Two chock men throw chocks behind the mainwheels but the starboard wheel slides and the port chock is knocked aside

11 The aircraft tips backwards, falls into the ocean and sinks rapidly in 16,000ft of water

Graphic: Ian Bott BA www.ianbottillustration.co.uk

ABOVE: A quartet of VA-56 "Scooters" during an exercise. Curiously, the example furthest from the camera is uncoded and without the unit's distinctive rudder flash. The A-4E introduced the more powerful Pratt & Whitney J52 engine as well as greatly improved avionics, including a toss-bombing computer.
US Navy via Skyhawk Association/www.a4skyhawk.org

BELOW: Safety aboard an aircraft carrier is paramount — this card aimed to keep crew aware of errors as discreetly as possible. *via author*

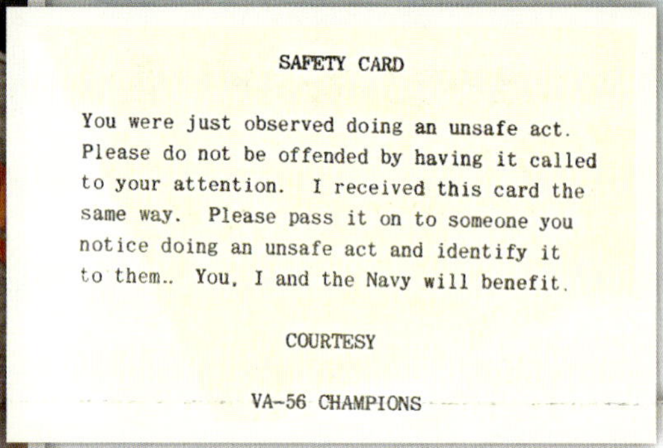

```
              SAFETY CARD

You were just observed doing an unsafe act.
Please do not be offended by having it called
to your attention. I received this card the
same way. Please pass it on to someone you
notice doing an unsafe act and identify it
to them.. You, I and the Navy will benefit.

                 COURTESY

              VA-56 CHAMPIONS
```

LEFT: A VA-56 Skyhawk on the *Tico's* No 2 elevator, from which Webster and his A-4E fell. The elevator projected some 40ft (12·2m) from the carrier's port side, a yellow diagonal line being painted 18ft (5·5m) from the edge of the hangar deck, marking where the aircraft must come to a stop. *via author*

"compromise" American operations and create an "adverse effect" on American national security interests.

As for the bomb itself, the Pentagon said in 1989 that: "Structural failure [of the weapon] occurred before it reached the ocean floor at 16,000ft, exposing nuclear material to the hydrosphere". The report concluded that "the high explosives contained in the bomb, which initiate a nuclear explosion, would have been corroded by sea water" and that "the nuclear material itself would dissolve in a relatively short time". It was so dense that "...it probably settled quickly on the ocean floor, and mixed with other sediment".

Douglas Webster's mother Margaret reportedly learnt the details of her son's death in early 1966 from a taxi driver, rather than through official channels. Many years later she visited Washington DC and was distressed not to find his name on the Vietnam Veterans

BELOW: The Tico is accompanied by replenishment-at-sea (RAS) ship *USS Mount Baker* off the coast of California in September 1965, shortly before the carrier's departure for Hawaii and the Far East. One of the Skyhawks ranged on the forward and angled decks may well be "472". *via author*

066 AVIATION CLASSICS: AMERICAN COLD WAR STORIES

ABOVE: Douglas Webster, whose gravestone resides at Arlington National Cemetery in Virginia.

ABOVE: Skyhawk "401", BuNo 150030, of VA-56 flies over the Sierra Nevada mountain range straddling California and Nevada, in 1964. The unit's home port when not at sea was NAS Lemoore, California, the Champions having moved in when the base was opened in the summer of 1961 — before that the unit's land base was NAS Miramar. *TAH Archive*

SMALL BOMB, BIG IMPACT

The B43 was developed as a low-drag parachute-retarded shock-resistant variable-yield nuclear bomb for high-speed low-altitude delivery, work beginning on the weapon at the Los Alamos National Laboratory in 1955. Originally designated TX-43, the bomb was intended to fulfil two distinct requirements, the first being the penetration of hard targets and the second the classic airburst method of delivery. For the former a special nose, designated Mod 0, incorporating a steel spike to penetrate a hard surface before a delayed surface burst, was fitted, the alternative Mod 1 nose carrying an airburst radar-fuzed system. The weapon's explosive yield varied from 70 kilotons of TNT to 1 megaton of TNT.

Following an extensive test programme, the weapon was put into production as the B43 in 1960, the Mod 0 entering service in 1961, the Mod 1 following a year later. Cleared for internal or external carriage on the Boeing B-52, Vickers Valiant, English Electric Canberra, Douglas A-4 Skyhawk, Grumman A-6 Intruder and others, the B43 was progressively updated, and training versions (BDU-6, BDU-8, BDU-18 and BDU-24) were developed.

Production of the B43 ended in 1965, after completion of some 2,000 examples. It remained on the inventory, however, until its retirement in the 1980s in favour of the newer B61 and B83 weapons.

ABOVE: B43 bomb *Greg Goebel*

Memorial Wall. The official position is that his death was outside Vietnamese waters and not a combat operation, so does not qualify.

Since the basic details of his death became public, some of Webster's shipmates and friends have worked to have his service and sacrifice formally recognised and lift the veil of secrecy that fell over the incident as soon as his A-4 disappeared beneath the sea.

In 2006 Webster's friends succeeded in having his name added to a memorial book kept at the Wall site. Nearly five decades later many questions remain unanswered. Doug Webster's squadron mate Randy Wilson says today: "I believe something funny went on out there". We may never know precisely what. •

Acknowledgments

The author wishes to thank Randy Wilson, George Floyd and other members of VA-56 and the crew of the USS *Ticonderoga*, and also Dennis Palmer. Thanks also to Chika Falconer and Peter B. Mersky for their invaluable help with the preparation of this feature. The author's book, also called *Broken Arrow*, published by Casemate in March 2019, contains further information and additional photgraphs.

BELOW: A view from the bridge of the *Tico* of the USS *Constellation* beyond the Skyhawks of VA-56 at San Diego in 1966, after the Tico's return to home waters. *Peter B. Mersky Collection*

Anything, anywhere, anytime – professionally

In 1965 British student JONATHAN POTE volunteered to spend his "gap year" with a medical team in Laos as part of the Colombo Plan – an experience which provided an unrivalled opportunity to see the work of the CIA's "secret airline", Air America, in South-east Asia at close quarters. Here he details the origins of Air America and how its pilots and groundcrew in Laos lived up to its motto.

Even before the Pearl Harbor débâcle which brought the USA into World War Two in December 1941, President Franklin D. Roosevelt had serious concerns about the USA's intelligence-gathering activities, and had appointed William J. "Wild Bill" Donovan, a lawyer, to advise him. Donovan was no stranger to war; as a Lieutenant Colonel commanding the 165th Infantry Regiment in late 1918, he had led from the front and been awarded the Medal of Honor.

Back in uniform, he formed the Office of Strategic Studies (OSS) in June 1942. As well as the collection and analysis of intelligence abroad, the OSS was permitted to "conduct special operations not assigned to other Agencies". It did indeed conduct military activities during World War Two (not only in French Indochina) and was involved in disagreements with both the military intelligence services and the Federal Bureau of Investigation (FBI) as a result.

In October 1945, very soon after VJ-Day, the OSS was disbanded owing to pressure from these organisations, and its functions were transferred to other State Departments.

It had, however, performed useful functions, and the by-now Major General Donovan successfully lobbied for "an organisation which will procure intelligence by overt and covert methods and will at the same time provide intelligence guidance, determine national intelligence objectives and correlate the intelligence material collected by all government agencies".

THE NATIONAL SECURITY COUNCIL

It was also to conduct "subversive operations abroad". As a result, the National Security Act of 1947 led to the formation of the National Security Council, and ultimately to the Central Intelligence Agency (CIA) under its direction.

The accountability of the CIA became cloaked in 1949, when it was decreed that funds could be acquired from other government organisations secretly, and that there was no requirement for the CIA to disclose the names or salaries of its personnel (nor even indicate their numbers).

In time, the CIA developed profit-making subsidiaries (including Air America) to provide additional funds, but by 1949 the die was cast for an organisation that could fulfill all the covert military activities that the American government required, but for which it could not use the conventional Military Services. So nebulous did "The Agency" become that when Richard Helms became its head in 1966 and asked the seemingly simple question of how many aircraft and of what types were available to the CIA, it took three months of urgent investigation to provide an approximate answer, with the rider that the number fluctuated from day to day.

"The Central Intelligence Agency is an independent United States Government Agency responsible for providing national security intelligence to senior US policymakers", so the organisation's Mission Statement blandly states. One could be forgiven for thinking that this mission did not require fighting wars on behalf of the USA, but "plausibly deniable" military activities were its routine fare. This is exactly what happened in Laos from 1954 to 1974, the largest such paramilitary operation the CIA ever attempted.

Air America was a major component in the "Secret War", which was kept from the American public for most of that time. The airline was only one of several used by the Agency (others included Inter Mountain, Southern Air Transport and Bird & Sons, which became Continental Air Services Incorporated on September 1, 1965), but was uniquely wholly owned by the CIA after 1950 via several holding companies.

TOP: Air America Douglas C-47B "147" prepares for one of the thrice-weekly "milk run" flights at Thakhek East in mid-1966. This aircraft went on to become one of the last to leave Saigon in April 1975 as the city fell to the North Vietnamese. *Jonathan Pote*

LEFT: Air America Helio Courier XW-PEA (c/n 541) departs the typically primitive airstrip at Thakhek West in September 1966. In keeping with Air America's deliberately confusing and obscure registration system, this identity was also applied to at least two other Couriers at the same time, while all three were based at the airport in the Lao capital, Vientiane. *Jonathan Pote*

THE EARLY DAYS

The story of Air America starts with General Claire Lee Chennault. Retiring as a Captain from the United States Army Air Corps in 1937, Chennault went to China to advise the country's nascent air force. Soon after, Japanese incursions into China developed into a full-scale invasion. From his former compatriots, he recruited the American Volunteer Group (AVG – better known as the "Flying Tigers") to assist the fledgling Chinese pilots. The AVG (its Curtiss P-40 Kittyhawks adorned with distinctive "shark's mouth" markings) was inducted into the United States Army Air Forces, after Pearl Harbor, as the 23rd Fighter Group.

Post-war, the now retired Gen Chennault formed CAT (Civil Air Transport) as a cargo operator supplying the Nationalist areas of China. At first CAT ranged across the vast Chinese mainland, but with General Chiang Kai-shek finally banished to Formosa (now Taiwan) by Mao Tse-tung, it became seriously underused. The nascent CIA – already a customer – seized the chance to buy CAT outright, keeping it ostensibly still a civil

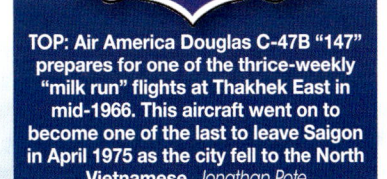

ABOVE: The unmistakably craggy-faced General Claire Lee Chennault beside a shark-mouthed Curtiss P-40 of the American Volunteer Group.

ABOVE: Showing the often atrocious condition of the landing strips, or "Lima sites", Air America's fleet of STOL aircraft were required to to operate from, this photograph of Helio Courier XW-PEA was taken at Thakhek West on July 22, 1966. Air America's Couriers in Laos were finished in bare metal with the registration in black midway up the fin and sported a black triangle under the port wing, the apex of which pointed towards the trailing edge. *Jonathan Pote*

LEFT: As commander of the USAF's 1095th Operational Evaluation Training Group during 1960–62, Major Harry "Heine" Aderholt was instrumental in developing the Lima sites in Laos for Air America's STOL aircraft operations.

airline but with the CIA now as the number one customer and with first priority.

The Korean conflict of 1950–53 provided much work, as did the closing days of French rule in Indochina. Fairchild C-119 Flying Boxcars (hurriedly transferred from USAF stocks and painted in French colours) were flown by CAT crews to help re-supply the doomed garrison at Dien Bien Phu in Tonkin. Several were battle-damaged, and one flown by American World War Two ace James B. McGovern (otherwise known as "Earthquake McGoon") was shot down.

Morale among CAT personnel deteriorated and the administration remained too chaotic for the CIA's liking, so at the end of March 1959 CAT was reorganised and renamed Air America by its own board; a seemingly oddly obvious name for such a clandestine organisation. It was perhaps hoped that it would send out the message that America was there to stay, and to help, but it was regretted in later years when the situation had changed. The airline soon developed its own unconventional *modus operandi* and camaraderie which lasted until it followed CAT into oblivion in 1975.

THE BUILD-UP

As early as September 1955, a year after the French débâcle at Dien Bien Phu, three Curtiss C-46s of CAT had begun to drop rice in mountainous north-eastern Laos to avert famine. The USA foresaw a great need to alleviate hunger in order to contain the further spread of communism; and, for added measure, leaflets were also dropped in communist areas of influence.

The arrival of Douglas C-47A B-817 in the Lao capital of Vientiane on June 30, 1957, was the start of 20 remarkable years of "airline" activity.

The American embassy felt the need to have its own ▶

> At the end of **March 1959** CAT was reorganised and renamed **Air America** by its own board; a seemingly oddly obvious name for such a **clandestine organisation.**

BELOW: Sikorsky UH-34D Choctaw H-12 of Air America on the football field at Luang Prabang in north central Laos, until the communist takeover in 1975 the royal capital and seat of government of the Kingdom of Laos. Initially Sikorsky H-19 Chickasaws were used by Air America in Laos but, after the (non-fatal) loss of an H-19 at Na Nhom in May 1960, the type was withdrawn and replaced by the UH-34, which itself struggled in the hot and humid climate. *Jonathan Pote*

The Land of a Million Elephants

Modern Laos, a landlocked country of some 91,500 square miles bordered by Burma and China to the north-west, Vietnam to the east, Cambodia to the south and Thailand to the west, traces its heritage back to the 14th Century kingdom of Lan Xang, the "land of a million elephants". In 1893 France made a unified Laos part of French Indochina, the country becoming independent in 1953. Its proximity to Vietnam made it an important part of the USA's anti-communist containment policy of the 1950s and 1960s. Central and southern parts of Laos later became vital sections of communist North Vietnam's supply lines — the Ho Chi Minh Trail — hence Air America's "plausibly deniable" presence in Laos.

Map by Maggie Nelson

AVIATION CLASSICS: AMERICAN COLD WAR STORIES   071

ABOVE: Curtiss C-46D N1383N (c/n 33641, built in 1945 as 44-78245) was acquired by Air America in 1963 and is seen here at Wattay, Vientiane, in 1966. This aircraft had been damaged in January 1965 when a nearby T-28 exploded, and in March 1970 one of its "kickers" fell out of the cargo door in flight – and survived. *Jonathan Pote*

ABOVE: Passengers aboard C-47B "994" during a milk run flight from Vientiane to Thakhek in February 1966. The author recalls: "The seats were extremely uncomfortable, especially on the ground with the tail down". Note the cargo packages roped together in the centre. *Jonathan Pote*

aircraft in the mid-1960s), but it needed to be: During 1960–61 there were some 26 crashes, seven from enemy action. More than 200 Air America aircrew would be lost before 1975.

CIVIL WAR IN LAOS

The Geneva Accords of 1954 had ceded the north-eastern provinces of Sam Neua and Phong Saly to the pro-communist Pathet Lao pending re-unification of the Country after the proposed elections of 1956. In 1959 civil war flared again and elections in Laos produced a massive right-wing win. The following year Captain (soon to be General) Kong Le of the Royal Lao Army failed in a coup intended to bring politics to the middle road, and proceeded to annex some 10,000 troops as part of a neutralist army, causing an upsurge in political and military activity on all sides.

> *Company pay was good ($50,000-plus annually to fly a light aircraft in the mid-1960s), but it needed to be: During 1960–61 there were some 26 crashes.*

aircraft to distribute supplies as the future Minister of Economic Planning in the new coalition was to be Prince Souphanouvong, a communist, whom it was thought might misappropriate American aid. From that point there was a steady build-up of aircraft and hours flown, and by 1966 Air America's fleet of more than 100 aircraft was flying tens of thousands of hours a year. The tasks ranged from pure civil aid to genuine military action by company personnel, and included the supply of most of the military equipment and ammunition needed by the Royal Lao Government forces.

There was no distinction between civil and military work; aircraft and crews switched from one to the other as needed. Some aircraft were bought on the open market, others "bailed" from the USAF or US Army for a nominal dollar. The crews were almost all ex-military, usually with recent experience in South Vietnam, so it was as simple to find someone who could use a North American T-28 to deadly effect over enemy territory as to find a pilot for a C-47 on a "milk run" (a conventional internal airline schedule), although more covert missions were restricted to a small cadre of pilots.

Air America competed for business against Bird & Sons, which was bought out by Continental Airlines to form Continental Air Services Inc (CASI) in 1965. Apart from hoped-for savings from competition, nobody was fooled that CASI was anything other than the CIA's "other airline". Company pay was good ($50,000-plus annually to fly a light

The same year, Air America acquired its first helicopters, four Sikorsky H-19s, which were found unsuitable and replaced within months by four Sikorsky UH-34s. The construction of "Victor" sites (renamed "Lima" sites from May 16, 1964, to avoid confusion with those in South Vietnam), to accommodate the small fixed-wing STOL types then entering the Air America inventory, also began in earnest. Created in mountainous terrain with only hand tools, these were perforce rudimentary. Built in a week or less, with a slope of up to 45° and a bend of 20° allowable, a runway of 100–200yd (92–184m)

072 AVIATION CLASSICS: AMERICAN COLD WAR STORIES

was considered adequate for a Helio Courier or, later, a Pilatus PC-6 Turbo Porter, the Courier being withdrawn around 1968.

The Courier had a troubled start in service, initially proving unreliable and unpopular with its single engine. On a proving flight to a new strip at Phong Saly in April 1960, Courier B-833 was detained by Pathet Lao troops overnight, but allowed to leave next day. Such gentlemanly conduct did not last long. The pilot, Major Harry C. "Heine" Aderholt, would rise to General rank as the war progressed, as would one of his passengers that year, Major Pao, later General Vang Pao, leader of the Hmong mountain tribal people.

The North Vietnamese also became involved in Laos as the 919th Air Transport Regiment of the Vietnamese People's Air Force (formed at Gia Lam near Hanoi on May 1, 1959, later moving to Dong Hoi) began airdrops (using Antonov An-2 *Colts*, Lisunov Li-2 *Cabs* and Ilyushin Il-14 *Crates*) to road-construction teams in eastern Laos working on the nascent *Truong Son*, or Ho Chi Minh trail. It soon added Mil Mi-4 *Hound* helicopters to its fleet to supply communist forces on the Plaine des Jarres. In December 1960 Soviet pilots, also using Il-14s, openly flew some of Kong Le's forces from Vang Vieng (barely 50 miles, 80km, north of Vientiane) to the Plaine des Jarres as he regrouped and sided for a time with Communist forces.

THAILAND, TIBET AND BURMA

The upsurge in activity was not only in Laos; at Takhli, 145 miles (240km) north-west of Bangkok in Thailand, CIA – and to a lesser extent USAF – clandestine operations built up. Lockheed C-130 Hercules flying over Tibet and Burma supported anti-communist elements there while Lockheed SR-71s and U-2s provided strategic reconnaissance over Asia. In the case of the Hercules, a USAF crew would arrive in Thailand for ten days of special ops, their aircraft assuming a new identity overnight. Its mission complete a week or so later, the faithful C-130 seemingly magically changed back to its previous (legitimate) identity while the crews slept off their fatigue.

In 1965 the author heard (still unsubstantiated) claims that Air America sent Fairchild C-123 Providers on similar temporary duties, to be used as bombers in northern Burma; reportedly, 500lb bombs were rolled out of the rear doors by hand. Certainly, Air America based its first unequivocally offensive aircraft at Takhli at this time: the Douglas B-26 Invaders acquired for Operation *Mill Pond*, the object of which was to bomb the Plaine des Jarres, although ultimately this operation came to nothing.

On March 9, 1961, Pathet Lao forces took the village of Sala Phou Khoun, strategically placed where Route 7, from North Vietnam via the Plaine des Jarres, meets Route 13, the major road in Laos, running north-south near the Mekong, in this case halfway from Vientiane to the royal capital of Luang Prabang. American patience ran out. With the country cut in half and both those cities threatened (and the "domino theory" of communist strategy accepted as gospel) President John F. Kennedy reacted. He immediately sanctioned the transfer of 16 Sikorsky UH-34s from US Marine Corps stocks in South Vietnam to Air America in Laos, and ten days later mobilised all United States Forces in the Pacific. The transition to an all-out east-west war had started.

The standoff continued, but in May peace talks started between the various powers in Geneva. As these continued, Air America reconnoitred the country, and especially the Plaine des Jarres and the Ho Chi Minh trail complex, with RB-26C Invaders as part of Operation *Black Watch*. The company's UH-34s and Curtiss C-46 Commandos were involved with clandestine airdrops over North Vietnam as well as delivering more legitimate rice supplies to the mountain peoples, principally the Hmong, of north-east Laos. The legendary Edgar "Pop" Buell, an Indiana farmer working for the US Operations Mission (USOM), covered the mountains largely on foot before organising drops of rice by the C-46s of Bird & Sons.

THE GENEVA ACCORDS FAIL

On July 23, 1962, after more than a year of negotiations in Geneva (during which the ▶

BELOW: Air America Fairchild C-123B Provider N5005X has its engines run up to full throttle in the background as Royal Lao Air Force C-47s prepare to pull troops out of Thakhek West after the successful conclusion of the Battle for Thakhek in November 1965. *Jonathan Pote*

American military stance had been relaxed), an "agreement" was reached and named *The Declaration & Protocol on the Neutrality of Laos*, which stated that all military forces would leave. President Kennedy's hope was that Laos could remain genuinely neutral, safe from the war in neighbouring Vietnam. To that end, the International Control Commission (ICC) was reactivated to oversee the situation. Six UH-34 helicopters were transferred from Air America and painted white, to be flown by French pilots and carrying observers from Poland, India and Canada to investigate alleged breaches of the Protocol by either side.

The USA's Military Assistance & Advisory Group (MAAG) was formed in 1961 from the Program Evaluation Office (PEO), which moved across the Mekong to Thailand, USOM becoming USAID (the US Agency for International Development). North Vietnam claimed that it had never had more than a handful of troops in Laos, and less than 100 of its 7,000 troops dutifully headed homeward past the ICC team on the North Vietnamese border. The rest remained in Laos.

The Americans were not quite as naïve as it may seem. While the notoriously murky PEO had been disbanded, USAID formed a Requirements Office (RO), which would serve as a conduit for military supplies to pro-Western forces. Air America was clearly going to have an increased workload if a bigger conflict ensued. It did, becoming known as the "Secret War".

Five USAF C-123B Providers (N5003X–N5007X) were bailed to the organisation. Bailing was a latter day Lend-Lease arrangement: for a nominal dollar, complete freedom of use of an aircraft was transferred to Air America, with the sole proviso that the aircraft be returned if no longer required – and still in one piece.

The company's first Dornier Do 28s were acquired and a de Havilland Canada DHC-4 Caribou (designated CV-2 in US Army service) was lent on a trial basis from the US Army. Caribous B-851 and B-853 were then obtained new from de Havilland Canada and several more were later bailed from the US Army. The dangers ahead were driven home when, on November 27, 1962, Provider N5004X was shot down while dropping rice.

In 1963 it was deemed prudent to establish a Flight Information Center, the prime function of which was to maintain an up-to-date plot of anti-aircraft weapon sites and brief crews accordingly. When the author flew in the British embassy's Scottish Aviation Pioneer CC.1 XL665, on detachment from No 209 Sqn, the pilot showed me the red chinagraph pencil marks on his map; there were communist anti-aircraft weapons sited not far east of our hospital in Thakhek.

A SLOWDOWN FOR AIR AMERICA?

In 1963 it seemed as though the company's workload was decreasing; some UH-34s were transferred to the Royal Lao Air Force as surplus, and the management felt that Air America should perhaps leave Laos, deferring to rivals Bird & Sons in the airlift role. The latter used C-46 Commandos, one load of rice from which could feed 1,000 people for nearly a month. The rice was triple-bagged and dropped on pallets without a parachute from about 800ft. By using up-slopes as drop sites, accuracy increased and the scattering or bursting of bags decreased. (In 1970 a tipping platform was devised to be fitted to the C-46's side door, so that the "kickers" no longer had to lean dangerously out of the door to the limit of their restraints to release bags, which were also less likely to hit the tailplane).

The Provider crews developed a dramatic drop technique; the entire load was freed, bar one large strap attached to the forward end. The pilot would ring a loud bell when he judged it correct, hauling back on the yoke simultaneously. The copilot would apply full power. As the nose rose steeply, the "kicker" would cut the strap and the entire load would slide down the roller bed and out over the ramp. Any failure by the crew, of either engine or of the load to exit cleanly, would cause a fatal stall. It never did.

The lull was brief, however, and American military aid to Laos totalled some $14m in 1964. Being low-cost materiel such as rifles, artillery pieces and ammunition, this made up a large tonnage. In 1964 CV-2A Caribous "392" (61-2392) and "401" (61-2401) were bailed to Air America, to be used for hauling petrol drums to suitable strips in the mountains, among other tasks. This allowed helicopters and light aircraft to refuel closer to their own operational areas. With its rear ramp open, the Caribou need not stop; with their restraints undone, the drums were pushed out of the back as the aircraft commenced take-off if time or enemy fire dictated urgency.

ABOVE: A Royal Lao Air Force T-28 over the author's house at Thakhek after a strafing run on communist positions during the fighting there in November 1965. Note the black band on the undersurface of the wing, painted to make it harder to see if a bomb was still on the rack. Communist troops were bolder once the bombs had been dropped! *Jonathan Pote*

> **American military aid** to Laos totalled some **$14m** in **1964**. Being low-cost materiel such as **rifles, artillery pieces** and **ammunition**.

ABOVE: Air America C-123B Provider N5007X unloads at Luang Prabang in June 1966. Originally built as 55-4555, the aircraft was quickly incorporated into the Air America fleet as "555" and later N5007X. Note the low cloud on the hills in the background. Following its upgrade to C-123K standard with the addition of pod-mounted General Electric J85 jet engines on the wings, this aircraft was lost on August 27, 1972, when it hit a ridge in cloud near Vang Vieng, killing nine. *Jonathan Pote*

BELOW: Seen here with the Civil Air Transport logo on the rear fuselage, de Havilland Canada DHC-4A c/n 52 was given the Taiwanese registration B-853, later shortened to just "853" in Air America service. Used as a commissary aircraft, it operated from Don Muang in Thailand in 1965 and was a regular visitor to Lima sites in Laos from 1966. *TAH Archive*

A BRAND NEW ROLE

With increasing Communist activity, an entirely new role was found for Air America. North American T-28s were coming into use with the Royal Lao Air Force in the ground-attack role. These had to be maintained by Air America engineers at Udorn, in north-east Thailand, there being no suitable facilities in Laos. With the T-28s being American-supplied and often flown (in Lao colours) by Thai mercenary pilots, it was a small step to make some available for Air America to operate when pinpoint or high-value targets were located. At first five pilots were transferred to T-28 operations, but soon the number doubled, this cadre being named "The A Team". Thai and Lao pilots made up the "B" and "C" teams respectively.

The US Ambassador, Leonard Unger, had to comply with strict rules of engagement for the Air America T-28s, but on July 18, 1964, UH-34 "H-19" was shot down while attempting to rescue the Thai pilot of a Royal Lao Air Force T-28 downed by communist fire. A helicopter crewman was killed in the crash. The Thai pilot was killed by gunfire but Air America pilot William A. Zeitler survived and evaded. With no time to refer the matter to the Chiefs of Staff in Washington DC, Unger took the decision to authorise the "A Team" to use napalm against the communist troops to effect a successful rescue of their colleague. That the Thai pilot was Capt Iriyapong Tavashi (base commander at Udorn and nephew of the Thai Prime Minister) may have been a factor. The US Ambassador's action was retrospectively approved by the US Government and Admiral John S. McCain, Commander-in-Chief of the Pacific Fleet (CINCPAC) was heard to say "Laos is a SECSTATE war", by which he meant one run by the Secretary of State rather than the Secretary of Defense.

Washington further agreed for Air America aircraft to be used on an *ad hoc* basis for the rescue of downed American pilots, the company's helicopters often being coincidentally close enough to the downed pilot to effect a quick "snatch" before communist troops arrived. Some 30 USAF and US Navy aircrew owe their lives to Air

ABOVE: Aero Commander "2714" at Lima Site 40 – Thakhek West – where it was based during operations against the Pathet Lao in November 1965.
Jonathan Pote

BELOW: The remarkable STOL performance of the Pilatus PC-6 Turbo Porter made it an ideal candidate for Air America service in Laos. This example, XW-PCL (c/n 583, formerly N13202), begins its take-off run down the slope of Lima Site 20 at Sam Thong in January 1966. It later served with CIA-sponsored Lao airline Boun Oum Airways. *Jonathan Pote*

> With increasing **Communist activity**, an entirely **new role** was found for **Air America**. North American T-28s were coming into use with the **Royal Lao Air Force** in the ground-attack role.

America, but sadly, of some 700 American personnel missing in action in Laos (unlike the prisoners in North Vietnam itself), none came home in 1975.

Nevertheless, the USAF did what it could for its own pilots over Laos. Apart from the 37th Aerospace Rescue & Recovery Squadron (ARRS), based at Nakhon Phanom in Thailand, close to where the author worked, there were also other Sikorsky HH-3E "Jolly Green Giants" on readiness at Ban Na Khang (LS36) in the far north-east of Laos, near Hanoi. As USAF helicopters lacked air-to-air refuelling capability at the time, it was the only way they could cover the northern part of Laos and North Vietnam. Hence the site was resolutely defended against North Vietnamese attempts to over-run it. Indeed, it became known as "The Alamo".

The Jolly Green Giants could come and go as the action ebbed and flowed, but to Air America pilots in their trusted UH-34s fell the task of replenishing the defenders and their supplies. Ban Na Khang finally fell to the communists on March 1, 1969.

THE BATTLE FOR SALA PHOU KOUN

By early 1964 General Kong Le had become disillusioned with the communists and had realigned his forces with the Royal Lao Army. As a result, it was possible – and desirable – to recapture Sala Phou Koun, where Route 7 met Route 13 between Vientiane and Luang Prabang. This would re-open the north-south route and give access east towards the Plaine des Jarres.

Air America inserted and supplied friendly forces to allow a three-pronged attack on the village, while "A-Team" T-28s, controlled by Aero Commander 560 "2714", gave close air support as fighting started on July 22. Both Route 13 and a significant stretch of Route 7 towards Muong Soui were cleared of the enemy. The Aero Commander would have been designated a U-4B had it ever officially been on the USAF inventory. It was reputedly a gift from President Eisenhower to the King of Laos, which has led some sources to claim – erroneously – that it was the aircraft used by Eisenhower to commute from his Gettysburg ranch to Washington DC; the smallest ever Air Force One. In reality Eisenhower's aircraft (55-4647) is on display in the Presidential Gallery of the National Museum of the USAF in Dayton, Ohio.

ABOVE: The interior of Caribou "392" en route to Vientiane in April 1966. *Jonathan Pote*

In 1965 Pilatus PC-6A Turbo Porters were introduced in country, and became very popular despite mountain bases having to stock Avtur for the new turboprop-powered aircraft, in addition to keeping stocks of Avgas for the other piston-engined aircraft. Further Dornier Do 28A/Bs also arrived.

The same year, Air America pilots built on the experience of using the Aero Commander by employing Cessna U-17As (military version of the 185 Skywagon), Turbo Porters and even RLAF Cessna O-1 Bird Dogs as forward air controller (FAC) aircraft (with "Butterfly" call signs) for the T-28s flown by the company and the RLAF, the latter never developing its own FAC expertise, perhaps because American forces were keen to do it for them.

In 1966 Gen William W. Momyer, Commander of the US Seventh Air Force in Saigon, learnt that his own fast jets were being controlled tactically by FAC personnel who were not only non-pilots, but also not even officers (although many had been before joining Air America). Overnight the "Butterflies" were grounded and soon replaced by the more aptly named "Ravens". These were individuals who had completed a tour as forward air controllers in South Vietnam and were offered a chance to volunteer for service in Laos. If they accepted, they were "sold" a Cessna Bird Dog for a dollar and flew themselves to Laos.

At first, there was no maintenance available for their aircraft, Air America later taking the responsibility for them – but not the pilots. As "sheep-dipped" USAF personnel, they were legally self-employed civilians on a contract – mercenaries. In reality their USAF careers continued secretly, in line with their peers, promotion and pension included. This was fine until lives were lost – and many were.

> *Air America C-130 Hercules with Air America crews flew **ammunition** and other **clandestine supplies** from **Thailand** into the **Lao airfields** bordering the Mekong and up to **"Alternate"** (Long Tieng, the **secret airbase**) in the mountains.*

Aero Commander 560 c/n 214 was initially registered N2714B, thus becoming "2714" in Laos. It bore the Royal Lao Air Force "Erawan" national insignia. During the author's year in Laos, the RLAF seemed to have taken over the use of this aircraft to transport very senior officers and it was based at Savannakhet. It was later returned to Air America, still in RLAF markings, and eventually survived the war to be allocated civil registration N92619, which it never took up.

SAR OPERATIONS

Air America responded to all potential search and rescue (SAR) situations to the best of its ability, but understandably its greatest efforts were expended when one of its own aircraft was down.

BELOW: Caribou "392" at Thakhek West on April 18, 1966. The aircraft was serving as a stand-in on the milk run as the regular C-47 had hit a buffalo and was undergoing repair. *Jonathan Pote*

078 AVIATION CLASSICS: AMERICAN COLD WAR STORIES

On October 13, 1965, soon after the author arrived in Laos, UH-34D "H-32" was reported missing east of Pakse in the south of Laos. Four people were aboard. Immediately every possible asset was deployed for an SAR mission which lasted several days. Initially several Do 28s (including some from rival CASI), Helio Couriers, a Beechcraft Baron and Caribou "853" (the commissary aircraft – the beer and mail would have to wait) were used in the search, but it was a sister UH-34D that found "H-32" the next day.

An Air America C-123B Provider flying overhead provided on-scene co-ordination throughout the search. The Caribou carried Lao paratroops ready to be dropped to secure the area if necessary. Three T-28s flown by Air America pilots were fully armed and on standby at nearby Pakse, although none was needed in the event. Sadly all aboard "H-32" were dead, but the response could not have been bettered by a national air force. Air America, however, was an airline in name only. In reality, it was an air force.

During 1965–67, flying continued at a brisk pace. Three C-47s – "147" and "994" having joined the veteran "817" – flew the milk runs north to Luang Prabang and south to Pak Sane, Thakhek, Savannakhet and Pakse thrice weekly, while the dozen or so Caribous, Providers and Commandos dropped or landed "soft rice" (food – 7,000,000lb a month, 85 per cent of which was airdropped) or "hard rice" (weapons and munitions). The UH-34s shuttled small numbers of troops around the mountains for maximum effect, and joined the many Couriers, Turbo Porters and Do 28s ferrying "customers" (CIA case officers) wherever they needed to go.

THE SECRET BASE AT LONG TIENG

Each aircraft down – and there were many – caused a flurry of activity until all personnel were accounted for. Air America-piloted T-28s attacked high-value targets under Raven control, and the B-26 Invader was back, this time in the form of On Mark Marksmen fitted with terrain-following radar (TFR) to perform low-level night drops to surveillance teams working beside the Ho Chi Minh Trail complex. Again, they were found wanting, and were replaced by de Havilland Canada DHC-6 Twin Otters (also fitted with TFR).

That the area was lethal was shown when a US Navy surveillance unit equipped with Lockheed OP-2E Neptunes (based at Nakhon Phanom on the Thai border) lost three aircraft (a quarter of its strength) in six weeks. Nightly, Air America C-130 Hercules with Air America crews flew ammunition and other clandestine supplies from Thailand into the Lao airfields bordering the Mekong and up to "Alternate" (Long Tieng, the secret airbase) in the mountains. Up to 280 armed Lao troops could be carried at once, owing to their small stature and the crews' disregard for weight limitations. •

Acknowledgments
The author would like to thank Dr Joe F. Leeker for his help during the preparation of this feature.

ABOVE: Hercules with Skyhook. *TAH Archive*

AIR AMERICA & THE SKYHOOK

The Caribou took on a new role in 1965 when Air America acquired two sets of Fulton Skyhook equipment to permit the pick-up of agents or downed aircrew by an airborne aircraft. A pack containing a helium cylinder and a balloon with a harness attached (by a long stretchable rope) was dropped to the downed crewman. Once he was attached by the line to the inflated balloon aloft, the aircraft would snag the rope between two nose-mounted prongs aimed just below the balloon. Alarmingly, the crewman left the ground vertically initially before being trailed behind the aircraft until winched into the open rear doors. Whether Air America actually ever used this equipment remains difficult to clarify, but the role was probably taken over by the USAF as at least two Hercules with Skyhooks were seen at Udorn in 1966.

BELOW: Dornier Do 28A XW-PCG (c/n 3026) at Thakhek West in November 1965. Note the dragom motif on the fuselage and a UH-34D, probably of the Royal Lao Air Force, in the background. *Jonathan Pote*

Air America
– the Tet Offensive and its aftermath

With air combat over Laos ceasing, and other organisations shouldering the responsibility for food and munitions drops, Air America found itself increasingly removed from the centre of operations. JONATHAN POTE concludes his look at the history of 'the CIA's secret airline.

The status quo changed forever in 1968. On December 24, 1967, a USAF TACAN (Tactical Air Navigation) beacon sited just east of Savannakhet in central Laos, one of half a dozen illegally located in that country to aid the war in Vietnam, was destroyed by North Vietnamese troops. Although this hampered air operations in the nearby northern area of South Vietnam, nobody realised the significance of this attack immediately. President Lyndon B. Johnson ordered a Christmas bombing pause over North Vietnam, hoping for talks with the regime there. He extended that pause when in January the North Vietnamese government announced that talks were agreed.

The South Vietnamese government and the Viet Cong also agreed a ceasefire over Tet, the Vietnamese Lunar New Year. This time, the American government had indeed been naïve. On January 31, the eve of the Tet celebrations, North Vietnamese forces attacked 36 out of 44 provincial capitals in South Vietnam, and the world looked on as American might was humiliated. The change in Laos was

ABOVE: Bell 204B N8513F was one of the first examples of the type acquired by Air America, in September 1965. It would go on to see a great deal of action in Vietnam and Laos throughout the conflict before being evacuated from Saigon aboard the USS *Denver* on April 29, 1975. *Mike Hooks Collection*

that henceforth all fighting would be done by North Vietnamese units and the Pathet Lao irregulars would be sidelined.

Fighting would also continue throughout the wet season as well as in the drier months, and the towns of Attopeu and Saravane in southern Laos would have to rely on air supply (largely by Air America) in the future. Both towns fell to the North Vietnamese in 1970. The increased tempo of North Vietnamese aggression greatly increased the number of refugees (to more than half a million), and, to feed them until they could produce crops once they were resettled, rice drops increased to 10,000,000lb (4,536,000kg) per month. Although there were some successes by Royal Lao Government forces, from now on the communists gained territory inexorably.

In March 1968 Phou Pha Thi (Lima Site 85) fell to an "at whatever cost" attack by North Vietnamese regular soldiers. This dramatically steep 5,000ft-high limestone karst, or outcrop, was in a strategic location near the North Vietnamese border and mounted a TSQ-81 radar and TACAN beacon to guide USAF aircraft in the Hanoi area. ▶

ABOVE: A characteristically anonymous Air America de Havilland DHC-4 Caribou taxies in at Lima Site 20, Sam Thong, on January 9, 1966. Among many Air America aircraft at Sam Thong that day was Prestwick Pioneer XL665, on loan from No 209 Sqn, based at Singapore, for use by the British Embassy. *Jonathan Pote*

AVIATION CLASSICS: AMERICAN COLD WAR STORIES 081

It was deep within enemy-held territory, entirely supplied by air and largely staffed by American civilians, many of whom died despite heroic rescue attempts by Air America helicopters. In an effort worthy of a Medal of Honor had they been in conventional military forces, Capt Kenwood held one skid of his Bell UH-1 Huey in contact with the clifftop, under effective communist fire, while Loy M. "Rusty" Irons assisted surviving technicians to climb aboard across the abyss below.

HELICOPTER VS BIPLANE

Air combat over Laos ended on January 11, 1968, as bizarrely as it had begun in 1961, with Communist Antonov An-2 *Colts* bombing the site being intercepted by a (civil-registered) Air America Huey, one or possibly both *Colts* being shot down by a hand-held machine-gun firing through the Huey's cabin door. The Air America crew members were immediately sacked, but then reinstated with commendations. (In 1961, Lt Khanpanth of the Royal Lao Air Force [RLAF] fatally damaged a Soviet-crewed Ilyushin Il-14 *Crate* over northern Laos, using his North American AT-6 Texan's air-to-ground rockets).

The pressure was on and (as in the wider conflict in South Vietnam) defeat loomed. Sikorsky UH-34s continued to shuttle troops, at times friendly soldiers in Pathet Lao uniforms. While inserting troops thus dressed was at times tense, picking up unknown, but believed friendly, troops in enemy uniforms at remote rendezvous points must have been very fraught indeed. In 1969 Vang Pao reoccupied the Plaine des Jarres for the first time in nearly a decade, capturing 25 Soviet-supplied PT-76 tanks, 200 lorries and thousands of tons of supplies – but it was a last gasp. The communist backlash in 1970 pushed his troops off the Plaine and pursued them south-west.

On March 13, 1970, a small elite North Vietnamese force captured Sam Thong, destroying the hospital and Air America facilities abandoned only hours before. The same year the "milk run", Air America's scheduled services to the major Mekong River towns using Douglas C-47s and de Havilland Canada DHC-4 Caribous, was terminated. The management of Air America felt obliged to tell its aircrew on other duties that they could refuse missions they deemed too dangerous. The memo listed the names of more than a dozen aircrew killed or missing in the previous year, and authorised crews to assess whether the risk of each mission was worth the potential benefits. Even "soft rice" (food) drops routinely drew anti-aircraft fire, although as the company had added "hot soup" (napalm canisters rolled out of freight doors over suspected communist troop concentrations) to its "menu", this was not surprising. In fact Air America stopped dropping rice altogether in 1971, as Continental Air Services Incorporated (CASI) offered a cheaper quote for the contract.

> The management of **Air America** felt obliged to **tell** its **aircrew** on other duties that they could **refuse missions** they deemed too **dangerous.**

TIMES GET TOUGH

Air America had to fight commercial competition as well as the communists and six of the now redundant Curtiss C-46 Commandos were sent to Tainan on Taiwan for storage. On December 27, 1971,

ABOVE: Vang Pao.

LEFT: The forbidding limestone outcrop of Phou Pha Thi, also known as Lima Site 85, where American forces operated a valuable radar station until it was overwhelmed by North Vietnamese troops in a hard-fought "at whatever cost" attack on March 10, 1968. *Jeannie Schiff/USAF*

Fairchild C-123 Provider "293" (originally C-123B 57-6293, by 1971 a C-123K) was lost without trace with four on board. As this loss was near the site of a road being built into northern Laos by the Chinese, it is likely that this new enemy was at fault. The purpose of this road was never entirely clear – from the southern border of communist China, it crossed some of the planet's most treacherous terrain and by the end of the war had reached Thailand. It seemed to have no relevance to the North Vietnamese struggle, other than Communist China being one of North Vietnam's major allies. It was an incredible engineering achievement, a proper all-weather road, unlike the Ho Chi Minh Trail, and was fiercely defended by Chinese anti-aircraft weapons, making it one of the most dangerous areas of Laos.

If the dangers of the task were not enough, Air America crews were occasionally murdered by their own side. On May 13, 1969, William J. Gibbs refused to take some Royal Lao Army troops aboard UH-34D "H-68" at Ban Dong Hene. As the helicopter lifted off, he was shot and fatally wounded. Fortunately for others on board, he was not the sole pilot. Not long afterwards, on August 19, 1969, Capt Ralph S. Davis was flying the short hop from "Alternate" (LS 20A, Long Tieng, the busy secret airbase on the other side of Skyline Ridge) to Sam Thong in Pilatus Turbo Porter N196X when he was fatally shot by "friendly" troops. All 13 aboard died.

There were still some innovations to come. North Vietnamese Ilyushin Il-28s bombed Ban Luang on the Plaine, and the Vietnam People's Air Force (VPAF) began using the captured airfield at Tchepone in south Laos after October 1968. On the night of December 6–7, 1972, a Hughes 500P (N351X or N352X) helicopter flew out of Thakhek to near Vinh (in North Vietnam) where a wire tap was successfully inserted for eavesdropping military telephone lines. A small device was attached to a telegraph pole and a relay station placed in a tree atop a high hill nearby. Once it was confirmed that the telephone conversations were being intercepted by American forces in Thailand or South Vietnam, the helicopter withdrew, still unnoticed. Night supply drops around the Ho Chi Minh Trail complex were made by de Havilland Canada Twin Otters using terrain-following radar. One once flew into North Vietnam, landing at Dien Bien Phu (the valley where the French were defeated in 1954) supporting a commando raid.

Of somewhat dubious value, a Caribou was used to drop millions of counterfeit currency notes over areas controlled by the Pathet Lao in an attempt to destroy an economy that probably did not rely on paper currency at all. However, the CIA had decided, on April 21, 1972, that air assets such as Air America were no longer a viable way to do business and that with the impending end of the war in south-east Asia they would be liquidated. Even with the death sentence pronounced (but not communicated to those on the front line), the year's budget exceeded US$40m and the company lost 12 aircraft and many crewmen that year.

PROVIDERS DOWN

On December 6, 1972, the four crew of C-123K Provider "648" had a remarkably lucky (or unlucky, depending on how you look at it) escape. With their aircraft disabled by anti-aircraft fire near Paksong in southern Laos, all were able to bale out within the small confines of a friendly area. Three were picked up by UH-34D "H-52", which suffered a tail-rotor tree strike with the third lift. With "H-52" forced to land in a minefield, "H-53" was near enough for a quick lift. However, "H-53" had extended on task for this snatch and soon had to put down, out of fuel. Finally turbine-powered Sikorsky S-58T XW-PHE brought everyone to Pakse,

ABOVE: Sikorsky UH-34D "H-F" of Air America lands at Sam Thong in January 1966. Most UH-34s used by Air America in Laos were serialled with the letter H followed by a number and it is probable that by the time the author arrived in country in 1965 "H-F" was a unique survivor of a previous identity system used by Air America in Laos. *Jonathan Pote*

where they were reunited with the fourth crew member – who had required just one helicopter rescue compared to their three.

On February 9, 1973, Provider "374" was shot down near Thakhek, with only one survivor. Less than two weeks later, on February 21, a ceasefire came into force and CASI (as the less "politically offensive" airline) took over most of Air America's contracts.

The company's forward air control Ravens immediately disappeared from the scene. Little else changed, however. The USAF used its full bombing inventory in the north of Laos now that it no longer raided North Vietnam and the 919th Air Transport Regiment of the VPAF continued to fly into airstrips in the north-

ABOVE: Curtiss C-46 XW-PBW, bare metal apart from Lao Erawan insignia on the fuselage and upper port wing surface and Lao flag on the tail, prepares to take off on a sortie from Vientiane in June 1966. Note the Sikorsky UH-34D of the International Control Commission, used to fly officials around Laos and Vietnam, parked opposite. *Jonathan Pote*

084 AVIATION CLASSICS: AMERICAN COLD WAR STORIES

east of Laos, principally at Sam Neua. The remaining Providers (by now all modified to C-123K status with auxiliary General Electric J85 turbojets) were transferred to the Royal Lao Air Force, although "524" was lost en route to Ban Houei Sai while still with Air America. The wreckage was not found for more than a week, despite intense searching, and even then could not be approached because of enemy ground fire. That it was again near the Chinese road was a probable explanation for the loss, the crew of five having lost their lives transporting a cargo of empty pallets.

Since 1966 Volpar N9542Z (a modified Beech C-45) had been used on 12hr photo-reconnaissance missions high over the Ho Chi Minh Trail area, using World War Two-vintage Fairchild cameras. On July 31, 1973, so close to the end of the chapter, the aircraft sustained severe damage from anti-aircraft fire. The pilot in command, Capt Pat Thorson, was fatally injured, although the copilot made a safe landing at Pakse. The author had seen N9542Z at Don Muang airbase (Bangkok) in 1966. Although the cameras were later updated, this ageing twin had provided almost all the photo-reconnaissance data required in Laos for a decade. It was replaced by Lockheed SR-71 Blackbirds and satellites – a quantum leap in technology.

THE FINAL DAYS

By November 1973 only half-a-dozen Air America aircraft remained in Laos; C-123K Providers used to convert RLAF crews and C-46 Commandos XW-PBV and 'PBW, which flew in Lao markings and did not publicise their ownership. On April 5, 1974, the communist Provisional Government of National Unity was formed. All American assets departed, although the embassy was closed for just one day before it was reopened by the new regime. On June 3, Caribou "389" crossed the Mekong River "at 1113Z" (around 1800hr local time) bound for Udorn in Thailand. The last Air America aircraft out of Laos, it was flown by Capt Fred Walker, who had flown C-47 B-817 of (then) CAT into Vientiane in 1957, to start the whole saga. The last telex from Air America's Lao office to that of the Chief Executive ended with the following: "And, in remembering, we will smile and look ahead to the next challenge. We grieve for those missing and dead in Laos and regret that they too could not have enjoyed today".

Air America operations from Udorn also rapidly wound down (from 14 aircraft in May 1974) and the last Air America flight out of the Thai airbase, on June 30, 1974, was Volpar N3278G on a ferry flight to Saigon, where the airline would continue to operate until that city fell on April 30, 1975. That last flight schedule document typed at Udorn bore a typed "Adieu" under the flight details, along with the following: "So ends the last sentence of the final paragraph of a saga which may have an epilogue but never a sequel. It has been to each participating individual an experience which varied according to his role and perspective. However, there is a common bond of knowledge and satisfaction of having taken part in something worthwhile and with a slight sense of pity for those lesser souls who could not, or would not, share in it. This last flight schedule is dedicated to those for whom a previous similar schedule represented an appointment with destiny."

In Saigon flight operations continued to the end. Indeed, Air America aircraft extracted the vast majority of those who fled that doomed city, both to Thailand and to aircraft carriers offshore. On April 29, 1975, the day before Saigon fell, C-47s "994" (originally 45-0994) and "147" (originally 43-16147) were among the last fixed-wing aircraft to leave. A decade before, in easier times, the author had flown in them several times around Laos.

AIR AMERICA PASSES INTO HISTORY

Bailed aircraft were returned to the American government. Legally-owned aircraft, 24 in all, and a large spares holding, were collected and valued for liquidation in a sale at Roswell, New Mexico; a C-46 Commando, "equipped with antique tube electronics", was valued at $20,000, a Caribou at $100,000. Some US$20m was eventually returned to the USA's treasury. Thus Air America passed into history. There has never been, nor ever will be again, anything like it. There was indeed no sequel, just as the last flight authorisation sheet prophesied. The USA ▶

> *Air America operations from **Udorn** also rapidly wound down (from 14 aircraft in May 1974) and the **last Air America flight** out of the Thai airbase, on June 30, 1974, was **Volpar N3278G** on a ferry flight to **Saigon**.*

BELOW: Douglas C-47B "994" at Thakhek East in 1966. The aircraft was polished bare metal with its identity repeated on the nose and "Air America" painted on the rear fuselage — this aircraft, C-47 "147" and Caribou "392" were the only Air America aircraft to bear the company name in Laos.
Jonathan Pote

AIR AMERICA AND THE NIGHTMARE OF PLAYING HARD AND FAST WITH IDENTITIES...

One of Air America's most interesting facets concerns the identity painted on each individual airframe. Each sovereign state has allocated prefixes to allow it to maintain an internationally recognisable register of its civil aircraft. Likewise, its military authorities can allocate serials which are complemented by recognised national markings which are also internationally acceptable. Air America did not see the need to comply with these protocols in Laos. Chiang Kai-shek's government in Taiwan used a simple "B" followed by a number for its civil aircraft, and Air America's aircraft in South Vietnam were on this register. In Laos, just as the Geneva Accords came into force in July 1962, the B prefix was removed both to further the aim of "plausible deniability" and because the Chinese Nationalist Government on Taiwan was politically unpopular in the area. Thus Air America used a simple three-figure number for each airframe (although from the mid-1960s some were placed on the Lao civil register, prefixed XW-). This number could be derived from a Taiwanese registration, the previous USAF serial number, the aircraft's constructor's number, or (it would seem) randomly drawn from a hat. The American FAA annotated the records of some Air America and other CIA aircraft as "File in locked drawer", presumably to avoid unauthorised investigation.

Thus Douglas C-47A B-817, the first Civil Air Transport aircraft into Laos, became "817" (but had reverted to B-817 when the author last saw it in Saigon in 1966). If the USAF serial was the basis, usually the "last three" appeared (for example C-47B 45-994 became "994"). Occasionally any three were used (e.g. C-130A 56-0510 became "605". This aircraft was lost on approach to Lima Site 20A, Long Tieng, on April 10, 1970, when it hit Phou Bia, a 7,500ft-high mountain). In 1971 the Royal Australian Air Force (RAAF) gave C-47 A65-16 to the Royal Lao Air Force. Originally built as 42-24136, it became "998" from its constructor's number, 9998, probably because there was already an RLAF aircraft marked "136". Although this was an RLAF aircraft, it is very likely that Air America at Udorn in Thailand prepared it for service and chose its number. A considerable benefit of Air America running its own company register was that any aircraft lost would not be subject to any inquiry by authorities outside the company itself. Because there is no record of international recognition of these identities, quotation marks have been used to identify them in the main text.

Even these dubious identities were further corrupted at times. Sometimes, more than one aircraft carried the same identity, the Lao civil marks XW-PEA being known to have been carried by three separate Helio Couriers simultaneously. Aircraft used on the more covert missions changed identities to provide alibis for known Air America aircraft. Constructor's plates as well as exterior markings were removed from some airframes and engines when this level of evasiveness was reached; a nightmare for engineers maintaining powerplants of unknown variant or hours run. Constructor's plates were further abused; an aircraft could be destroyed and yet reappear, fully serviceable, on the flight line within days. In this case a replacement airframe would have been obtained from the American military, repainted as the lost aircraft, and the constructor's plate transferred. This ploy was used to "prove" that the original destroyed aircraft could not have been in Air America service. Most of Air America's aircraft bore no paint bar their number, which aided rapid changes of identity: "All you need is a tin of paint and three hours" was one quote referring to this frequent event.

In an ironic double bluff, USAF crews flying unmarked USAF C-130s out of Takhli in Thailand were issued with Air America flight suits and badges. Better to be seen as part of the airline that should not be there rather than the USAF, which definitely should not be carrying out a covert task!

ABOVE: In April 1965 Continental Air Services Inc (CASI) was formed as a subsidiary of Continental Airlines with a view to "helping" Air America with its commitments in Laos; in reality Continental wanted a share of the government's subsidies for such work. CASI operated Lockheed L-382s into Laos for a brief period during 1965–66. *Jonathan Pote*

> This **history** is dedicated to the **243 men** of **Air America** who were **killed** in service, mainly in **action**.

still has clandestine work to be done, but it uses other methods.

This history is dedicated to the 243 men of Air America who were killed in service, mainly in action. Undoubtedly I met some of them, and like many other Americans I knew in south-east Asia, they were brave men who gave their all in a cause they truly believed in, however harshly history has subsequently judged them. ●

Acknowledgments
The author would like to thank Dr Joe F. Leeker for his help with the preparation of this two-part history of Air America in Laos. Professor Leeker is the custodian of the Air America Collection at the University of Texas in Dallas. For more information on the murky but fascinating world of Air America visit *www.utdallas.edu/library/collections/speccoll/Leeker/history/index.html*

BELOW: Caribou "393" was one of several C-7As bailed from the US Army, with which it was serialled 61-2393. Here it thunders down the runway at Sam Thong in January 1966. Sam Thong was typical of the primitive strips from which Air America aircraft operated, offering little margin for error and a requirement for superb airmanship. *Jonathan Pote*

AIRCRAFT IN LAOS
SEPTEMBER 1965 – AUGUST 1966

Beech C-45 and derivatives

XW-TAP	C-45 Silver overall, VTE 24 Sep 65
XW-TBC	C-45 Silver overall, parked VTE, rarely flown
XW-TBD	ditto 'BC
XW-TBF	ditto 'BC
F-OAGB	C-45 Silver overall, white decking, blue cheat line. Tricoleur on rudders. AMBASSADE DE FRANCE above windows. Black inner nacelles. Ld TK West 6 Mar 66
N801T	Possibly mis-ident for N906T
N906T	Super H-18, c/n BA667. Yellow and cream, Air Vietnam insignia on tail, blue boar head insignia of 390th Tactical Fighter Squadron (Vietnam) on fuselage. Seen VTE 23 Jan 66 (for o/haul)
N5454V	C-45 Light grey overall, silver control surfaces. Black registration rear fuselage only. VTE 30 Jan 66
N7591C	Used by Air America. Ambassador's aircraft, USA flag behind cockpit. Deep blue and silver. Minor prang TK West 19 Jan 66
N9664C	As '91C but "64C" repeated on nose. First seen VTE 18 Apr 66

Curtiss C-46 Commando

Air America

136	TSN, 6 May 66. Air America, aluminium overall
136	Curtiss C-46F, c/n 22465, 44-78642. "To CAT 1953, destroyed Pha Khao 13 Aug 61, 6 killed" – but seen as above
138	VTE and TSN, 6 May 66. Air America, aluminium overall
138	Curtiss C-46F, c/n 22500, s/n 44-78677. Possibly at Takhli 61, at VTE 64, TSN 66, Taiwan 71.
910	VTE 24 Sep 65 and 27 Sep 65. Air America, aluminium overall
924	VTE 2 Oct 65. Air America, aluminium overall
N1361N	VTE. Air America, aluminium overall
N1383N	VTE and flew SKT–VTE 11 Aug 66. Air America, aluminium overall
N1383N	Curtiss C-46D, c/n 33641, 44-78245. To Air America Oct 1963, damaged at VTE 24 Jan 65 when T-28 exploded. Kicker T. Homhuan fell out 26 Mar 70 and survived, rescued by UH-34 "H-62". N1383N became RP-C1461 in Philippines 1975, wfu 1980
N1386N	VTE and flew VTE–SKT 16 Oct 65. Air America, aluminium overall. Crashed EFATO SKT 25 Nov 68; 23 pax, three crew killed, two pax survived
N1386N	Curtiss C-46D, c/n 22265, 44-78442. To USAID VTE 1964. Parachutist killed 3 Sep 64, 'chute did not open. 25 Nov 68 crashed after take-off at Savannakhet, two miles from runway at 1530hr local. Engine failed, wing burned, aircraft broke up. "24 killed"
N9458Z	VTE 8 Jan 66, Air America, aluminium overall, AF O-477589 erased but visible (possibly ex-44-77589)
N9458Z	Curtiss C-46D, c/n 32985, 44-78589 (NB different from above). To Air America Nov 65, to South Vietnam 1971?, left TSN on 29 April 75 as Saigon fell, flew to Taiwan. Became RP-C1462 in Philippines Bird & Sons/ Bird Air
N65561	
N67961	VTE 27 Sep 65. Blue cheatline
N4871V	VTE Brown cheatline. Cannibalised, less outer wing panels and engines
N7560Z	VTE
N9473Z	VTE 2 Oct 65, 4 Jun 66
N9473Z	Curtiss C-46F, c/n 22293, leased by Air America ex Bird & Sons, crashed after engine failure, Phu Cum (LS 50), with CASI, 13 Aug 67. Port engine hit by enemy fire, forced-landed off airfield, one crew seriously injured, four pax, other crewman OK
N9760Z	VTE 27 Sep 65, 2 Oct 65. Blue cheatline
N9760Z	Curtiss C-46F, c/n 22574, leased by Bird & Sons to Air America 1964. To "Tri-9 Corp" in Phnom Penh, destroyed by rocket 26 May 72

Lao Register

XW-PBV	VTE 27 Sep 65. Bare metal, Erawan insignia
XW-PBV	Curtiss C-46D, c/n 22232, s/n 44-78409. Used for arms drops in Cuba 17–20 April 1961, before Bay of Pigs invasion. Became B-914 after, to Laos 63 as XW-EAA. Air America to USAID, then to Royal Lao govt as 'PBV in 1964. Damaged in storm at VTE 24 Mar 76, then registered RDPL-34040
XW-PBW	VTE 4 Jun 66. Bare metal, Erawan insignia
XW-PBW	Curtiss C-46D, c/n 33451, s/n 44-78055. At Bay of Pigs, Cuba, 1961, with false Guatemalan Air Force serial "1887". To USAID and then Bird & Sons, VTE, as XW-EAB. Became XW-PBW in 64, to Royal Lao Govt 1 Dec 73, crashed 75 miles NNE of VTE 15 Oct 74
XW-PCU	VTE 13 Feb 66, Royal Air Lao, ex-Air Vietnam; white decking, deep blue upper cheatline, red lower cheatlines, overall gloss grey. Nacelles black under wing. Believed ex-B-517

Lisunov Li-2 Cab (Russian licence-built Douglas DC-3)

01	Silver grey overall, derelict at VTE since Phoumi's Coup in 1960
611	Olive drab overall, ex-Aeroflot, derelict VTE since Phoumi's Coup 60
627	As 611
651	As 611

Douglas DC-3/C-47 Skytrain Royal Lao Air Force

Fin markings as noted by author

21057	SKT 8 Sep 65
127	SKT 8 Sep 65
51127	TKE 16 Jul 66. Marked as 51127 (not as 127), s/n 45-1127A by plate. Neutral grey overall
48157	SKT 8 Sep 65
O-48159	TKW 18 Nov 65 and 20 Feb 66. VC-47D s/n 43-48159 by plate, but bare interior with parachute rails though still soundproofed. White decking, grey belly, cheatline above and below windows
24178	VTE 29 Jan 66 with Thai football team, TKE 8 June 66 with British Ambassador and other VIPs. 20-seat airline VIP interior. C-47A s/n 42-24178 by plate. Silver/grey overall
O-15316	VTE 29 Jan 66. VC-47D s/n 43-15316 by plate. Grey belly
356	VTE 2 Oct 65
49356	PSE 2 May 65. Landed. Grey overall
374	SKT 8 Sep 65. Also TKE. C-47D s/n 43-19374 by plate
375	SKT 8 Sep 65. In hangar, all centre fuselage skin removed
O-316375	SKT 2 May 66. Blue serial and cheatline. Rudder and elevators removed
O-23398	SKT and PSE 8 Sep 65. TKW 15 Nov 65, TKE Jun 66, Day-Glo arrow on nose, black cowlings and fairings, grey belly
869429	PSE 8 Sep 65
501	SKT 8 Sep 65, TKW Nov 65, 20 Mar 66
O-15519	SKT 8 Sep 65, PSE 2 May 66, brought spares to repair "633" at TKE Jul 66. White decking. Also TKW November battle
633	VTE 24 Sep 65, TKW Nov 65, crashed and repaired TKE 1 Jul 66 onwards, s/n 43-45633
656	SKT 8 Sep 65 and TKW November battle
374656	SKT 8 Sep 65
47658	PSE 8 Sep 65
15666	TKW 12 Nov 65, LP 1966 C-47A s/n 43-15666 by plate
30678	TKW 1 Mar 66. Probably C-47A 30678 by plate. Silver/ grey overall, upper inner nacelles and lower fairings black
685	TKW 19 Nov 65 bringing Prince Souvanna Phouma, Prime Minister; C-47D s/n 43-48685 by plate. Royal/ Prime Ministerial aircraft of the RLAF. Airline interior. White decking, markings outlined in yellow
806	TKE 23 Mar 66
956	unconfirmed
47965	PSE 8 Sep 65, blue cowlings. Was later marked O-47965 at TKW in Nov 65. C-47A s/n 43-47965A by plate, sole RLAF C-47 with nose art, actually on upper fuselage side behind cockpit, on port (and possibly starboard) side – a stylised cooking-pot and fire with Kim Gia above and Burner Special below (Col Burner was US Military Attaché – USMA – in VTE). Based VTE, seen there 24 Sep 65. NB Air America had C-47 "965" (silver overall) at VTE on 8 Oct 65. Possibly same aircraft between two colour schemes
108976	TKE. Newly repainted, no national markings, RLAF lettering painted over, black cheatlines above and below windows. Col Burner, USMA, aboard
976	c/n 13608, ex-42-108976 Stored at Udorn 1973 still in RLAF markings
991	SKT 8 Sep 65. TKW Nov 65. C-47A s/n 43-45991 by plate
Nil	TKW 18 Nov 65. Completely unmarked, "corroded aluminium" overall with sanded-off old-style USAF markings and serial O-00979 plus a badge still discernible. Believed to be C-47A-75-DL s/n 42-100979
998	42-24136, ex-RAAF A65-16, VH-AFF, donated by Australia to RLAF 28 Aug 71. RLAF serial from c/n 9998

Air America

147	Aluminium overall. No marks, initially bar serial on fin. Milk-run regular
147	Douglas C-47B c/n 20613, s/n 43-16147A. Bailed from USAF to Air America 61. Damaged at VTE on 24 Jan 65 when T-28 exploded. More damaged than "817". To South Vietnam late 66. Struck steel bundle while landing at Ban Loc, Jan 69; lost starboard wheel, prop and tailwheel. Back in service Feb 69. Port mainwheel collapsed Ban Me Thuot East 71. Repaired. Due for return to USAF June 75, fled Saigon 29 Apr 75, the day before South Vietnam fell. To RTAF initially as 147, then L2-53/19. SOC 81
817	As "147" but with B-817 discernable on fin. Milk-run regular until early 66. Seen in Saigon 6 May 66 freshly overhauled and marked as B-817 again
817	Douglas C-47A c/n 19256, s/n 42-100793. To CAT 52 as B-817, sank in mud in Laos 60, hit truck VTE 61, taxy collision 63, premature undercarriage retraction 64, damaged by exploding T-28 at VTE 65, battle damage 66 while on training flight, mortared at Da Nang 67, rocket damage at TSN 68, to Khmer Air Lines 73 as XU-AAE
879	Grey overall, fitted with cargo/rice rollers on floor. VTE 23 Jan 66 and a few other rare occasions
879	Douglas C-47B c/n 34325/17058, s/n 45-1055. Previously B-879, used to drop to "Road Watch Teams" out of Udorn, late 60s. To China Airlines 74 as B-1555. WFU 77
965	Aluminium overall, seen VTE 8 Oct 65. Possibly 47965/O-47965 of RLAF
994	C-47B. As "147"
994	C-47A, c/n 34259, 45-994. (USAAF serials states C-47B). Bailed to Air America 60. To South Vietnam late 66. Due for return to USAF June 75, escaped from TSN on 29 Apr 75 to BKK as Saigon fell. To RTAF as L2-54/19

In mid-June 1966 "147" and "994", the remaining milk-run regulars, were given a polish, their serials repeated on the nose, and a stylised "Air America" painted on the fuselage sides

United States Air Force

348311	VTE 15 Oct 65. First seen at Don Muang, BKK, 1 Sep 65 as a US Navy R4D, then in VTE as the Bangkok US Air Attaché aircraft. White decking
45-1093	VTE, 8 Oct 65 and 15 Oct 65. Full USAF colours
O-16364	VTE, 1966. Possibly USMA aircraft

L'Armée de l'Air

49821	VTE 8 Oct 65. Callsign F-SDLR, French Air Attaché. White decking. Named Chateau de Wattay. Tricolore on fin. TKE to collect French professors for home leave mid-66. Beneath paint Iraqi Air Force markings and code letter "H" discernible

Royal Australian Air Force

A65-70	VTE 66. 2 Sqn RAAF. Silver with white decking, roundels above and below wings, fin flash and lightning insignia also on fin. See also RLAF "998"

Royal Air Lao

XW-TAD	VTE. Red and white colour scheme
XW-TAE	scheme as XW-TAD
XW-TAF	BKK, VTE, PSE, LP. Scheme as XW-TAD
XW-TAH	scheme as XW-TAD

Others

XW-PAP	C-47, ex-N7780C, USAF marks discernible, very scruffy, white decking, no underwing reg. Cargo rollers in cabin. PSE 8 Sep 65, TKW 20 Mar 66
XW-PAR	VTE 24 Sep 65. Red, white and blue flash. Operating with French airline Cie Veha Akat
XW-PCP	C-53 Skytrooper or DC-3 (small door). Arrived VTE about 26 Dec 65 as B-1533, with light grey control surfaces and wing underside, and Air Vietnam insignia on tail. N155A was discernible on rear fuselage under paint. Repainted as XW-PCP and in service by 29 Dec 65
XW-PDA	VTE 21 May 66. Operating with Cie Veha Akat
N560	VTE 24 Sep 65. Green cheatline
N560K	VTE 8 Jan 66. Continental Air Services Inc (CASI)
N64910	VTE 24 Sep 65. CASI. Ex-Frontier Airlines. Possibly N64810
N8744R	TKW Nov 65. CASI. Silver, white decking, green cheatline

Douglas DC-4/C-54 Skymaster

XW-TAG	Royal Air Lao, silver with emerald-green nacelles. VTE 2 Oct 65.

Fairchild C-123B Provider

All Air America aircraft; C-123Bs in 65–66, with underwing droptank lugs, aluminium overall, identity on fin only, red propeller warning bands. All surviving C-123Bs converted at Fairchild to C-123Ks with additional jet pods during 68–69

"293"	VTE 3 Jun 66
"374"	VTE 24 Sep 65, TKW Nov 65, ex-84374
"538"	TKW 17 Nov 65
"613"	VTE 18 Apr 66
"617"	VTE 1966
"655"	VTE 24 Sep 65, TKW Nov 65
"671"	VTE 66
N5003X	VTE 8 Sep 65
N5003X	c/n 20234, s/n 55-4573. Ex-347th Troop Carrier Squadron (TCS), Pope AFB, as "510", then N5003X in 62. Ground collision 64, blew over several a/c 29 Oct 64 during run-up, crashed on go-around at LS 20A, Long Tieng, 3 Oct 65. Copilot Frank Muscal killed
N5005X	TKW Nov 65
N5005X	c/n 20206, s/n 55-4545. Ex-347th TCS, Pope AFB, 1962, as "530", became N5005X. Landed short Jun 64, engine fire near Takhli. Was Victor control 13 Oct 65 for crash of "H-32" near Saravane. Became "545" Jun 66. Starboard mainwheel collapse Nam Bac (LS 203) 18 Oct 65. To C-123K at Fairchild 68. Nosewheel collapse at Ban La Tee (LS 190). Caught fire Udorn 71. Severe battle damage 28 Dec 71. Double engine fire out of Ban Houei Sai 24 May 73, one prop blade through fuselage and hit opposite jet. Repaired, to RLAF 1973
N5007X	VTE 2 Oct 65. LP–VTE Jun 66
N5007X	c/n 20216, s/n 55-4555. Ex-347th TCS, Pope AFB, 1962, as "550", became N5007X. Crewman Rizal Alomares fell out on to runway Udorn 65, killed. Became "555" in Jun 66. First Air America C-123B converted to C-123K, Apr 68. Hit by anti-aircraft fire despite civil registration 71. On 27 Aug 72 en route Vang Vieng (LS 20A) hit top of ridge in bad weather, nine killed

Lockheed L-382B (civil C-130) Hercules

N9260R	TKW 30 Nov 65. CASI.
N9261R	TKW, later than '60R. CASI.

These two civil Hercules (the first to be built) were ordered by Alaskan Airlines but taken over by CASI. Arrived VTE Nov 65, contract cancelled mid-66

de Havilland Canada DHC-4/ CV-2A/C-7A Caribou

All Air America aircraft; bare metal overall, except "853" with identity on fin

"389"	VTE 27 Sep 65
"392"	VTE 24 Sep 65. s/n 61-2392. Sam Thong–VTE 9 Jan 66 and TK–PSN–VTE milk run 18 Apr 66
"393"	VTE 8 Sep 65
"401"	24 & 27 Sep 65 & 7 Oct 65
"430"	VTE 8 & 24 Sep 65 & 2 Oct 65
"851"	VTE 8 Oct 65
"853"	DM 1 Sep 65, SKT 8 Sep 65, Sam Thong 9 Jan 66. Commissary aircraft, light grey overall

The author's eyewitness listing of aircraft seen operating in Laos during September 1965 to August 1966. Although by no means a comprehensive list, it is, we believe, one of the most thorough yet published.

Contemporary eyewitness record compiled by Jonathan Pote, Volunteer in the Colombo Plan Medical Team, September 1965–August 1966, revised and added to from other sources

(Notes in italics are added from Professor Joe Leeker's research)

Sikorsky UH-34D Choctaw

Air America

All olive drab overall with white identity on fin. No other markings

"H-F"	Sam Thong 9 Jan 66. Believed to be sole survivor of earlier series of UH-34D identities
"H-12"	TKW 23 Jul 66, carrying Pathet Lao defectors. LP May/Jun 66
"H-14"	
"H-15"	TKW 1 Mar 66, refugee evacuation
"H-22"	TKW–Ban Na Koke–Ban Na Ken (north-east of Thakhek) 27 Apr 66, visited Japanese colonel. Helo missing for three days with CIA case officer aboard. Reason for absence not known
"H-27"	VTE 8 Sep 65, Sam Thong 9 Jan 66
"H-28"	Sam Thong 9 Jan 66
"H-29"	
"H-30"	PSE 8 Sep 65. Code "N9" discernible under paint
"H-31"	TKW 6 Mar 66
"H-33"	TKW, Nov 65. Ex-Bu Aer 149368 of US Marine Corps unit HMM-363, unit code YZ64 discernible beneath paint
"H-34"	VTE 2 Oct 65
"H-35"	Sam Thong 9 Jan 66
"H-36"	TKW 15 Mar 66
"H-37"	VTE 8 Sep 65, Sam Thong 9 Jan 66
"H-38"	27 Apr 66. First of five "new" helos, "H38"–"H42", with dorsal antennae
"H-40"	
"H-41"	TKW 20 Jul 66, CIA case officer aboard

Royal Lao Air Force

Olive drab, Erawan on fuselage, white serial on fin

"1332"	SKT 8 Sep 65, TKW with Crown Prince 14 Sep 65, TKW Nov 65, landed twice in hospital grounds, presumed casevacs
"1335"	Based VTE, there 8 Oct 65, TKW 14 Sep 65 with Crown Prince
"3846"	TKW 9 Mar 66, "E3" and US markings discernible beneath paint

International Control Commission

White overall, based VTE for CIC (Commission Internationale pour/de Contrôle) Large "CIC" on fuselage, serial on fin.

"CIC 4"	VTE 24 Sep 65
"CIC 5"	VTE 24 Sep 65
"CIC 6"	

North American T-28

All T-28s light grey overall, serial on fin. Many serials started O-13xxx, but this could not be written down for each aircraft as time was too short (aircraft side by side, seen from moving C-47). Many had an eagle insignia. Probably all had Erawan. Serials listed here In order of last three digits, unless full serial known. Believed disposition of RLAF T-28s at the time: SKT 15; VTE 9; PSE 6; LP 3; others including Long Tieng 9; total about 42–45

???	Wreckage on strip CF4, Phou Khou Khouai, about 62 miles (100km) north-east of VTE
"1225"	
"331"	SKT 8 Sep 65
"345"	SKT 8 Sep 65
"351"	SKT 8 Sep 65
O-00374 (?)	Took off VTE 13 Feb 66, one of formation of nine
O-13465	SKT 8 Sep 65, 16 Oct 65, low over Thakhek 11 Nov 65
"467"	SKT 8 Sep 65, 16 Oct 65
"469"	SKT 8 Sep 65
"472"	SKT 8 Sep 65
"506"	SKT 8 Sep 65
O-13507	SKT 16 Oct 65
"508"	SKT 8 Sep 65, 16 Oct 65. Bombed target nine miles (15km) east of Thakhek 12 Nov 65
O-13518	
"531"	SKT 8 Sep 65, 16 Oct 65
"538"	SKT 8 Sep 65, 16 Oct 65
"608"	SKT 8 Sep 65
O-13617	
"7622"	SKT 16 Oct 65
"647"	SKT 8 Sep 65
O-13656	SKT 8 Sep 65
"668"	SKT 8 Sep 65
O-13743	Took off VTE 13 Feb 66. Formation of nine aircraft
"0765"	
O-13768	Wreckage (tail only) seen at VTE 13 Feb 66, believed to have crashed during low-level roll
"3771"	Took off VTE 13 Feb 66. Formation of nine aircraft
"774"	SKT 16 Oct 65
"7777"	SKT 16 Oct 65
O-17779	SKT 16 Oct 65
O-13791	Took off VTE 13 Feb 66, one of formation of nine aircraft. Possibly O-13719

(Also O-17778 was seen at at Pochentong, Phnom Penh, serving with the Royal Khmer Air Force)

de Havilland Canada DHC-2 /L-20A Beaver

Royal Lao Air Force

82046	SKT 16 Oct 65. Olive drab
"2052"	SKT 8 Sep 65. Grey overall. Serial 82052 in cockpit. Based VTE, at TKW 22 Feb 66. Seen SKT 2 May 66, minus rudder and elevator
82052	c/n 1384, ex-58-2052
82053	Olive drab, yellow serial on fin, RLAF on fuselage, western script on port, Lao on starboard. Often at TKW, based there during Battle of Thakhek, Nov 65. Carried 0·5in machine-gun in port cabin door, plus four small bomb racks under wings
82053	c/n 1385 ex-58-2053 RLAF. Returned to US Army, later became N577V, still current in Alaska in 2010

XW-TBB	Silver overall, Royal Air Lao markings. Based VTE, seen there 24 Sep 65, 2 Oct 66
F-OAIV	French Embassy aircraft, based VTE. Silver, white top, tricolor on tail. VTE 24 Sep 65, Sam Thong 9 Jan 1966, TKW 24 Feb 66

Helio 395 Courier

All Air America aircraft. Bare metal overall bar serial on fin and black triangle under port wing, apex to rear

"166"	VTE 8 Sep 65
"169"	Ex-13169
"183"	
"524"	VTE 30 Jan 66
"541"	See XW-PEA
"839"	VTE 13 Feb 66, buckled rear fuselage; crated and sent to USA
"845"	VTE 24 Sep 65
"857"	VTE 11 Aug 66, brand new
"865"	VTE 24 Sep 65
"869"	
"965"	VTE 8 Oct 65
XW-PBS	
XW-PBT	VTE 2 Oct 65
XW-PBX	
XW-PBY	VTE 18 Apr 66, and remains at VTE 11 Aug 66
XW-PCA	Sam Thong 9 Jan 66
XW-PEA	TKW 23 Jul 66, "541" discernible under paint

Cessna L-19/O-1 Bird Dog

Royal Lao Air Force

"666"	SKT 16 Oct 65, yellow overall, also TKE 1 Jul 66 after crash of C-47 "633"
"4364"	SKT 8 Sep 65. Olive drab overall
"6468"	TKE 1 Jul 66 after crash of C-47 "633"
???	TKE. Abandoned fuselage, yellow overall, beside TKE all year. Ex-51-12650, c/n 23374

Pilatus PC-6A Turbo Porter

Air America

No standard colour scheme, all in individual markings

XW-PBL	VTE 8 Sep 65, crated for USA after crash near LP; 2 killed
XW-PCB	VTE 24 Sep 65, Sam Thong 9 Jan 66
XW-PCC	Mid grey overall, black cheatline
XW-PCD	
XW-PCE	Sam Thong 9 Jan 66
XW-PCK	VTE 26 Dec 65. Grey overall
XW-PCL	Sam Thong 9 Jan 66. White, blue cheatline and rudder mass balance
XW-PCN	VTE 26 Dec 65. Mid-grey overall
XW-PCO	Sam Thong 9 Jan 66. Mid-grey overall, black cheatline
XW-PCQ	Mid-grey overall
XW-PCR	VTE 21 May 66. Mustard yellow overall
XW-PDC	VTE 4 Jun 66. Yellow and white
N12235	LP 3 Jun 66. Blue and silver
N9444	VTE 11 Aug 66. Wrecked

Dornier Do 28

XW-PCG	PSE 8 Sep 65, TKW15 Nov 65. Dull silver overall, maroon stripe, Vietnamese dragon on fuselage. Do 28A-1 c/n 3026, built Friedrichshafen, initially N4222G. Used by Air America
XW-PCT	See N9184X
XW-PDB	See N4228G
XW-TBJ	VTE 8 Oct 65, SKT 14 Dec 65, again in VTE late Dec 65 following crash. Used by Air America
N4224G	VTE 8 Sep 65. Used by Air America
N4228G	Do 28A-1. VTE Jan 66 on overhaul, then seen damaged. Silver overall. Seen re-registered as XW-PDB at TKW 22 Jul 66 and later
N9180X	Do 28B-1. VTE 8 Jan 65; c/n 3085, built 64. VTE–Sam Thong 9 Jan 66
N9181X	Do 28B-1 c/n 3086
N9182X	Do 28B-1 VTE 8 Oct 65, TKW Nov 65; c/n 3087
N9183X	Do 28B-1 VTE 23 Jan 66; c/n 3057
N9184X	Do 28B-1 VTE 23 Jan 66, c/n 3058. Seen again PSE 2 May 66, silver overall, registered as XW-PCT
N9185X	Do 28B-1 VTE 23 Jan 66; c/n 3059
N9186X	Do 28B-1 VTE 23 Jan 66; c/n not noted

NB N9180X–N9186X were all red and cream. N9183X–N9186X were all built in 1965 and arrived at VTE on 23 Jan 66 after a ferry flight in loose formation. 541lit overload tanks fitted for delivery

Cessna U-17A (Cessna 185 Skywagon)

64-14867	TKE 17 Jun 66. Light grey overall, Erawan on fuselage, full serial in black on fin, "867" underwing
64-17797	VTE 2 Oct 65. Written off VTE 12 Oct 65, burnt out after take-off crash. Pilot unhurt. Wreckage remained in VTE. Colours as 64-14867
65-10853	VTE 1 Jan 66 and later. Colours as above, but serial painted in light blue instead of black

Aero Commander 560

2714	Often seen VTE but based SKT. At TKW during Nov 65 fighting for Thakhek. Blue and white colour scheme, with fuselage Erawan; c/n 214, built Oklahoma March 1955

Beech L-23D Seminole

76061	VTE and TKW. US Army Attaché's aircraft. Red and white colour scheme

Republic F-105F Thunderchief

38365	12 Oct 65. Stores pylon only, in army camp at K15

	Mahaxay Mil Mi-4 Hound
14108	VTE all year. Derelict but complete, on north side of Wattay, with four Li-2s. Presentation aircraft from Soviet Russia 60

Prestwick Pioneer CC Mk 1

XL665	Arrived VTE 2 Oct 65. British Embassy aircraft, detached from 209 Sqn, Singapore; c/n 126. Camouflaged. Often used to bring British embassy staff to TKW, including Ambassador, Sir Frederick Warner, during the November fighting for Thakhek.

Scottish Aviation Twin Pioneer

XW-PBJ	VTE 8 Jan 65, scruffy blue colour scheme. Used by CASI and fitted for cargo dropping. Built 1958, "PAL" (Philippine Air Lines) discernible beneath paint
XW-PBP	VTE 16 Oct 65, and Sam Thong 9 Jan 66. White top, grey belly, wide black or deep blue horizontal stripe including windows and in front of cockpit. Neat. Also ex-PAL

Wren 460 (Cessna 182G)

N3790U	VTE 24 Sep 65; c/n 182-55190

Piper PA-24 Comanche

N3267P	VTE 24 Sep 65

Piper PA-23 Apache

N2267P	VTE 11 Dec 65, CASI

Beechcraft Baron 55

N1349Z	VTE 2 Oct 65, TKW 15 Nov 65 during fighting

Boeing 307 Stratoliner

F-BELV	VTE 15 Oct 65. International Control Commission; c/n 1996, ex-TWA NC19905, later C-75 42-88624
F-BELX	VTE 23 Jan 66 International Control Commission; c/n 1999, ex-TWA NC19907, later C-75 42-88625

NB For full information on the South-east Asian careers of these former TWA airliners, see the author's From Penthouse to Workhorse feature in The Aviation Historian Issue No 1

Lockheed L-188A Electra

VR-HFN	VTE 23 Jan 66. Cathay Pacific Airways, second production Electra

Jodel D140B

XW-PCV	VTE 4 Jun 66. Red and cream colour scheme

Notes on serial numbers etc

AF	USAF serials
"O"	e.g. "O-12345" is for "Obsolescent", and not a zero
B-XXX	(e.g. B-607) Chinese Nationalist/Formosa/Taiwan register
"by plate"	The stenciled full aircraft serial number (including fiscal year of order) behind cockpit on port side
c/n	Constructor's number. Many C-47s were allocated the wrong number by some admin error, and thus have a number on the maker's plate different from that allocated
"xyz"	e.g. "991". Any (usually three-figure) number not thought to be a legitimate full serial, possibly the last three of a legitimate identity, or last three of a c/n, or just plain fiction (Air America types mainly), referred to as "identity" to indicate possible lack of legality. Serials, registrations and c/ns are considered legal identities

Discernible: possible to make out previous markings etc either under new paint or on a stripped area
"Silver/aluminium/light grey": Could be any of these, not specific

Abbreviations

BKK	Bangkok
CASI	Continental Air Services Incorporated
DM	Don Muang, Bangkok
EFATO	Engine failure after take-off
Erawan	Royal Lao Air Force national insignia (3 x elephants & parasol)
LP	Luang Prabang
LS	Landing site (LS 20A etc)
PSE	Pakse
RLAF	Royal Lao Air Force
RTAF	Royal Thai Air Force
SKT	Savannakhet
TK	Thakhek, East or West
TKE	Thakhek East. Usually known as K6 (Kilometer 6) locally. Wet weather alternate to TKW/K2 (see below)
TKW	Thakhek West. Usually known as TK2 (Kilometer 2) locally, flooded in monsoon
TSN	Tan Son Nhut, Saigon, (Ho Chi Minh City)
VTE	Vientiane (Wattay/Vattai etc)

New year on Skyline Ridge

Following on from his recollections about Air America in Laos, JONATHAN POTE remembers being invited in January 1966 to celebrate the Meo Lunar New Year at Sam Thong, reached via an unforgettable flight from Vientiane to Lima Site 20, a remote airstrip buried deep in the Lao jungle…

In September 1965 I left school and volunteered for what would now be called a "gap year" before studying medicine. It was only appropriate that I should be sent to work on a medical team, but extremely fortunate for me that it should be in Laos in South-east Asia. Then, as now, it was a little-known country; at Heathrow nobody at BOAC seemed to have heard of it, but eventually I walked across the apron with the other passengers bound for Bangkok, Thailand, and boarded Boeing 707 G-APFE.

On the flight out I was invited to sit in the cockpit for some time, although even then I was not allowed to sit in the First Officer's seat. (A few months later, in turbulence over Mount Fuji, Japan, this aircraft's fin failed and all aboard perished.) At Bangkok I boarded Douglas DC-3 XW-TAF of Royal Air Lao before temporarily returning to the tarmac while a large hammer and some slightly more sophisticated tools were applied to one of the Pratt & Whitney Twin Wasps. Eventually we were airborne, heading north towards Laos through the turbulent monsoon clouds. The aircraft leaked, to the extent that I had to use a waterproof over my head to deflect the rainwater to one side. A visit to the toilet had added interest, as a large inspection panel in the rear bulkhead was missing and I could look through the tailwheel aperture to the drenched jungle not far below. The turbulence was severe, and to an impressionable 18-year-old it could have been Burma in 1944 below. In fading light, we circled Wattay (Vientiane airport) beside the Mekong. In the gloom I saw many Douglas C-47s and Curtiss C-46 Commandos parked around. Yes, I thought, this is going to be a very interesting year.

AN INNOCENT ABROAD

Into the complex, confusing and, above all, conspiratorial situation that was Laos in 1965 I had blundered with a camera and a diary,

090 AVIATION CLASSICS: AMERICAN COLD WAR STORIES

but I was received almost everywhere in a friendly and helpful manner.

By the time I arrived Aviation Lao had become the Royal Lao Air Force (in 1960), Civil Air Transport had transformed into Air America Inc (1959) and the Office of Strategic Studies had become the Central Intelligence Agency (in 1947). The few original airfields had been supplemented by many new airstrips. The older airfields were given "L", or "Lima", numbers, these signifying Laos, not "Landing". "Victor" airfields were those located in neighbouring Vietnam (initially, strips in Laos used the "Victor" prefix, but this was soon changed). Newer, and almost invariably smaller, strips were prefixed by "LS" for "Lima Site", these eventually totalling several hundred.

Many of these strips served genuine civilian projects of USAID, the United States Agency for International Development; many were rather more sinister in their use. Several had alternative strips suffixed with an "A", for "Alternate", the primary site being unusable in the wet season. However, one such site – LS 20A – was merely LS 98 renumbered as a cover for Long Tieng (a secret airfield), LS 20 at Sam Thong nearby being all-weather; LS 20A was usually called just "Alternate". Rumours suggested there was a 10,000ft (3,000m)-long earth strip on the Plaine des Jarres for Boeing B-52s damaged over North Vietnam. If there was, it was never used. There were numerous American military personnel in the country, some 50 accredited to the Embassy as "Assistant Military Attachés", but many more were even less accountable.

Everything in Laos was illogical and blurred. The US Ambassador personally controlled all military and USAF assets. "Civil" airlines such as Air America, Continental Air Services Inc (CASI) and Bird & Sons flew the secret or "black" missions, the Royal Lao Air Force did the smuggling and there were more foreign than Lao troops in the country by far (despite the indigenous three-way civil war within the broader East–West conflict).

While some very good personal accounts of those years have appeared in print, official American records regarding Laos are sealed for 75 years, far longer than those for Vietnam. When these files are opened in 2050 there will be nobody who was in Laos during the "secret war" still alive to interpret them. Records of the Kingdom of Laos are presumed destroyed by the victorious Communists. Presented here is my recollection of just one small episode in the oft-forgotten secret war in Laos.

TO THE MEO CAPITAL

Each year, for dubious political benefit, Air America, aided by other companies, was contracted to fly all the diplomatic staffs in Vientiane to Sam Thong, to watch the indigenous Meo (later Hmong) people's Lunar New Year celebrations, or Pi Mai Meo. By chance I was in Vientiane on that day, January 9, 1966, and officially on the Embassy staff even if at the lowest level.

An invitation card secured, I headed off to Wattay airport in the early morning with three companions. Showing our invitations in lieu of passes, we were directed towards an Air America Fairchild C-123B Provider. Luckily, one of our group (and the only Lao national employed by the medical team) was the daughter of Touby Lyfong (Conseiller du Roi and the most important Meo personage). She headed instead for a very smart Dornier Do 28B-1, N9180X, (one of a quartet owned by Boun Oum Airways and used for VIP work by the American Embassy). The pilot accepted us as his load without question or noting our names and left immediately. We taxied past neat lines of perhaps two dozen aircraft – Helio Couriers, Pilatus Turbo Porters, Do 28s, de Havilland Canada Caribous, Douglas C-47s and Providers – clearly this was a "maximum effort" operation, and were soon airborne.

As the ground war had see-sawed back and forth across the Vietnam/Laos border the communists had inexorably pushed the American-supported Meo southwards off

LEFT: Spending his "gap year" with a medical team in Laos as part of the Colombo Plan, the author was afforded the opportunity to take numerous photographs of the exotica to be found in South-east Asia in the early days of the Vietnam conflict. One example was de Havilland Canada DHC-2 Beaver "82053" of the Royal Lao Air Force, snapped at Thakhek West in November 1965. *Jonathan Pote*

ABOVE: Dornier Do 28B-1 N9180X (c/n 3060) parked beside DHC-4 Caribou "392" at Sam Thong. Operated by Bird & Sons, in whose distinctive red-and-cream colour scheme it is seen here, N9180X later went missing en route from L 54 (Luang Prabang) to L 25 (Ban Houei Sai) on April 6, 1967, with six aboard. *Jonathan Pote*

their mountaintop villages, their "capital" of Xieng Khouang (on the Plaine des Jarres) falling to the enemy. A new administrative capital was established at Sam Thong, just to the south-west of the Plain.

Nearly 4,000ft (1,200m) above sea level and only connected to the outside world by almost impassible tracks over tortuous terrain, Sam Thong had accumulated more than 4,000 inhabitants in less than four years, boasting a teaching hospital with 250 beds, a comfortable chalet for Air America crews staying overnight and many other large buildings. A single driveable dirt road headed south-east over "Skyline Ridge" to Long Tieng or "Alternate" (LS 20A), the busy secret military base with a population of some 40,000. It was the headquarters of General Vang Pao and the base for a huge CIA/Air America operation, including the Meo (Hmong) North American T-28 strike force after 1967. Accidental visitors were held at gunpoint and flown out blindfolded. Dire threats were made to dissuade them from speaking later of their experience.

We cruised northwards, a lone aircraft at some 7,000ft (2,100m), towards distant peaks 10,000ft (3,000m) high and still partly shrouded in morning mists. The view of the finest remote country I was to see in Southeast Asia was superb through the large bulged windows of our cabin, with just four seats, two facing forward and two facing

BELOW: Illustrating the primitive nature of the airstrip at Sam Thong, this photograph shows Scottish Aviation Twin Pioneer XW-PBP (c/n 567) at Lima Site 20 on January 9, 1966. Although the aircraft is painted in Philippine Air Lines colours, and was indeed registered to the airline as PI-C434, it never served with the company. It was acquired by CIA cover airline Bird & Sons in December 1963 before being transferred to another CIA surrogate, Continental Air Services Inc, in September 1965. It was damaged beyond repair in a thunderstorm at Vientiane in March 1968. *Jonathan Pote*

BELOW: Not for the faint-hearted — an Air America Pilatus PC-6 Turbo Porter whistles down the 800yd (730m) heavily-sloped runway at LS 20 during the author's visit. The other visiting aircraft are parked in the limited space at the foot of the runway. *Jonathan Pote*

aft. We passed over the couple of Couriers that had left before us. Far below, they seemed too low to clear the tree-covered razorback ridges. We also passed over Phou Khao Khwai, where an abandoned T-28 lay wrecked beside the dirt strip. It was slowly being stripped of its aluminium skin by villagers using it to fashion various implements. We had visited the area by Land Rover some weeks previously.

From then on there was no sign of human habitation except the very occasional hilltop village comprised of a few simple Meo huts. Had we continued northwards, only hours later would we have seen "civilisation" again – deep in communist China, having crossed the easternmost foothills of the Himalayas. Suddenly, however, the aircraft banked to port and I could see a small network of jeep roads, a barracks with parade ground and an orderly western-style settlement.

UP ON SKYLINE RIDGE

We flew low along a ridge, sending birds aloft, and then turned steeply through 180°. For the first time, LS 20 was visible, an irregular earth scar on a steep slope. The Do 28 touched down and stopped in less than 100yd (90m). We climbed out into the warm dusty air, and watched our taxi take off immediately, leaving the strip almost deserted.

Lima Site 20 was in a large bowl in the mountains, what was known as "Skyline Ridge" prominent to the south-east. A bare patch of earth a few hundred yards across, it was approached over a lip several hundred feet above the valley floor. Beyond the flat area, it continued up a steep slope as a narrow runway. There was a flat turning area at the top.

All buildings were on the south side, as was a large limestone outcrop. While lighter aircraft could land easily on the wide lower level, larger aircraft were committed to touch down at the edge of the lip and run on up the slope, their oleos visibly compressing as the gradient steepened. Full power was applied to avoid running backwards down the slope, which was then negotiated with idle power and heavy braking after turning around on the top platform. This was not a place for faint-hearted pilots – it was very marginal for larger types at 4,000ft elevation, overshooting being precluded by a ridge just beyond the upper

> *This was **not** a place for **faint-hearted pilots** – it was very **marginal** for larger types at **4,000ft elevation**, overshooting being precluded by a **ridge** just beyond the **upper end.***

end – but landings were great sport to watch.

Additionally, there was always the possibility of communist anti-aircraft machine-guns on the ridge. On August 19, 1969, Pilatus PC-6C N196X of Air America crashed with the loss of all on board after the pilot was killed by a rifle bullet fired from Skyline Ridge, in this case by a disaffected Meo soldier. While the weather was perfect that January day, I did

ABOVE: An abandoned North American T-28 of the Royal Lao Air Force at Phou Khao Khwai in December 1965. The locals quickly reduced the aircraft to a hulk, taking anything usable to make tools and other useful items. *Jonathan Pote*

ABOVE: The six Sikorsky UH-34Ds of the *Commission Internationale de Contrôle* (two of which are seen here), flown predominantly by French pilots, were tasked with supervising the neutrality of Laos, and were all maintained by Air America at the latter's repair depot at Udorn in Thailand. Note the Helio Courier already well airborne by the end of the runway at LS 20. *Jonathan Pote*

wonder just how difficult it would be when the monsoon filled the bowl with cloud and turned the strip to mud.

Constructed in 1965 and finally overrun by communist forces on March 19, 1970, Sam Thong/LS 20 became probably the busiest dirt strip in the world at that time. More than 100 landings daily were averaged over the year, 70,000 US gal of fuel being flown in each month. Later, during 1969–70, in the final months before Sam Thong fell, two Lockheed C-130A Hercules –"704" and "605"/56-510 – used the strip at night in addition to Long Tieng and the Mekong valley airfields. Except at Vientiane, their engines were never shut down in case sudden communist shelling made an immediate departure essential.

As I waited, the strip began to fill rapidly with more aircraft; it was a truly eclectic collection. The Air America aircraft mainly left for a further load as soon as they could, dragging themselves up the slope for a take-off downhill, but the other aircraft stayed

BELOW: Another of Air America's stalwarts in Laos was the Fairchild C-123 Provider, which proved invaluable owing to its capacious fuselage and outstanding short take-off and landing capabilities. This example, "655" (originally 54-0655 in USAF service) was photographed by the author at Thakhek West in November 1965. *Jonathan Pote*

and were scattered around the edge of the lower plateau. They included de Havilland Canada DHC-2 Beaver F-OAIV, no doubt with the French Ambassador: l'Armée de l'Air wisely did not try to get its ambassadorial C-47, 49821/F-SDLR, named Château de Wattay, into this strip. The British Embassy's aircraft, Prestwick Pioneer XL665, on loan from No 209 Sqn in Singapore, brought our Ambassador, His Excellency Sir Frederick Warner. Scottish Aviation Twin Pioneer XW-PBP (later damaged beyond repair), formerly registered to Philippine Air Lines, now with CASI, was an unexpected arrival, as was a lone American-registered C-47.

The International Control Commission fielded its three available white Sikorsky UH-34D helicopters, CIC 4, 5 and 6. Air America UH-34D Choctaw "H-F", the last one in Laos still bearing the earlier letter-only codes from 1961, seemed to be resident. Added to these were many Couriers, Turbo Porters, Caribous and Providers of Air America. With all this activity (including reciprocal take-offs on the same narrow strip as the landings) there was no form of control until a pilot sat atop his Courier and used a hand-held radio to establish some order in the chaos.

Interesting as all this was for me, I had to leave soon and proceed towards the arena. Here all were personally met by Touby Lyfong as the senior Meo personage. We were handed an apologies slip from General Vang Pao ("Le Général de Brigade"), regretting his inability to greet us as Savang Vatthana, the King of Laos, was his personal guest. If one has to be passed over by Le Général, then in favour of the King himself is an acceptable reason.

There was much ceremony that day, mainly military, and good food. The bullfight was just that – two large bulls fighting it out in a gully until one broke away and ran through the closely gathered crowd, hotly pursued by the other. Suddenly, the airstrip seemed the least danger of the day!

Perhaps too readily, I moved back to the airstrip and faced a tantalising problem: I could choose just one of almost any of the aircraft parked around for my flight back to Vientiane. The C-123 still did not appeal; an engine failure before crossing Skyline Ridge would not be survivable. In the end, I chose Caribou "392". In some ways I came to regret my choice, as some time later I had a flight in the same Caribou on one of Air America's "milk run" scheduled services to the Mekong villages. However, on that day it suited me admirably, clearing the infamous Skyline Ridge in a sprightly fashion. The view out was good; below, the lone jeep road wound over the ridge and down to "Alternate" at Long Tieng, duly photographed in the distance as I flew back to Vientiane.

> With all this **activity** (including reciprocal take-offs on the same **narrow strip** as the landings) there was no **form of control** until a pilot sat atop his Courier and used a **hand-held radio** to **establish** some **order** in the **chaos.**

THE CALM BEFORE THE STORM

That day was merely a sop to the world, as represented by the diplomatic staffs of many countries. There was great sadness to follow. The King and his family would later die in a Communist "re-education camp" after the fall of Laos. The Meo people – later known as the Hmong ("Meo" was a pejorative word) – would be hunted off their mountaintop refuges into near-annihilation. They were abandoned by the USA, to the great disgust of the Americans who had recruited, trained and fought alongside them. Author Dr Jane Hamilton-Merritt has written from her own experiences the desperately sad story of the Hmong in her excellent book *Tragic Mountains: The Hmong, the Americans and the Secret Wars for Laos 1942–1992* (Indiana University Press, 1993). Ray S. Cline, Chairman of the United States Global Strategy Council in 1992 and former Deputy Director of Intelligence at the CIA, said in his review of the book that this was "a classical tragedy of heroic proportions… not only is it a useful contribution for the benefit of the brave Hmong people, but will also encourage more thoughtful strategic planning in Washington and more compassionate government policy for protecting foreign ethnic groups who perform great service for the USA". So even those at the top finally realised and admitted that they had got it wrong, allowing the Hmong and other ethnic groups to be destroyed and abandoning Laos to its fate. ●

BELOW: Arrival on Skyline Ridge — Air America Caribou "393" rolls to a stop up the runway at LS 20. Landing the bigger aircraft at the primitive strip required a high level of skill from the Air America pilots, the wheels having to touch down on the very edge of the ridge's lip. *Jonathan Pote*

Operation Bolo & project Silver Dawn

In January 1967 the USAF undertook its most intensive MiG-hunt of the Vietnam War. Well-known as a masterpiece of American tactical skill and leadership, Operation Bolo has never been explored from both the USAF and Vietnamese perspectives, or in terms of the vital secret role played by the recently declassified Silver Dawn project. ALBERT GRANDOLINI takes a look at the full story for the first time.

In a conflict in which close air combats were relatively sporadic, the USAF's Operation *Bolo* is one of the better-known examples of the Vietnam War, and is celebrated in the USA as an object lesson in tactical innovation, technological superiority and leadership, rewarded with success. It was to be a fragile success, however, for in the following weeks the MiGs of the *Khong Quan Nhan Dan Viet Nam* (Vietnam People's Air Force – VPAF) made an aggressive return to the fray, overcoming their difficulties by devising new tactics. *Bolo* also highlighted the difference between two opposing conceptions of how to fight an air war.

The USA initially anticipated a swift conclusion to the conflict by unleashing the entire might of its air power against its third-world adversary. America's air arms quickly found this strategy frustrated, however, and were forced by their leadership into a gradual, cautious and costly protracted campaign aimed at denying North Vietnamese support to the communist insurgents in the south. The USA found itself on a collision course with China as early as the start of Operation *Rolling Thunder*, the air campaign against North Vietnam, in March 1965. Beijing sent several anti-aircraft artillery (AAA) divisions to bolster the fledgling North Vietnamese air-defence system, with Chinese troops donning North Vietnamese military uniforms.

To their alarm, the Americans also found themselves facing surface-to-air missiles (SAMs) operated by Soviet technicians, as American signals intelligence (SIGINT) intercepts would reveal. All was in place for a replay of the Korean conflict, in which the USA had not only faced the Korean People's Army Air Force, but also entire Soviet and Chinese air divisions. Less than three years after the Berlin and Cuban missile crises, the probability of a global – and possibly nuclear – conflict, at least with China, had to be taken seriously by President Lyndon B. Johnson.

GUERRILLA AIR WARFARE

It was within this context that North Vietnam invested a substantial part of its economic and military resources in setting up an integrated air-defence system which, once completed, would replace the Chinese units. The initial plan was to cover main urban centres like Hanoi and Haiphong, as well as some industrial sites such as the Thai Nguyen steel mill and the coalmines at Hong Gai and Cam Pha.

A second phase would see the system expanded to cover the whole of North Vietnam, particularly the vital logistic routes that channelled men and equipment towards South Vietnam. With limited resources, not least in educated and qualified personnel, North Vietnam was forced to restrict the development of the VPAF, instead devising an original doctrine in which air power was seen only as an adjunct to its ground-based air-defence assets. Deploying only two fighter regiments of MiG-17s (Nato reporting name *Fresco*) and MiG-21s (*Fishbed*), a total of around 100 fighters, the VPAF had no illusions about its ability to secure air superiority against 1,500 American combat aircraft. The main task of its interceptors would be to harass and disperse American attack formations, making the latter more vulnerable to SAM and AAA units as part of a "guerrilla air warfare" strategy. If, by making firing passes, the VPAF's fighters could succeed in forcing the American fighter-bombers to release their bombs before reaching their intended targets, the mission could be deemed a success. The ability of the VPAF's inexperienced pilots to create such a nuisance grew over the months, despite heavy losses, forcing American pilots to recognise the courage and determination of their opponents.

By the end of 1966 the American air campaign was gaining momentum, but it seemed to have no tangible effect on the Hanoi leadership and its determination to continue the war. Receiving foreign journalists, Chairman Ho Chi Minh reaffirmed his determination to continue the struggle for "ten, 20 or even 30 more years, for the total reunification of the country", a task presented to his people as a national crusade.

In the USA the Pentagon set about reorganising its air tactics. From the first intermittent strikes undertaken during the second half of 1964, the attacks evolved into a sustained and continuous day and night campaign. In April 1966 North Vietnam was divided by the Americans into tactical Route Packages (RPs), which delineated the operational areas of the USAF and US Navy. The latter was tasked with operations over RP-II, RP-III, RP-IV and RP-VIB, which covered the North Vietnamese coastal zones, including Haiphong and the eastern part of the Red River Delta areas. The USAF was to operate over RP-I, just north of the Demilitarized Zone (DMZ) separating the two Vietnams; RP-V, covering the western part of North Vietnam, and importantly, RP-VIA, which included the well-defended Hanoi area. In addition, two specially restricted zones were put in place over the strategic harbour of Haiphong and the North Vietnamese capital. Strikes inside these zones required authorisation from the highest American authorities. Finally, a 9–12-mile (15–19km) no-fly zone was imposed along the Chinese border after several accidental crossings into Chinese airspace.

ABOVE: A haggard President Johnson (centre) confers with his team over a model of Khe San in 1968.

ABOVE: The USA's Secretary of Defense, Robert S. McNamara, in 1967. An accountant by training and temperament, McNamara was one of the prime architects of the USA's policy in Vietnam and based his strategy on a statistical approach, i.e. "they will run out of soldiers before we do".

OPPOSITE PAGE: Colonel Robin Olds, CO of the 8th Tactical Fighter Wing and mastermind behind Operation *Bolo*, is lifted aloft by members of his unit on the occasion of the completion of his last combat mission over Vietnam in September 1967.

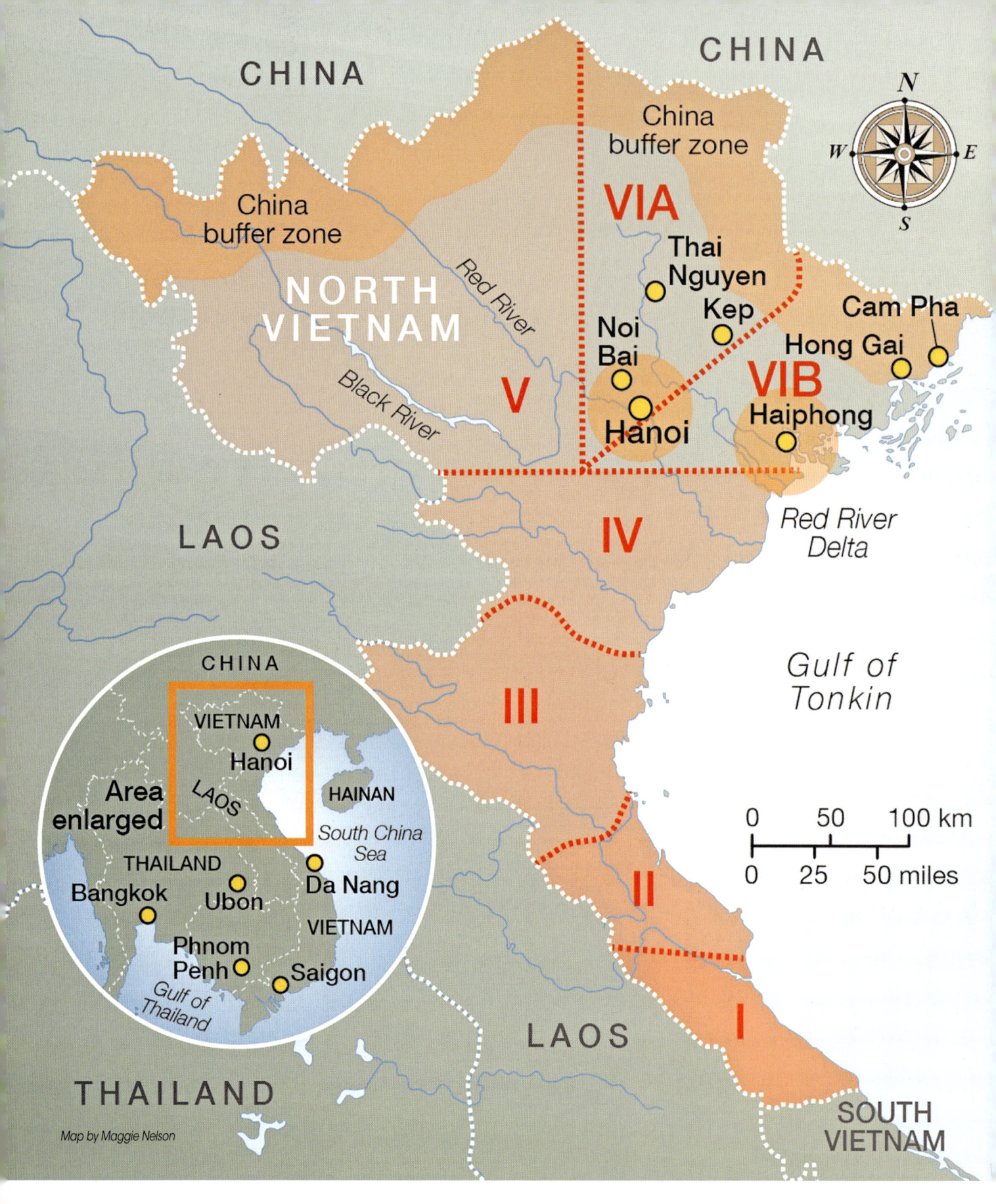

The USA's strategy combined air attacks with secret diplomatic missions to convince the Hanoi leadership of the futility of its war aims, as a prelude to imposing on it, by force if necessary, an accord that guaranteed the survival of a non-communist South Vietnam. Furthermore, the purpose of the air campaign was to demonstrate to the North Vietnamese that the more they attacked in the south, the more they would be exposed to greater destruction in the north.

One of the most significant escalations of the American air offensive was the series of attacks undertaken against petrol, oil and lubricant (POL) depots throughout the country, along with the bombing of storage areas, railway stations and bridges in the Hanoi and Haiphong areas in June 1966. However, after two years of incessant American air strikes, many military and civilian leaders in Washington DC began to doubt the efficacy of the policy. Indeed, it was difficult to evaluate the impact of these strikes on the reduction of the military and economic capacities of North Vietnam, a country that imported most of its goods from its communist allies. The same could be concluded about the impact of the continuous air attacks on the morale of its population, which was completely organised and mobilised by a totalitarian state system.

Nevertheless, the USA's Secretary of Defense, Robert S. McNamara, one of the staunchest supporters of the air offensive in Vietnam, persisted with his strategy in the strong belief that Hanoi was on the brink of total collapse. McNamara had created a complex evaluating system to assess the effectiveness of the campaign, using the number of sorties flown and targets attacked each week, as well as the tonnage of bombs dropped, as a metric. However, using such statistics as a basis for a coherent airpower strategy did not necessarily bring about the desired results.

The most tangible result of the air campaign up to that point was the increasing effectiveness of the North Vietnamese air-defence system, which by this time was enjoying greatly improved co-ordination between MiG and SAM/AAA operations. The VPAF began to deploy its first MiG-21Fs (Nato reporting name *Fishbed-C*) in November 1965 – with more advanced MiG-21PF *Fishbed-Ds* arriving in April 1966 – in a new fighter regiment manned by 33 pilots under the command of Maj Tran Manh, with Capt Dinh Ton as Operations Officer. The decision to set up the new unit had been taken in the spring of 1965, when 12 MiG-17 pilots and 24 newly graduated cadets were sent to Krasnodar in the southern Soviet Union for conversion to the MiG-21. Three of the pilots were "washed out", however, and were reassigned to the MiG-17.

ABOVE: The commander of the VPAF in January 1967 was Lt-Col Dao Dinh Luyen, a former infantry officer and one of the first North Vietnamese fighter pilots to be trained in China in the late 1950s. *Albert Grandolini Collection*

ENTER THE FISHBED

The unit chosen to operate the new supersonic fighter was the 921st Fighter Regiment (FR), named *Sao Do* (Red Star), the first and at that time only VPAF fighter unit, which transferred its MiG-17s to the newly created 923rd FR. Only a small cadre of experienced personnel stayed with the 921st FR to help with conversion on to the MiG-21. The VPAF's fighter force commander, Lt-Col Dao Dinh Luyen, thoroughly trained his men on the new aircraft and set about devising suitable tactics for using it. Owing to the inexperience of most of his pilots, he wisely decided to begin with a period of "on the job" training, simulating attacks on American formations and assessing their results. Accordingly, American airmen began to report sighting elusive MiG-21s making passes but breaking off quickly, as if they were on a training

> The **VPAF** began to deploy its first **MiG-21Fs** (Nato reporting name Fishbed-C) in **November 1965** – with more advanced **MiG-21PF** Fishbed-Ds arriving in **April 1966.**

BELOW: The Vietnam People's Air Force received its first Mikoyan-Gurevich MiG-21F Fishbed-Cs in November 1965. This example of the 921st Fighter Regiment is seen at Noi Bai armed with a pair of Soviet-designed R-3S (AA-2 Atoll) infrared short-range air-to-air missiles, essentially a reverse-engineered version of the American AIM-9 Sidewinder. *Albert Grandolini Collection*

ABOVE: The McDonnell Douglas F-4 Phantom II formed the backbone of the USAF's fighter units at the beginning of the Vietnam conflict. They were, however, also used in numbers for the ground-attack role in addition to the Republic F-105s. This F-4D of the 435th TFS, 8th TFW, refuels before heading north on a bombing mission in 1968. *Vern Barton via Warren Thompson*

cycle, trying to improve their technique.

The next stage was to attack Ryan Firebee drones used for surveillance and as SAM-bait, and attempts were also made to intercept high-flying Lockheed U-2s. These tactics seemed desultory at first, but the Americans were expecting the North Vietnamese MiG-21s to engage soon, and took such a threat very seriously.

The type's first combat occurred on April 26, 1966, when a USAF McDonnell Douglas F-4 Phantom II shot down a VPAF MiG-21. Initially, the VPAF combined mixed formations of MiG-17s and MiG-21s in low-level dogfights with haphazard results, the American fighters usually having the upper hand. The MiG-21 proved to be a poor dogfighter, owing to a restricted field of vision for the pilot, especially to the rear and below the nose. As a result, the MiG-21 pilots were ordered to disengage as soon as they found themselves in a disadvantageous position. Several aircraft were lost after running out of fuel while trying to outrun the American fighters patrolling over their bases or along the Chinese border, cutting off all potential escape routes.

An important issue for the VPAF was the close co-ordination required between the Ground Control Interception (GCI) officer and the pilots who relied on him for target guidance, a serious problem being the limited avionics of the MiG-21. The MiG-21PF's RP-21 Sapfir radar had a practical detection range of only 4–8 miles (7–13km), while the MiG-21F had only a radar rangefinder, making both variants completely dependent on ground control for target vectoring. By comparison, the F-4C's AN/APQ-100 radar had a detection range of around 37 miles (60km).

The MiG-21's weapons system was also very limited, comprising two R-3S (Nato reporting name AA-2 *Atoll*) infrared guided missiles (the MiG-21F had an additional Nudelman-Rikhter NR-30 30mm autocannon). A copy of the AIM-9B Sidewinder that equipped the Phantoms, the R-3S suffered from the same weakness, namely a narrow acquisition cone from the rear of the target for its infrared homing system. During one early engagement, a flight of MiG-21s expended no fewer than six *Atolls* against a group of USAF Republic F-105 Thunderchiefs without scoring a single hit. The North Vietnamese tried to alleviate the problem by deploying mixed formations, the leading MiG-21 being armed with two R-3S missiles while his wingman carried two pods of R-5M air-to-air rockets. The latter's task was to finish off the target with a salvo of rockets, but the results were mixed at best. Nevertheless, the VPAF claimed at least three kills with the unguided rockets, downing an F-105 on June 7, 1966, and two F-4s on September 9 the same year.

The MiG-21s became more aggressive during the summer of 1966, claiming two F-105s in July against two *Fishbeds* shot down by Phantoms. By the autumn the VPAF had begun to launch co-ordinated attacks with MiG-17s and MiG-21s, maintaining combat air patrols (CAPs) along the enemy's main approach routes to the Hanoi area. The incoming American fighter-bomber formations were initially engaged by SAMs before being disrupted and forced into low-level dogfights with MiG-17s at low level. The MiG-21s would then pounce on the rear of the American formations, trying to pick off isolated flights or aircraft by making supersonic passes and firing their *Atolls* at a distance of 5,000–6,500ft (1,500–2,000m). The MiG-21s would then dive to low altitude, where the radars of the Phantoms could not pick them up.

In December 1966 the MiG-21s began to expand their operating zone beyond the Red River Delta area in the heart of North Vietnam. They now operated from four bases, the main base being Noi Bai (Phuc Yen for the Americans), north-west of Hanoi, with detachments at Gia Lam in the suburbs of the North Vietnamese capital, Cat Bi near Haiphong and Kep, north-east of the Red River Delta.

Encounters with MiGs intensified considerably in September 1966, some 37 combats taking place, 25 of which were against F-105s. The strength of the two VPAF fighter regiments was increased by 60 per cent with the arrival of newly graduated pilots returning from training in the Soviet Union, and air combats became a daily occurrence during October–December. ▶

*Encounters with MiGs **intensified** considerably in September 1966, some **37 combats** taking place, **25** of which were against **F-105s.***

ABOVE: The F-105D undertook the lion's share of *Rolling Thunder* missions against North Vietnam, the type being able to carry an impressive bomb package, but lacking the agility of the Phantom. This example wears the "JJ" tailcodes of the 34th TFS, based at Korat in Thailand, and carries an AN/ALQ-71 ECM pod on its outboard pylon.
Bernard Reck via Warren Thompson

ABOVE: The upgraded MiG-21PF *Fishbed-D* was introduced into VPAF service in April 1966. One of the first was "4225", an early production example completed with the original fin — a broader version was fitted to later production aircraft to improve stability. The PF variant incorporated extra fuel tanks behind the cockpit, giving it a "fatter neck". *Albert Grandolini Collection*

Nearly a quarter of the Thunderchiefs delivering attacks in the RP-VIA area aborted their missions and were forced to drop their bombs off-target when intercepted. Most of the effort was undertaken by the MiG-17s but the MiG-21s also increased their attacks, claiming some 13 kills during September–December. (The Americans, however, acknowledged only three aircraft destroyed and two probables due to the *Fishbeds*.)

During the same period, the MiG-21s made efforts to bring down Douglas EB-66 Destroyer electronic countermeasures (ECM) aircraft tasked with jamming North Vietnamese radar and radio communications. Although the MiG-21s were not successful – these precious assets were zealously guarded by a barrier of Phantoms – the USAF was forced to move its jamming orbits further back, decreasing their efficiency.

> *Various American and South Vietnamese air units participated in strikes against North Vietnam, but the main effort was undertaken by the two USAF Wings of Thunderchiefs based in Thailand and two Wings of F-4 Phantoms.*

Various American and South Vietnamese air units participated in strikes against North Vietnam, but the main effort was undertaken by the two USAF Wings of Thunderchiefs based in Thailand and two Wings of F-4 Phantoms, the latter comprising the 366th Tactical Fighter Wing (TFW) at Da Nang, South Vietnam, and the 8th TFW "Wolf Pack" at Ubon, Thailand. The 8th was also assigned escort duties for the fighter-bombers, which meant gaining and maintaining air superiority over North Vietnam. However, the unit was becoming increasingly distracted from this important task because of a growing demand for bombing missions.

SETTING THE TRAP

To sustain the increasing mission rate required by the Pentagon, it was decided that the 8th TFW should be engaged on night-attack missions as part of Operation *Rapid Roger*. Up to this point, night operations had been assigned to specialised USAF Martin B-57 and US Navy Grumman A-6 Intruder units. With no additional resources, the 8th TFW was forced to undertake a high number of missions for several weeks, ultimately bringing it to the verge of collapse. The pilots, living in primitive conditions, alternated day and night missions without proper recuperation time, their mechanics working to the point of exhaustion and sleeping when possible in the hangars.

The Seventh Air Force, which ran the air war in South-east Asia, fired the Wing's overzealous CO, Col Joseph Wilson, as a scapegoat. He was replaced on September 30, 1966, by Col Robin Olds, a Second World War ace with 12 kills, well known for his independence of mind and for leading his men by example. His previous assignment had been as CO of the 81st TFW at RAF Bentwaters in the UK, a unit equipped with McDonnell F-101C Voodoos specialised for the nuclear strike role beyond the Iron Curtain.

After converting on to the Phantom in the USA, Olds arrived in Thailand to find a demoralised Wing which had lost ten F-4Cs in less than two months over North Vietnam. Characteristically, Olds went into action immediately, flying as many missions as possible, particularly the most difficult, to ▶

ABOVE: Wearing the "FO" tailcodes of the 435th TFS, a pair of F-4Ds heads out for a bombing mission in North Vietnam. By the end of 1966 most of the 8th TFW's Phantoms were engaged on ground-attack missions.
James Wood via Warren Thompson

RIGHT: Col Robin Olds. *USAF*

ABOVE: Four pilots of the 923rd FR walk along a line of the unit's MiG-17s before a mission in 1967. From left: Luy Huy Chao (six kills), Le Hai (seven), Mai Duc Tai (two) and Hoang Van Ky (five – KIA on June 5, 1967).

evaluate the unit's working conditions and tactics and to assess his new team. During his one-year tour, Olds flew some 152 sorties, many over the dangerous Hanoi area, as against his predecessor's total of 12. The new CO suspended all nocturnal sorties and placed MiG-hunting at the heart of his Wing's activities.

Olds quickly realised that most of his young pilots had not yet accrued the fundamentals of air combat or become versed in the art of dogfighting. Citing great progress in the development of radar and air-to-air missile technologies, the USAF had reduced the close-combat element of its training syllabus. The time dedicated to such training had been reduced to around ten per cent of what it had been a decade previously. The emphasis was now on the interception of enemy aircraft beyond visual range (BVR) with AIM-7D/E Sparrow radar-guided missiles. However, like the short-range infrared-guided Sidewinder, the Sparrow's reliability in combat proved disappointing.

Olds set about honing the skills of his men, and arranged training sessions with the RAAF's resident No 77 Sqn, the latter's CAC Sabre Mk 32s playing the role of enemy MiG-17s. After several weeks of practising, the Wolf Pack became one of the few units in theatre, along with some US Navy Vought F-8 Crusader squadrons, that could be considered truly proficient in air combat. With his pilots' morale restored, Olds began a campaign to obtain permission for a major MiG-hunt.

POLITICAL CONSIDERATIONS

Since the beginning of Operation *Rolling Thunder*, the Americans had envisaged destroying the VPAF at its bases. However, a reluctance to risk casualties among the Soviet and Chinese advisors on the bases precluded this scheme. To the great frustration of the American pilots, the Pentagon chose not to react when a group of North Korean pilots became involved, flying VPAF MiGs. The US Government's fear was that, once the VPAF had been eliminated, China might send its air force into North Vietnam as part of a new phase of escalation. Indeed, a clause in the secret military accord signed between Hanoi and Peking in February 1964 had explicitly envisaged the deployment of Chinese air units to North Vietnam in the case of hostilities with the USA. However, despite North Vietnam's repeated requests, the Chinese government deferred its obligation in a gesture of appeasement.[1] The only way to destroy the MiGs would be to entice them into combat.

ABOVE: MiG-21PF "4228" was one of the seven shot down during Operation *Bolo*, the pilot, Vu Ngoc Dinh, ejecting safely. The aircraft is seen here with a typical armament load of an R-3S (AA-2 Atoll) air-to-air missile on each wing and a 490lit (107 Imp gal) PTB-490 centreline fuel tank. *Artwork by* TOM COOPER

104 AVIATION CLASSICS: AMERICAN COLD WAR STORIES

The most recent reports indicated that the MiGs prioritised the F-105s, which had become less manœuvrable since being equipped with newly deployed AN/ALQ-71 (QRC-160) ECM pods to jam the radars of the SAMs. The "Thuds" were forced to fly rigid four-aircraft formations to maximise their electronic jamming capability, substantially increasing their vulnerability. Olds devised a plan to make his agile Phantoms look like cumbersome bomb-laden F-105s, in order to lure the MiG-21s into a dogfight. A similar trick had been used on July 4, 1965, when four F-4Cs enticed four MiG-17s to attack them, the Phantoms shooting down two of the *Frescos*. Olds envisioned a far more ambitious plan to catch as many of the elusive MiG-21s as possible.

Olds gathered a small planning team around his Operations Officer, Capt John B. Stone, including Maj James D. Covington, Capt Ralph Wetterhahn and Lt Joe Hicks. It appeared that the North Vietnamese GCI stations had an advantage in being able to vector their interceptors undetected at low level towards the American formations, the interceptors then popping up to make a surprise firing pass. At this point, American radar stations in South Vietnam, Thailand and aboard US Navy ships did not have the required range to cover the strategic Red River Delta area. The USAF's Lockheed EC-121D Warning Star early-warning aircraft could not detect the MiGs below 10,000ft (3,000m), and, when the latter were higher, the EC-121Ds could not ascertain an exact altitude.

SILVER DAWN

Olds, however, learnt that the National Security Agency (NSA) was eavesdropping on North Vietnamese radio communications as part of the top secret Project *Silver Dawn*, using specially configured Lockheed C-130B-IIs of the USAF Security Service's 6988th Security Squadron. The unit's operators were able to detect when a North Vietnamese take-off order had been given, when the MiG pilots had American aircraft in sight and when they were ordered to attack; invaluable information for the Phantom pilots – if they could access it. Olds was told, however, that the NSA would not potentially compromise its intelligence operations for purely tactical considerations. Nevertheless, he persisted and was finally authorised to include the use of the C-130B-IIs for his plans.

The next challenge for Olds would be the installation of ECM pods on the F-4Cs to simulate the electronic signature of the F-105s. After drafting an outline of his plan, he flew to Baguio in the Philippines, where a General Staff conference was being held. Once there, Olds went directly to see the commander of the Seventh Air Force, Gen William W. Momyer, but without success. Olds continued to plead his case up the ladder of command until the idea began to arouse interest. Finally, on December 22, 1966, his plan was approved and christened Operation *Bolo*.[2] Olds was granted the required support and could borrow the ECM pods for one week.

Bolo would be the biggest MiG-hunt to date, and would involve the deployment of two main Phantom forces. First, a formation of 20 Da Nang-based F-4Cs of the 366th TFW would penetrate North Vietnam from the Gulf of Tonkin to cover the eastern part of the Red River Valley and Kep airbase, and act as a barrage along the Chinese border in order to prevent VPAF MiGs escaping across it. The main striking force would comprise 28 Ubon-based 8th TFW F-4Cs, which would cross into North Vietnam from Laos and head directly into the Hanoi area. These would entice the MiGs to come up by masquerading as a formation of lumbering F-105Ds, the Phantoms carrying the same ECM pods. A third force of 24 F-105D/Fs would clear the way for the Phantoms by attacking SAM sites around the main VPAF bases at Kep, Cat Bi and Noi Bai. Supporting elements included four EB-66s with their eight escorting F-4Cs, one EC-121D Warning Star, two NSA RC-130B-IIs, several Boeing KC-135 tankers and a cadre of Sikorsky HH-3 Jolly Green Giant rescue helicopters and their accompanying Douglas Skyaiders. The whole force would be covered by 16 Lockheed F-104C Starfighters while withdrawing from North Vietnam.

The planners determined that if the MiGs took the bait, their fuel endurance from take-off to landing would be a maximum of around 55min. Accordingly, the arrival times of the Phantom flights over the targeted airfields were set 5min apart, to ensure continuous coverage and provide maximum opportunity for engagement in the target area, the idea being to run the MiGs out of fuel by preventing them from landing. The mission was also planned so that no other American aircraft would be active in the area, allowing the first three flights of F-4s "missile-free" engagement without first having to identify the target.

BOLO IS GO!

It was not until December 30, 1966, that the

> The National Security Agency (NSA) was **eavesdropping** on North Vietnamese **radio communications** as part of the top secret **Project Silver Dawn**, using specially configured Lockheed **C-130B-IIs.**

BELOW: A pair of Lockheed C-130B-IIs similar to this example were employed for the first and only time in a tactical role during Operation *Bolo*. The 6988th Security Squadron crew (or "Bats" as they were known) comprised linguists and translators who eavesdropped on orders issued by the VPAF controllers and passed the information on to the USAF pilots. *USAF*

participating pilots were informed about the forthcoming operation. Details of the plan were meticulously gone over, particularly the need to adhere strictly to the specified flight parameters, in order to simulate convincingly the performance of the lumbering Thuds. It would be the first time the pilots had used the ECM pods. Olds also charged his maintenance crews with inspecting, cleaning and repairing all equipment on the aircraft assigned to the mission, and fine-tuning each missile. The crews worked non-stop for 27hr. As soon as the F-4s were fitted with the ECM pods, the date of the operation was set for January 1, 1967.

The mission was delayed, however, owing to bad weather, and rescheduled for the next day. Olds authorised a small party to celebrate the New Year although Stone, the operation's main planner, was tense and nervous and slept poorly. The mission was launched during the afternoon of January 2, despite the latest weather forecast indicating a solid overcast over the Hanoi area.

The North Vietnamese radars detected the incoming aircraft as they were being refuelled over Laos to the west and the Gulf of Tonkin to the east. Flying low over the latter were the two C-130B-IIs of the NSA, carrying Vietnamese, Chinese, Russian and Korean translators, who monitored the North Vietnamese radio frequencies. The North Vietnamese air-defence system was on full alert.

Leading a flight that bore his name, Olds was the first to arrive over Noi Bai airbase at 1500hr local time. Flying south-east along the ingress route used by the F-105s at 480kt, with its ECM pods turned on, the flight drew no defensive reaction and turned northwards to clear the area. Usually, the VPAF maintained a CAP over the airbase, with another further north and another west of Phuc Yen, over the Red River, during Thud attacks along that penetration route. If the engagement developed favourably for the North Vietnamese, additional MiGs would be launched. This time the air-defence commanders seemed confused, probably owing to the strikes taking place against radar and SAM sites by EF-105Fs. The commanders thus delayed the launching of their interceptors and awaited a clearer situation.

A frustrated Olds and his flight continued northwards, wondering if the enemy had taken the bait and seriously considering whether to cancel the mission. After about 15min a VPAF order was given for a force of MiG-21s to take off. The NSA operators immediately sent a warning to Olds on a pre-selected radio channel, but the message failed to get through owing to defective radio equipment in Olds's Phantom. Fortunately, the commander of the East Force, then arriving from the Gulf of Tonkin, received the NSA message and forwarded it to Olds, who immediately dropped his external tanks and turned back towards Hanoi with full afterburner, forbidding any BVR missile engagements, as per the plan, to avoid hitting friendly aircraft coming the other way.

Captain Ralph Wetterhahn, callsign *Olds 2*, was the first to obtain fleeting radar contact ahead. Suddenly, a MiG-21 popped up from the thick overcast at 7,000ft (2,100m) just behind the *Olds* flight and was seen by the arriving *Ford* flight, which sounded the alarm. Breaking hard, the *Olds* flight evaded this first enemy pass, after which Olds spotted another MiG-21 emerging from the cloud at his 11 o'clock, at which he fired two Sparrows, neither of which hit its target. Closing in, he fired an AIM-9B which also did not guide. A third MiG-21 popped up at Olds's ten o'clock position. Olds barrel-rolled to starboard and found himself above the third MiG, half inverted. He held his position until the MiG-21 had finished its turn, and moved into position 1,500yd behind the MiG. With a deflection angle of 20°, Olds launched two Sidewinders, one of which hit the MiG and tore off its starboard wing.

PUT 'EM UP
Meanwhile, Wetterhahn had lined up behind a MiG-21 pursuing Olds, and fired a pair of Sparrows that turned the MiG into a ball of fire. At roughly the same time, Capt Walter S. Radeker III, *Olds 4*, spotted a MiG-21 tracking his element leader and manœuvred to engage it. Unable to acquire a consistently good tone (indicating a missile lock) Radeker launched a Sidewinder that guided perfectly anyway, and struck the *Fishbed* forward of its tail, sending it into a spin.

Next it was the *Ford* flight's turn to be engaged by three MiG-21s, which also attempted a pincer attack; one closed in from the six o'clock position and two from the ten o'clock position. The latter pair tracked the two leading F-4Cs, which broke hard. Captain Everett T. Raspberry Jr, *Ford 2*, performed a barrel roll that placed him in a perfect position behind the trailing MiG, which he brought down with a Sidewinder.

The NSA translators now heard the angry and worried voices of the MiG pilots explaining that instead of the expected F-105s, they were facing AAM-equipped Phantoms. One MiG pilot even requested authorisation to land. It was too late. In the confusion of the moment, additional *Fishbeds* were launched, a total of 14 MiG-21s taking off. *Rambler* flight, led by Stone, arrived over Noi Bai to be confronted head-on by

> **Wetterhahn** had lined up behind a **MiG-21** pursuing Olds, and **fired** a pair of **Sparrows** that turned the **MiG** into a ball of fire.

BELOW: *Fishbed-Ds* are pushed out at Noi Bai in the spring of 1966 in preparation for another air-defence mission against the USAF. The VPAF took the bait during *Bolo* and scrambled the equivalent of an entire squadron, the MiGs suffering accordingly. Note "4228", lost during *Bolo*, in the forground. Albert Grandolini Collection

ABOVE: McDonnell Douglas F-4C 63-7680 was the Phantom flown by Col Robin Olds during Operation *Bolo*, armed with AIM-7E Sparrows mounted in underfuselage troughs (two forward and two aft) plus a pair of AIM-9B Sidewinders on each wing. The AN/ALQ-72 ECM pod fitted for *Bolo* is shown beneath the tail. Olds's Phantom was yet to be marked with the "FP" tailcode of the 497th TFS, 8th TFW.
Artwork by TOM COOPER

four MiG-21s, followed by two more slightly below and two miles (3km) behind. Stone put his Phantom into a dive and launched a Sparrow, which failed to ignite. He fired a second, then a third Sparrow which locked on and hit one of the MiGs. Seconds later, a MiG-21 crossed in front of *Rambler 2* (Lawrence Glynn), who fired a pair of AIM-7Es – one of which turned the *Fishbed* into a ball of flame and debris, which slightly damaged his Phantom. Finally, *Rambler 4* (Maj Philip P. Combies) also fired two AIM-7Es against a MiG-21, one missile hitting its tail, forcing the pilot to eject. The American aircraft were now targeted by SAMs and Olds ordered everybody to withdraw towards the Laotian border. The entire combat had lasted 12min.

The final four flights of 8th TFW aircraft arrived to find the engagement over and, wary of the SAM threat, departed the area. The Da Nang-based East Force assessed the weather conditions and decided against penetrating North Vietnamese airspace. Two Phantoms of the Ubon-based West Force had aborted the mission for technical reasons, and ultimately only 26 of the 56 assigned fighters entered the target area; of those only 12 had engaged.

The triumphant return of the Phantoms was awaited at Ubon. All the pilots performed their traditional victory rolls except Stone, who, exhilarated that his planning had worked as planned but exhausted, did not want to push his luck and landed directly. Olds organised a huge party for all involved, taking care to thank the groundcrews for their efforts too.

The USAF claimed a record seven MiG-21s shot down on a single engagement during *Bolo*. The American missiles, well maintained and upgraded for the operation, had worked well, achieving a kill ratio of 20 per cent for the AIM-7E Sparrow and 33 per cent for the AIM-9B Sidewinder, compared to an average kill ratio of eight per cent and 15 per cent respectively during Operation *Rolling Thunder*. North Vietnamese sources, however, acknowledged only five aircraft shot down, with all their pilots being able to eject safely.[3] Did the Americans exaggerate their claims despite each claim being thoroughly analysed? A likely explanation is that the two other MiG-21s were almost certainly flown by North Korean pilots, as recorded in the NSA SIGINT intercepts.[4]

ABOVE: Captain Walter Radeker of the 555th TFS poses with an "FG"-coded Phantom of the 433rd TFS at Ubon in Thailand in early 1967. The Phantoms were pooled for *Bolo*, and only those deemed best were used. *Walter Radeker III via Warren Thompson*

OPERATION BOLO: THE USAF VICTORIES
COMPILED BY ALBERT GRANDOLINI

The following table summarises the 8th TFW's seven MiG-21 victories during Operation Bolo, January 2, 1967

Squadron	Callsign	Aircraft Commander*	2nd Pilot	Missile
555th TFS	Olds 2	Capt Ralph F. Wetterhahn	1st Lt Jerry K. Sharp	AIM-7E
555th TFS	Olds 4	Capt Walter S. Radeker III	1st Lt James E. Murray III	AIM-9B
555th TFS	Olds 1	Col Robin Olds	1st Lt Charles C. Clifton	AIM-9B
555th TFS	Ford 2	Capt Everett T. Raspberry Jr	1st Lt Robert W. Western	AIM-9B
433rd TFS	Rambler 4	Maj Philip P. Combies	1st Lt Lee R. Dutton	AIM-7E
433rd TFS	Rambler 1	Capt John B. Stone	1st Lt Clifton P. Dunnegan Jr	AIM-7E
433rd TFS	Rambler 2	1st Lt Lawrence J. Glynn Jr	1st Lt Lawrence E. Cary	AIM-7E

* In 1967 all USAF F-4s were crewed by two rated pilots, with the more experienced flying the front seat as "aircraft commander". The use of rated navigators as Weapon Systems Officers began in 1969

THE AFTERMATH

Despite its losses, the VPAF's 921st FR continued operations over the following days, including trying to shoot down weather-reconnaissance aircraft over North Vietnam. Olds took the opportunity to set another trap, despatching two F-4Cs flying in close formation to appear as the usual weather-reconnaissance RF-4C, on January 5, 1967. The North Vietnamese did not take the bait on this occasion, but on a repeat mission the next day four MiG-21s were launched to intercept, two of which were shot down.

After this new setback, the VPAF decided to suspend MiG-21 operations for more than three months in order to analyse these engagements and develop new tactics. The VPAF High Command recognised that it had acted too boldly, becoming overly self-confident in its ability to conduct operations in a changing tactical situation, making the mistake of launching the equivalent a full squadron of MiG-21s. It was realised that the VPAF should restrict itself to its own "guerrilla air warfare" doctrine, i.e. use its interceptors only in favourable conditions or give up and wait patiently to fight another day. Its pilots, despite being eager to fight, were still too inexperienced to face highly trained American veterans of the Second World War and Korean conflict.

Among the pilots involved in the dogfight of January 2 was Capt Nguyen Van Coc, who ejected from his stricken aircraft and landed by parachute back at base. He immediately requested another MiG-21 be made ready so he could continue the fight. He was calmed down, but swore that he would avenge this defeat, and over the following months would claim nine kills, with seven acknowledged by American sources, placing him at the top of the scroll of aces of the Vietnam War.

Olds scored three more aerial victories as the head of the 8th TFW. Reportedly, he passed up several opportunities to achieve another kill to become the first American ace of the conflict, not wanting to be sent back to the USA before the end of his tour of service in South-east Asia. After his departure, Olds's achievements in improving air-combat training were not adopted by the USAF, which preferred to focus on technology developments, such as the introduction of the AIM-4D Falcon air-to-air missile, which proved to be a great disappointment. The NSA's C-130B-IIs were not used again in a tactical role despite their clearly proven value. Their capabilities were partly filled by a new electronic device, the QRC-248 interrogator, installed on EC-121Ds from October 1967, which enabled the Warning Stars to read the MiGs' IFF transponders, detecting them even at low altitudes.

The MiG-21s returned to front-line operations in April 1967 with new tactics. After suffering heavy losses, particularly in May, the North Vietnamese once again overcame their difficulties. In this ongoing duel, both sides constantly refined and adapted their tactics to each new development. The previously unassailable superiority of the Phantom was increasingly in jeopardy. The North Vietnamese fighter force regained the

> The VPAF's 921st FR continued operations over the following days, including trying to shoot down weather-reconnaissance aircraft over North Vietnam. Olds took the opportunity to set another trap, despatching two F-4Cs.

ABOVE: Bearing a red star victory marking on its intake splitter plate, F-4C 64-0838 was photographed a few weeks after Bolo, when it was flown as *Rambler 4* by Maj Philip Combies of the 433rd TFS, and during which it shot down a MiG-21. This Phantom still exists and is displayed at the US Space & Rocket Center at Huntsville, Alabama, USA. *USAF*

ABOVE: Olds (left) before he had grown his distinctive but strictly non-regulation moustache, alongside Capt John B. Stone, the operations officer responsible for planning *Bolo*. *USAF*

initiative at the end of the *Rolling Thunder* campaign, inflicting serious losses on attacking enemy air-craft, claiming 22 per cent of the total of those shot down, anti-aircraft artillery accounting for most of the rest. The wheel had turned and the ratio of kills to losses, at one point three to one in favour of the Americans, had declined to a mere 0·85 to one. By January 1968 the ratio had shifted to five to one in favour of the MiG-21s. It took the Americans several more years to deal with this threat by improving technologically, and tactically by devising a new air-combat training programme. ●

BELOW: In the wake of the Operation *Bolo* setback, the VPAF grounded its MiG-21s for several weeks before returning to combat with revised tactics, which inflicted heavy losses on the Americans in the last days of the *Rolling Thunder* campaign, which ended in 1968. Here VPAF ace Nguyen Nhat Chieu (far left) relives a combat. *Albert Grandolini Collection*

ENDNOTE REFERENCES

1 The secret military accord signed between North Vietnam and China in February 1964 envisaged the deployment of the People's Liberation Army Air Force in case of American air attacks undertaken against the North. Hanoi was bitterly disappointed when Beijing did not fulfil its promise. However, the VPAF's MiGs could seek asylum on Chinese air bases across the border.
2 Bolo — a traditional large knife, like a dagger, carried by Philippine warriors.
3 Pilots involved were Bui Duc Nhu, Nguyen Danh Kinh, Nguyen Duc Thuan, Nguyen Van Coc and Vu Ngoc Dinh.
4 By monitoring the radio frequencies used by the VPAF, the 22 linguists aboard the two C-130B-IIs recorded conversations of the following cumulative lengths during Operation Bolo: 27hr in Vietnamese; 10hr in Korean; 3hr 10min in Chinese; 20min in Russian. These totals comprise the initial phase before the arrival of the American aircraft, the actual combat and its immediate aftermath. The implication of the North Korean is obvious.

The Scarface Klan:
The Bell HueyCobra & HML-367 in Vietnam, 1969–71

When US Marine Corps helicopter unit HML-367 — "The Scarface Klan" — exchanged its Bell UH-1E Hueys for the same company's altogether more formidable AH-1G HueyCobra in late 1969, it lost no time in getting to grips with the famously fearsome helicopter gunship. WARREN E. THOMPSON profiles the unit's 18-month campaign in Vietnam and explains why "when you're out of Scarface, you're out of gun…"

In early December 1969 US Marine Corps (USMC) helicopter unit HML-367 moved to Marble Mountain, south of Da Nang in Vietnam, where it gave up its Bell UH-1Es and took on a full complement of the same company's AH-1G HueyCobra gunships. This move put the squadron in the heavy firepower mode, with the ability to fire a devastating load of 2·75in rockets along with a turret-mounted 7·62mm minigun and, when needed, a stub-wing-mounted 20mm cannon.

Formed in March 1968 when Marine Observation Squadron VMO-3 was redesignated as Marine Light Helicopter Squadron HML-367, the unit used the callsign *Scarface*, much better reflecting its new aggressive role than VMO-3's original *Oakgate* moniker, used during 1966 and the first half of 1967. With the delivery of 24 AH-1Gs in December 1969, HML-367 was ready to begin operations – its helicopters would support just about every type of rotary-wing operation then being flown by the US Marines. There were also numerous missions flown in support of the US Army and Korean Marines.

POINT-BLANK FIREFIGHTS
The commanding officer for all USMC helicopter operations in Vietnam was Col Haywood R. Smith of Marine Aircraft Group 16 (MAG-16). Having completed his tour in Vietnam in 1970, Smith had the following to say about the "Scarface Klan": "I flew many missions with HML-367 in AH-1Gs and I firmly believe that the 'Cobra was the best close-air-support weapon when it came to covering the insertion and extraction of friendly troops into hostile territory. Lieutenant-Colonel Harry Sexton was '367's

BELOW: A Bell AH-1G HueyCobra of HML-367 closes in on a suspected Viet Cong hideout in 1970. The HueyCobra incorporated the powerplant, transmission system and rotor of Bell's tried-and-trusted UH-1C Huey, the new dedicated gunship variant making its first flight on September 7, 1965, a mere six months after development had started. *Barry Pencek via author*

commanding officer during my tenure and he was one of the best leaders that served under my command.

"The main reason the 'Cobras were so effective was that they had the longest loiter-time over a hot area and they backed it up with some awesome firepower. Every one of the pilots in the squadron experienced a point-blank firefight with Viet Cong [VC] and North Vietnamese Army [NVA] troops on a regular basis. It is my belief that the 'Cobra was probably the most respected and feared weapon by the VC and NVA regulars during the war."

Smith continued: "No matter what their mission was, you could be assured that they were going to drum up a lot of groundfire. In early June 1970, '367 became involved in a unique mission that called for tactics quite different from those it was used to. A few days before the missions, one of our recon teams was able to capture a Viet Cong prisoner. Once they put him through a lengthy interrogation session, he talked and revealed where the HQ of the VC was in the Que Son mountains. This was a mountainous area laced with caves. We attended several high-level meetings to determine the best way to attack the target. The final plan called for 16 Sikorsky CH-53Ds. However, with this large an attack force, it only required one heavily-armed 'Cobra from HML-367."

This mission would result in one of the longest flights – 5hr 48min – flown by a CH-53 during the Vietnam War, the average being around 3hr. Each of the big

ABOVE: Colonel Haywood Smith, Commanding Officer of MAG-16 and all US Marine Corps helicopter operations in Vietnam, smiles for the camera beside one of the "Scarface Klan's" HueyCobras. *Col Hayward Smith via author*

helicopters was loaded with 15 x 55 US gal drums of napalm, equating to some 6,000lb (2,700kg) of napalm per helicopter or a grand total of 96,000lb (43,500kg) for the full attack force. The final plan called for the CH-53Ds to hover above the cave complex and drop their loads simultaneously, at which point the HueyCobra was called in with its 54 x 2·75in rockets. Seconds later, the rockets hit home and the entire area erupted in a massive fireball. The VC Commanding General of I Corps, along with a undetermined number of VC troops, was killed. This tactic was not used many times, but it was the heavy-hauling CH-53s and firepower of the HueyCobra that made this type of mission so successful.

The HueyCobra was used in many ways by the USMC during the Vietnam War, dynamically changing the posture of the North Vietnamese and their tactics against American ground and air units. As former HueyCobra driver Capt "Skip" Massey explains, "to be a 'Cobra pilot, it was necessary to perform the following duties: airborne forward air control; close air support; medevac escort; helo resupply escort; BDAs [bomb-damage assessments]; recon insert and hunt-and-destroy missions". There was a progression of experience required to become a section leader – mission commander of two 'Cobras – or division leader, when several AH-1Gs were used.

First Lieutenant Roland Scott recalls a dangerous mission in Vietnam's Quảng Nam province in July 1970: "I was a section leader of two 'Cobras, escorting two [Boeing-Vertol] CH-46 transports. We launched at 1500hr to extract a Marine reconnaissance team that was in contact with a numerically superior enemy force. After being briefed by a [North American Rockwell] OV-10, the team was in the process of moving down a small riverbed to a suitable helicopter-landing zone. This was accomplished under the cover of fixed-wing airstrikes on enemy positions. The OV-10 pilot warned the team that a thunderstorm was approaching from the south.

"The CH-46s dropped their teams on a sandbar, the aircraft retreating from the area owing to the storm. Within a few minutes the team radioed that it was surrounded by the enemy on all four sides."

Scott turned and flew directly into the low cloud and rainshower to help. He instructed his wingman to remain with the two CH-46s that were circling north of the rainstorm.

BELOW: A "snake" (HueyCobra) of HML-367 and a pair of US Marine Corps Boeing-Vertol CH-46s – nicknamed "Phrogs" in service owing to the type's appearance of squatting like a frog when on the ground— await the passing of a thunderstorm at Marble Mountain before undertaking a mission to drop USMC forces deep into enemy-held territory. *Barry Pencek via author*

Locating the team's position, Scott had to fly at a speed of 40–50kt (75–95km/h) at 20–50ft (6–15m) above ground level, making numerous attacks against the enemy forces using his 20mm cannon while only 100ft (30m) from the friendly force.

Scott also used his 7·62mm M134 minigun while only 50ft from friendly forces. The rainy weather continued to move out of the area and, with Scott's HueyCobra keeping the enemy pinned down, the CH-46s were able to get in and pick up the team. Meanwhile, Scott marked the enemy positions with phosphorous rockets. In recognition of his leading the charge to recover the team, Scott was awarded the Silver Star.

'COBRA BECOMES KINGFISHER

Almost immediately after converting to the HueyCobra, HML-367 became involved in *Kingfisher* missions, in which the unit aggressively searched out enemy troops before they had a chance to initiate a planned action. *Kingfisher* teams usually consisted of a rifle platoon, three CH-46s, two HueyCobras and an OV-10 plus a single UH-1E for primary command-and-control operations.

The idea was that the HueyCobras would be the "kingfishers", waiting above the assault team; when the enemy showed itself, the predators would pounce. The AH-1G's fuselage was a mere 36in (91cm) wide, with the pilot and copilot/gunner located in tandem. This gave the helicopter an extremely narrow head-on profile, a minimal cross-section and exceptional visibility from the cockpit. In addition, the type's stub wings were designed to carry a variety of state-of-the-art ground-attack weapons;

ABOVE: Spelling it out – the unit's nickname is written in ammunition on the hangar floor at HML-367's base at Marble Mountain. This head-on view shows the devastating firepower that each HueyCobra had at its disposal. The front turret is a standard M28 unit, equipped with a 40mm grenade launcher to port and an M134 minigun. *Barry Pencek via author*

BELOW: The port stub wing of this HML-367 AH-1G, adorned with an appropriate Cobra motif on the nose, is fitted with a 19-tube M159 2·75in folding-fin aerial rocket (FFAR) launcher inboard, with an M158 seven-tube FFAR launcher on the outboard hardpoint. *Barry Pencek via author*

these accumulated features made the HueyCobra the most valuable support aircraft in Vietnam.

According to former HueyCobra pilot Lt Deane Swickard, "we had a top speed of around 220 m.p.h. (355km/h). The stub wings could hold [four 19-barrelled M159] 2·75in-rocket pods or [two rocket pods and] a [single M195 Vulcan] 20mm cannon. The six-barrelled [M195] Gatling gun fired 2,000 or 4,000 rounds per minute. This weapon alone could cut down a 100yd [90m] swathe of thick-jungle hiding-places for the NVA. Although the *Kingfisher* attack group was tasked with getting in and out quickly, the enemy bodycount after a close-in firefight must have been extremely high.

"The pilot normally fired the wing stores and flew the aircraft, although the copilot/gunner also had flight controls and could fire the guns in the nose turret. When rockets were launched, turret fire was automatically interrupted. On *Kingfisher* missions, the 'Cobras would normally launch with two seven-shot rocket pods with 'Willy Pete' [white phosphorous – WP] warheads, two 19-shot rocket pods with 17lb [7·5kg] high-explosive [HE] warheads, a minigun turret armed with 4,000 rounds and a [wing-mounted] 20mm cannon with 300 rounds.

"Normally the crew would visually acquire a target, mark it with WP and attack it with HE rockets and high-volume fire from the other guns. Our 'Cobras were protected by 272lb [123kg] of armour. Research had shown where the armour should be put so that the engine compressor, fuel controls and crew seats were protected. Self-sealing fuel tanks, redundant hydraulics and an emergency oil-bypass system were also included. These features, combined with firepower, speed and profile, resulted in a potent gunship with high crew survivability."

Considering the low altitude at which the HueyCobras operated – often at treetop level – it is surprising how few were lost. Viet Cong and NVA soldiers put up a constant barrage of groundfire against the invaluable 'Cobra. For the Scarface Klan to be fully effective, the unit's HueyCobras had to stay low, especially during the exfiltration of troops using the larger helicopters. Lieutenant Bob "Robby" Robinson recalls such a mission: "The temperature in March was running over 100°F [38°C]. In that kind of heat, a loaded 'Cobra would struggle to get airborne; [it] would start its take-off down the runway while struggling to gain enough airspeed to enter translational lift. Many a pilot had to clean his pants after watching a fence or other obstacle at the end of the runway get bigger and bigger.

"On one flight that had us heading back towards Marble Mountain we heard an OV-10 talking to DASC [Direct Air Support Center]. He was looking for some guns as quick as possible. He had seen several VC run into a bunker and wanted to roust them out. His position was about 6km [four miles] south of Marble and we were only 10min away. We arrived overhead while the OV-10 was circling at 3,000ft [900m].

"He said the bunker was just north of the river and west of a large clump of trees and marked the location with a round of 'Willy Pete'. We lined up behind the OV-10 to get a good line of fire with our rockets. His marker hit close to the top of the entrance and he stated that my target was 50m [160ft] east of his mark. We lined up and I set up two rockets and fired; as they hit I lined up the crosshairs.

> "We had a **top speed** of around **220 m.p.h.** (355km/h). The stub wings could hold **[four 19-barrelled M159] 2·75in-rocket pods** or **[two rocket pods and] a [single M195 Vulcan] 20mm cannon.**

ABOVE: This view from the cockpit of an HML-367 HueyCobra was taken while protecting a CH-46 resupplying a remote USMC outpost – note the shadow of the "Phrog" on the slope facing the camera. Such resupply missions required acute vigilance from the Cobra, as the incoming helicopters were extremely vulnerable to groundfire. *Barry Pencek via author*

BELOW: HueyCobras of HML-367 in their revetments at Marble Mountain. *Barry Pencek via author*

AVIATION CLASSICS: AMERICAN COLD WAR STORIES 113

"I didn't want to make the 'snake' jerk when everything was ready. The opening in the bunker was in my sights and as I slowly squeezed the button on the cyclic, the 'Cobra jerked slightly as the two rockets launched from their tubes. Straight as an arrow, the two rockets sped towards the bunker opening. I must have done everything right. I adjusted the crosshairs on my sight; the impact area was just above the target. I fired the next two rockets and, to my amazement, one of them went right into the small hole that the VC had used to enter the bunker. I pulled the cyclic back and started my climb, straining to see what damage had been done. A beautiful orange mushroom secondary explosion erupted from the bunker. It was an impressive sight and after we had expended our ordnance we headed back to Marble Mountain.

"From that day on, I considered myself a master at shooting rockets. It took probably another 500 rockets to be really good consistently, but I did become a master in delivering them right where I wanted them."

OUT IN THE OPEN

One of the lowest-level roles that HML-367 undertook while in Vietnam was the *Pacifier* mission, the purpose of which was to flush out potential targets into the open and take prisoners if possible. The HueyCobras usually worked such missions in pairs, in concert with three UH-46 troop-carriers. Lieutenant-Colonel Bob Guay, a pilot in MAG-16, flew regular *Pacifier* missions and recalled: "On one of these missions the squadron CO, Lt-Col Harry Sexton, almost shot me down. I had spotted two boats crossing a stream. I went over to one to see who and what was in the boat. There were two young males and some packages. We were in 'free-fire country' and I was about to tell Sexton to go ahead and shoot the boat when he called me to get out of his way. He was in his gun-run and he sank the boat.

"Shortly after, I was coming out of Marble Mountain with two 'Cobras and some troop-carrying UH-46s, on my way to pick up some officers, when I spotted a farmer working in a rice paddy. This 'farmer' had command presence and football-player's legs – in other words he didn't have anything to do with farming!

"I told one of our 'Cobras to stop him by firing in his direction and had one of our UH-46s pick him up and take him as a prisoner. On interrogation, we found out he was a North Vietnamese Major.

"A few days later I spotted another man walking up one of the roads and he didn't look like a local. His clothes were spotless and he glared at me as I went by him at 10ft [3m]. I flew many of my *Pacifiers* at 10ft at a speed of around 60–80kt, as I liked to look into their eyes. As he came up to a rice paddy trail, he turned right off the road and started out into the paddy heading toward the mountains. I told one of the gunships to stop him

ABOVE: This view from an HML-367 HueyCobra's "office" shows the comparatively simple instrumentation in the gunship's cockpit. The instruments show the helicopter climbing through 4,000ft at 74kt; the apparently high altitude is deceptive, however, as much of the unit's work involved weaving through the Annamite mountains. *Barry Pencek via author*

> One of the **lowest-level roles** that **HML-367** undertook while in Vietnam was the **Pacifier mission,** the purpose of which was to **flush out potential targets** into the open and **take prisoners** if possible.

ABOVE: Captain Robert W. "Robby" Robinson was one of the Scarface Klan's "top-timers", having completed some 1,140 combat missions by the time the unit was rotated out of theatre. Robinson later published a highly-readable account of his experiences with the unit in Vietnam, entitled *Scarface 42* (Tailwind Publications, 2008). *Robert W. Robinson via author*

114 AVIATION CLASSICS: AMERICAN COLD WAR STORIES

RIGHT: An armourer loads the 7·62mm M134 minigun on the starboard station of the M28 nose turret. The mini-gun, a Gatling-style machine-gun with electrically-operated rotating barrels, was a scaled-down version of the M61 Vulcan 20mm cannon; the M134 was capable of delivering up to 4,000 rounds per minute without overheating. *Barry Pencek via author*

and a UH-46 picked him up. He turned out to be the second-highest-ranking officer in the NVA's I Corps.

"A few days later we were working the same area and I noticed a girl about 100yd away in a rice paddy. She had a 'diddy pole' on her shoulder equipped with two packages at either end. As one of our UH-46s approached her, she dropped the pole and started to run. They got her and let some troops out to recover the packages. It turned out that she was a VC courier and had $100,000 in piastres."

Pacifier missions picked up numerous VC and NVA soldiers, who then provided much valuable intelligence; in most cases, the 'Cobra did not have to fire a single shot. By 1970 HML-367 was operating at full capacity and, on April 24 of that year, the unit could boast of having all 25 of its AH-1Gs fully operational – the first time a helicopter squadron had attained 100 per cent serviceability in Vietnam. As a celebration, all 25 HueyCobras were put up for a formation flight over Marble Mountain. By the end of the 1970 fiscal year the unit had flown some 22,378hr.

In June 1971 HML-367 completed its combat tour in Vietnam and relocated to Okinawa, shortly thereafter re-equipping with Bell UH-1Es. Today, the "Cobra" name continues on in US Marine service with the twin-engined Bell AH-1W SuperCobra, which looks set to remain in service with the US Marines for the foreseeable future. ●

BELOW: A 'Cobra of HML-367 peels away towards the base at Marble Mountain after a lengthy patrol. The unit returned to Vietnam in the spring of 1975, its UH-1Es participating in the evacuation of Vietnamese and Cambodian refugees during the fall of Saigon. In 2009 HMLA-367's Bell UH-1Y Venoms deployed to Afghanistan. *Barry Pencek via author*

BELL AH-1G HUEYCOBRA DATA

Powerplant 1 x 1,400 s.h.p. Lycoming T53-L-13 shaft turbine (derated to 1,100 s.h.p.)

Dimensions
Length (fuselage)	44ft 5in	(13·54m)
(overall inc. rotor)	52ft 11½in	(16·15m)
Width (fuselage)	36in	(0·91m)
Height (overall)	13ft 5½in	(4·1m)
Stub-wing span	10ft 11½in	(3·34m)
Rotor diameter	44ft 0in	(13·41m)
Disc area	1,520ft²	(141m²)
Skid track	7ft 0in	(2·13m)

Weights
Empty	5,288lb	(2,399kg)
Fully loaded	9,500lb	(4,309kg)

Performance
Maximum diving speed	219 m.p.h.	(352km/h)
Cruise speed	196 m.p.h.	(315km/h)

Hovering ceiling
(IGE)*	7,200ft	(2,195m)
(OGE)**	4,500ft	(1,370m)

* In ground effect on an 80°F (27°C) day with fuel for typical 115-mile (185km)-radius mission + fuel reserve + 38 x 2·75in rocket projectiles and 8,000 rounds of ammunition

** Out of ground effect as above

Kellyinspirin'rich thinkin'skunkwork in'reconseein'two seatin'intelligence gatherin'J58drivin' JP7burnin'missileavoidin' MiGlosin'high-flyin' recordsettin'Mach-bustin'

Blackbird!

Giant Reach:
The Lockheed SR-71 in East Anglia, 1974-90

During the 1970s and 1980s the distinctive shape of the Lockheed SR-71 Blackbird always turned heads over the Suffolk countryside, despite being a regular sight for locals living within a J58's roar of the type's base at Mildenhall. BOB ARCHER documents the genesis and operational career of the 9th SRW's Detachment 4, which operated the mighty Blackbird from the base for some 16 years.

ABOVE: Looking like a malevolent insect, Lockheed SR-71A Blackbird 61-7962 makes its way from the parking area on to the taxiway at Mildenhall on December 6, 1984. Measuring some 107ft (33m) in length, the aircraft was powered by two huge 32,500lb-thrust Pratt & Whitney J58 turbojets. *Bob Archer*

In October 1989 the government of the USA withdrew all funding for Lockheed SR-71 flight operations, effectively grounding the type, including the pair located at RAF Mildenhall in eastern England. Even though the unique nature of the intelligence captured by the aircraft's sophisticated sensors was deemed vital to strategic-defence planning, operations with it were incredibly expensive, consuming millions of dollars annually in budgetary costs. Indeed, it was so expensive that senior officials with their hands on the financial tiller sought to axe the programme in favour of more glamorous fighter budgets. Despite attempts by politicians to restore the SR-71 to active duty, the type was ultimately "killed off" by a Presidential mandate. Thus ended a quarter of a century of aviation history performed by a truly exceptional aircraft.

SNAKES, BIRDS AND CROWNS
The SR-71 was a familiar sight in the skies of East Anglia for almost 16 years. It flew from RAF Mildenhall in Suffolk; the base was one of only three locations worldwide which regularly hosted this extraordinary aircraft, the others being Beale AFB in California and Kadena Air Base (AB) on Okinawa, Japan. Crews at the latter applied the nickname "Habu" to the type, as it resembled a deadly poisonous snake which inhabited the island. The locals around Mildenhall preferred the more familiar "Blackbird".

The SR-71 programme was codenamed *Senior Crown* for funding purposes, although the name was not widely known beyond official corridors. The appearance of the first SR-71 in the UK was widely publicised, however, as was its departure from service 16 years later; a period during which the

ABOVE: The first SR-71 to visit the UK was 61-7972, which set a new transatlantic time over distance record during its flight from Beale AFB in California to Farnborough on September 1, 1974. The aircraft is seen here six days later at the SBAC show at Farnborough. The previous record of 4hr 46min, set by an RAF Phantom between London and New York, was demolished by the Blackbird, which flew New York–London in 1hr 55min. *Bob Archer*

> A **new record** from London to Los Angeles, covering the **5,645 miles (9,084km)** in **3hr 47min 39sec** at an average speed of **1,480 m.p.h. (2,382km/h).**

SR-71 was a significant part of aviation in East Anglia, albeit shrouded in a veil of secrecy. Despite the latter, its missions from Mildenhall were fairly predictable, given the familiar telltale sights and sounds of a typical SR-71 departure: the early launching of Boeing KC-135Q tankers; the departure of each SR-71 mission precisely on the hour in complete radio silence, with a torch signal from the control tower to instigate take-off; and an earth-shattering roar from the two Pratt & Whitney J58 engines.

Blackbird missions to the Arctic or Baltic Sea regions were usually of 4–5hr duration, and the casual observer could easily work out an approximate time of return. An 0800hr departure usually signified a lunchtime return. Often the SR-71 would land back at Mildenhall around 1300hr, a perfect time for the astute photographer, particularly after training missions when the pilot and Reconnaissance Systems Officer (RSO) were happy to perform an overshoot. Ground support technicians much preferred to work on an aircraft which had cooled slightly, which an overshoot helped to produce. At altitude the external surfaces of the SR-71 heated up significantly, reaching temperatures of 500–1,000°C (930–1,830°F), the titanium used in its construction remaining hot once back on the ground.

Initially SR-71s were forward-deployed to Kadena from March 1968, for missions over North Vietnam and to monitor other potentially hostile nations in South-east Asia. Detachment 1 of the USAF's 9th Strategic Reconnaissance Wing (SRW) was established at Kadena to control the activities of the deployed SR-71s, a type which for many years was a total stranger to Europe.

The first recorded SR-71 transatlantic mission was completed in October 1973 during the Arab-Israeli Yom Kippur War, when an SR-71A flew from Griffiss AFB, New York, to monitor Egyptian, Jordanian and Syrian troop locations, enabling America's ally Israel to adjust its forces' tactics and turn the tide in its favour. The lengthy mission highlighted the need for the USA to be able to utilise air bases in Europe as forward-operating locations on an occasional basis.

The initial wish of Strategic Air Command (SAC) was to operate a small detachment of SR-71s from Torrejón AB in Spain, but the Spanish government refused to allow overt reconnaissance to be undertaken from its territory. The UK's Ministry of Defence (MoD) also declined to permit SR-71 operations from Mildenhall, worrying that such support for the USA might inflame relations with Arab nations and disrupt oil supplies. However, negotiations between the USA and the MoD for an "occasional" operating base in the UK were agreed in principle during 1974.

The feasibility of such operations still needed to be evaluated, though, and the Americans decided to send an example to England. To enable the operation to raise little suspicion as to the true nature of the visit, the flight was to be staged under the full glare of publicity. Two transatlantic legs were flown in an attempt to capture the fastest crossing times for the outward mission between New York and London, and between London and Los Angeles on the homeward section.

On September 1, 1974, Majors James V. Sullivan, pilot, and Noel F. Widdifield, RSO, crossed the starting line above New York in SR-71 61-7972 at approximately 80,000ft (24,400m) and at a speed of more than 2,000 m.p.h. (3,220km/h). Exactly 1hr 54min 56·4sec later, they had set a new world speed record. The aircraft averaged 1,817 m.p.h. (2,924km/h) over the 3,488-mile (5,612km) course, slowing to refuel just once from a KC-135Q. The SR-71 landed at Farnborough, where it stole the show as a static display exhibit at that year's SBAC show. It marked the first time the distinctive SR-71 had been on public display outside the USA.

Another historic speed record was set on the return journey, when pilot Capt Harold B. Adams and RSO Maj William Machorek set a new record from London to Los Angeles, covering the 5,645 miles (9,084km) in 3hr 47min 39sec at an average speed of 1,480 m.p.h. (2,382km/h). The difference in the two speed records was owing to refuelling requirements, and the need to reduce speed over major American cities. Despite precautions being taken, broken windows were reported in the Los Angeles area owing to the SR-71's sonic boom. The aircraft's arrival time in Los Angeles was almost four hours before its departure time from London, owing to the 8hr time difference between the UK and California. The departure airfield in the UK was RAF Mildenhall, which enabled personnel of the 9th SRW to conduct an unhindered and successful evaluation.

BLACKBIRD IN BLIGHTY

More important than the record flights was the completion of the feasibility study into operations from RAF Mildenhall. The USA notified the MoD that it would like to begin operations on an ad hoc basis. The MoD approved the request in principle, with the proviso that operational detachments be restricted to a maximum of 20 days in duration, and that ministerial approval would be required for each visit. Accordingly, SR-71 visits to the UK were rare and short in the early days.

The first operational Blackbird deployment to Mildenhall began when 61-7972 returned to the Suffolk base on April 20, 1976, for a ten-day stay. The station also housed a single Lockheed U-2R at the time, hangared on the south side of the airfield where it was taken immediately on landing, to enable its precious film to be extracted from the cameras.

ABOVE: Blackbird 61-7958 is towed into position as the star exhibit in the static display at the Mildenhall Air Fête on May 29, 1977, the first time an SR-71 was put on display at the Suffolk airbase. This airframe made a total of four visits to Mildenhall, the last being from September 1983 to June 1984. *Bob Archer*

> The historic **first mission** took place on **May 20,** to satisfy a US Navy request for **high-resolution radar imagery and electronic intelligence (ELINT)** sensor recordings of the **nuclear and conventional submarine operations** and port facilities in the **Murmansk area.**

The occasional SR-71 deployment was kept separate, although the two aircraft were housed within the same area.

The U-2R needed no aerial support, as its glider-like capabilities enabled 10hr missions to be flown with ease. In contrast, the SR-71 required the services of several KC-135Q tankers carrying the special JP7 fuel unique to the Blackbird. The 17th Bomb Wing (BW) operated the KC-135Qs from Beale AFB during 1975–76, until they were reassigned to the 100th Air Refuelling Wing (ARW) in September 1976. Eventually the tankers were amalgamated into the 9th SRW.

European SR-71 operations were ostensibly to coincide with major Nato exercises; but, as aircraft residency increased, so missions were specifically organised for dedicated intelligence-gathering requirements. The first operational strategic reconnaissance missions began in May 1977, when SR-71 61-7958 was flown to Mildenhall. The historic first mission took place on May 20, to satisfy a US Navy request for high-resolution radar imagery and electronic intelligence (ELINT) sensor recordings of the nuclear and conventional submarine operations and port facilities in the Murmansk area. The mission was a joint effort with 55th SRW RC-135V *Rivet Joint* 64-14846, which also flew from Mildenhall. The Top Secret mission was probably flown to enable the SR-71 to capture "emitter" traffic across the airwaves produced to monitor the *Rivet Joint* and for the *Rivet Joint* to do the same for the Blackbird.

The tasking of SR-71 missions was approved at the highest level of both the American and UK governments, with locations of primary interest being situated behind the "Iron Curtain", particularly East Germany and the Soviet Union. One particular focus of interest was the vast military complexes in the vicinity of the southern Barents Sea around the Kola Peninsula, chiefly around the Murmansk Oblast. Although the SR-71 had previously flown directly overhead North Vietnam to obtain data, overflights could not take place above eastern European countries or Russia. Therefore European Blackbird missions were restricted to observing activities from the peripheral safety of international waters, or above friendly territory. Nine visits to the area took place during the 1970s, although as the decade drew to a close the need for additional, lengthier stays began to become apparent.

One noteworthy Blackbird mission was undertaken during early March 1979 to monitor the situation between the Republic of Yemen and its Saudi Arabian neighbour. The Yemenis appeared to be on the brink of invading Saudi territory, with the American authorities anxious to gain intelligence on Yemeni intentions. Accordingly, faithful 61-7972 was despatched to Mildenhall to perform the lengthy mission. After two cancelled missions, '972 was airborne before dawn on day three, and completed its tanker rendezvous before streaking into the sunrise across the Mediterranean. Two more aerial refuellings were completed before '972 headed for the target area. A glitch in the automated navigation system resulted in the aircraft accidentally overflying the planned turning point, as the optical bar camera in the nose and the various individual cameras in the chine bays captured their imagery. The delay in completing the turn produced unexpected results, yielding much valuable additional data. The crew returned to Mildenhall after completing a 10hr mission.

This sort of mission was fairly uncommon, however, most being conducted to gather intelligence from the Soviet Union and its Warsaw Pact allies. Blackbird missions frequently involved departing Mildenhall and flying north around Norway before undertaking activities in the Barents Sea and White Sea areas. Others involved overflying the Baltic Sea to look deep into Poland, East Germany and Russia. Subsonic missions along the border between East and West Germany were also undertaken.

Blackbird 61-7979, which had arrived in mid-April 1979, departed Mildenhall for home on May 2 the same year, the day before the Labour government was swept from power and Margaret Thatcher became the new Prime Minister. The new administration was much more amenable to the USA extending its UK SR-71 operations, although initially this was undertaken on a gradual basis. The final UK Blackbird deployment of 1979 was of serial 61-7976, which arrived on October 18 and stayed for 26 days. Before this symbolic deployment, Detachment 4 of the 9th SRW had been formed at Mildenhall during March 1979. The unit also became responsible for the ongoing U-2R operation, with one aircraft almost permanently in residence, as well as the occasional SR-71 presence. European SR-71 operations were codenamed *Giant Reach*.

Throughout 1980 the duration of the SR-71's UK deployments lengthened and by the end of the year Det 4 was operating the type virtually full-time. This increased further during 1981 and, on April 5, 1982, the MoD received Prime Ministerial approval to allow Det 4 to operate on a permanent basis, with two SR-71s assigned. However, the MoD still retained final approval of the more sensitive missions. The aircraft continued to operate from the hangar complex on the south side, but it became evident that a permanent, more suitable pair of barns would have to be constructed. Work on these began in 1985, with 61-7962 having the honour of christening the new complex upon returning from a mission on August 8 that year.

THE BODØNIAN EXPRESS

Mildenhall was the SR-71's primary operating base in Europe, although the changeable weather conditions called for a number of diversionary airfields to be established. Blackbird missions frequently took the aircraft above the Baltic Sea, around the top of Norway into the cold Arctic region to monitor military complexes in northern Russia. Thus the USA approached the Norwegian government, which agreed in principle that, in an emergency, its bases could be used. The first occasion on which an aircraft was diverted was on August 13, 1981, when 61-7964 landed at Bodø AB, while on a combined mission/delivery to Mildenhall from Beale AFB. The aircraft suffered an oil malfunction in one of the engines. Rather than risk flying

ABOVE: Major Tim McCleary (pilot, left) and Lt-Col Stan Gudmundson (RSO) shake hands before the penultimate SR-71 return flight to the USA on January 18, 1990. Given the extreme altitudes at which the Blackbird operated, special pressure suits had to be worn by its crews. The David Clark S-1030 suit offered full protection in the event of a cabin depressurisation at altitude. *Bob Archer*

the ailing aircraft to Mildenhall, the crew elected to divert to Bodø.

A KC-135Q full of technicians and spare parts was hastily despatched from Beale and arrived at Bodø, within the Arctic Circle, at around 0700hr the next day. Repairs commenced immediately and continued late into the night. With no hangar available, '964 was left outside, a new experience for the California-based personnel. The technicians were back at work early the following day and eventually restarted one engine, although the other refused to ignite. With little fuel remaining in the SR-71's tanks, an orbiting KC-135Q, which had launched from Mildenhall to assist with the final leg of the journey, elected to land at Bodø. The overweight tanker ran off the runway, sank into the soft earth and had to be pulled out. Eventually both SR-71 engines started, and preparations were made for departure, but not before the name *The Bodønian Express* and a small white crab had been applied to the Blackbird's fins.

Detachment 4 increased to two aircraft on December 19, 1982, when 61-7971 arrived to join '972. With two Blackbirds stationed in the UK, the USAF began to undertake many more missions and expand its area of interest, acquiring more peripheral photography of eastern Europe and the Middle East. This enabled planners to increase the number of missions flown with a corresponding growth in the quantity of intelligence obtained. The aircraft could not fly supersonic overland, as the shockwave would have created catastrophic damage. However, missions over water could be accomplished at the aircraft's design cruise speed of Mach 3+. Although the need for

BELOW: With engines running, 61-7972 prepares to depart Mildenhall on September 12, 1974, having completed a USAF evaluation of the type's suitability for UK-based operations. Blackbird '972 was joint most frequent visitor to the UK, along with 61-7964, both being deployed six times to Mildenhall during the type's European operational career. *Bob Archer*

ABOVE: In August 1981 Blackbird 61-7964 became the first Det 4 SR-71 to divert to a foreign airfield when it suffered engine problems during a mission. Seen here at Mildenhall in November 1981, the aircraft has been "tagged" by Military Airlift Command groundcrew, who have chalked "MAC & Crew" and "For sale" on its port fin. *Bob Archer*

secrecy prevented details from emerging at the time, subsequent releases have highlighted that many missions to the militarised region of north-west Russia were on behalf of the US Navy.

Formerly classified documents have confirmed that the SR-71s frequently flew to an area off the coast of Murmansk to monitor the Soviet Northern Fleet's submarines. The strategic sub-marine base at Gadzhiyevo and the Northern Machine Building Production Association plant at Severodvinsk were of primary interest. The US Chief of Naval Operations, Adm James L. Holloway III, requested regular SR-71 missions to the region, having highlighted five naval bases of particular interest: Gadzhiyevo; Gremikha (now known as Ostrovnoy); Severomorosk; Vidyayevo and Zapadnya Litsa; between them they housed the Northern Fleet, which controlled the lion's share of Russia's nuclear submarine force.

On July 9, 1983, SR-71A 61-7962 settled on to the runway at Mildenhall after a lengthy ferry flight from Beale AFB. To the casual observer this was just another SR-71, unlikely to cause too much excitement, as the same aircraft had been deployed to Mildenhall before, having spent more than two weeks there during September 1976. Except that this was a clever subterfuge – it was not '962 at all. It was actually 61-7955,

the Palmdale-based test aircraft, which was evaluating the new Goodyear Advanced Synthetic Aperture Radar System (ASARS-1). The decision to apply a different serial for the duration of the stay in England was taken to mask the true purpose of a test aircraft flying a rare operational mission overseas. The subterfuge worked, and the full details stayed buried for more than a decade. The aircraft stayed long enough to complete the evaluation before returning home and reverting to its true identity; ASARS-1 was subsequently installed in Blackbirds for specific missions.

OPERATION EL DORADO CANYON

By the mid-1980s the belligerent sabre-rattling of Libya's leader Muammar Gaddafi had significantly increased, as the Colonel encouraged his supporters to become more aggressive to non-Muslim governments, and the USA in particular. Coupled with his financial backing of terrorist groups, Gaddafi and his regime became a thorn in the side of the American government. Confrontation seemed the only solution to silence this "loose cannon". A build-up of USAF tanker aircraft at RAF Fairford and Mildenhall heralded the likelihood of an air strike, and on the evening of April 15, 1986, the 20th and 48th Tactical Fighter Wings launched EF-111As and F-111Fs respectively from RAF Upper Heyford and Lakenheath. The latter were used to

strike targets in Libya while the EF-111A "Spark-Varks" provided electronic jamming.

Codenamed Operation *El Dorado Canyon*, the mission was moderately successful, and had the desired effect of silencing the vociferous Colonel. Post-strike photography was completed by the two Mildenhall-based SR-71s, with both aircraft being airborne simultaneously. A dual mission was flown on April 16 and on the two following days, as cloud cover hampered an effective take until the third mission. Images captured on film were taken from the aircraft and processed before being loaded aboard C-135C 61-2669, assigned to the USAF Chief of Staff. The imagery was deemed of such importance that the Chief of Staff himself, Gen Charles Gabriel, accompanied the film from Mildenhall back to Washington DC for analysis. This was the only occasion on which Det 4 flew both its aircraft together operationally.

Not all missions went so smoothly. On May 24, 1987, the pilot of 61-7973 managed to overstress the aircraft while on a mission. The Blackbird recovered safely to Mildenhall, but inspection revealed that temporary repairs would be required to enable a flight back to Palmdale for further analysis. The aircraft returned to the USA on July 22, although the prospect of the programme being terminated may have forestalled the expensive repair work being undertaken.

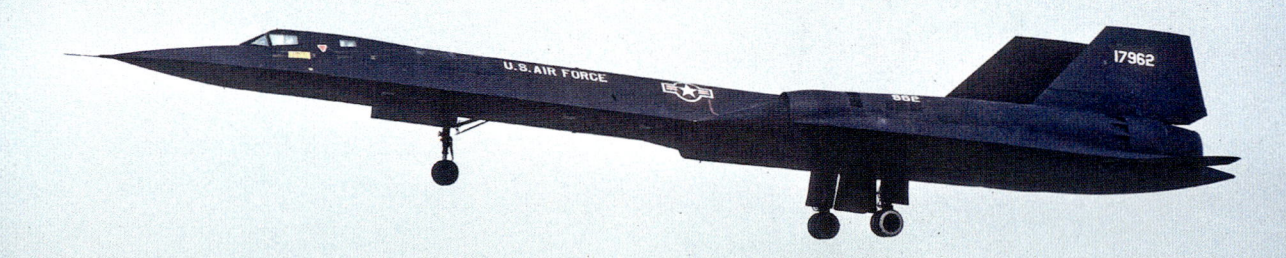

ABOVE: Just another routine landing at Mildenhall for 61-7962 – or is it? It is in fact the Palmdale-based test airframe, 61-7955, arriving in the UK under a false identity on July 9, 1983, a subterfuge that remained secret for more than a decade. The aircraft was in the UK to undergo trials with the new Goodyear ASARS-1 radar system. *Bob Archer*

120 AVIATION CLASSICS: AMERICAN COLD WAR STORIES

ABOVE: Blackbird 61-7975 on a mission over the USA in May 1982. This aircraft made only one sojourn to the UK to operate with Det 4, during July–October 1984. The SR-71A was painted overall in a black "iron ball" radar-attenuating finish which also helped to radiate heat away from the aircraft. The national insignia were applied in a specially-formulated heat-resistant paint. *Bob Archer*

On **October 1, 1989,** the first day of fiscal year (FY) 1990, the USAF issued an order **suspending** all **SR-71 operations,** except for proficiency flights.

The aircraft subsequently remained in storage with Lockheed at Palmdale, where it was later placed on display in the Blackbird Airpark.

Blackbird 61-7964 was no stranger to Norway. Having been the first to divert there in August 1981, the aircraft visited the country twice more while on operations. On March 6, 1987, '964 suffered a technical problem, requiring the crew to divert. Three months later, on June 29, the same aircraft landed in Norway again. The March visit obviously caused the technicians some extensive headaches, as the SR-71 was stranded in Norway for around 14 days. The second diversion must have been more straightforward to rectify, as '964 flew back to Mildenhall three days later.

Detachment 4 was never short of missions. The Middle East was frequently the target area, following the escalation of tension between confrontational nations. Missions to the region were also launched by Det 1 from Kadena. The French government characteristically refused authority to overfly its territory, resulting in Blackbird missions from Mildenhall being routed around the Iberian peninsula.

It was clear that the SR-71 was an extremely flexible reconnaissance platform, even though it was hugely expensive to operate. However, many senior USAF planners in the Pentagon were from the fighter community, and, owing to the classified nature of SR-71 operations, were largely ignorant of the type's precise capabilities. Some wanted the SR-71 to be killed off to save money, which, they argued, could be better spent on more useful programmes. General Jerome O'Malley, a former pilot with the 9th SRW, was one of the most staunch supporters of the SR-71 programme, as he clearly knew the capabilities and value of the Blackbird. He became Commander of Tactical Air Command (TAC) in 1984, and was widely tipped to become the USAF Chief of Staff. However, tragedy struck on April 20, 1985, when the T-39 Sabreliner carrying O'Malley crashed at Wilkes-Barre airfield in Pennsylvania, killing all aboard. Without guidance from O'Malley, the end for the *Senior Crown* programme hove into view. General Larry Welch, the C-in-C of SAC, eventually became Chief of Staff and set about eliminating the SR-71 from service. It was ironic that the single most vociferous opponent of *Senior Crown* had also been the head of SAC, its operating command, and therefore was more aware than most of its distinctive capabilities.

THE BEGINNING OF THE END
On October 1, 1989, the first day of fiscal year (FY) 1990, the USAF issued an order suspending all SR-71 operations, except for proficiency flights. On November 22 the same year all USAF SR-71 operations were terminated. Those at Det 4 had ceased two days earlier when 61-7967 had flown the last operational mission. The aircraft was fitted with an optical bar camera in the nose, which was unusual for the Mildenhall Blackbirds. The crew must have been aware that this was likely to be their last mission for a while, as they performed several overshoots before settling the giant aircraft on to the Mildenhall ▶

AVIATION CLASSICS: AMERICAN COLD WAR STORIES 121

ABOVE: Blackbird 61-7964 is prepared for its final journey home in one of Mildenhall's purpose-built barns on January 18, 1990. The barns were erected to house Det 4's two operational Blackbirds, and a large hangar provided accommodation for the reconnaissance interpretation equipment. Note the barn floor, awash with JP7 fuel – the SR-71 leaked like a sieve until the airframe heated up in flight and the joints tightened. *Bob Archer*

runway for the last time operationally.

The two Blackbirds remained securely tucked away in their barns for the next few weeks, while final plans were made for the Detachment to return the aircraft to the USA and disband. On January 16, 1990, both aircraft flew a functional check flight to ensure all systems were in order and working correctly.

Two days later the press was admitted to watch Lockheed technicians prepare 61-7964 for the journey home. Access to the barns was available to all, with the two crew members, Maj Tom McCleary (pilot) and Lt-Col Stan Gudmundson (RSO) freely chatting to the media. Shortly before lunchtime the aircraft spooled into life, and with all systems functioning normally, taxied to the Mildenhall runway for the last time. With a characteristic roar and with diamond shockwaves dancing in the clear winter air, the Blackbird gracefully lifted from the runway and flew a 360° pattern to perform a fast, very low fly-by, before McCleary pointed the nose skyward and headed for Beale. The next day 61-7967 departed, to considerably less fanfare, marking the end of a unique era. On January 26, 1990, an SR-71 decommissioning ceremony was staged at Beale, with Gen Welch, the main architect of the type's demise, in attendance.

Detachment 4 had flown a total of 894 operational missions, with a further 164 being functional, test or delivery flights. Blackbird 61-7960 earned the distinction of performing the most operational missions, completing a total of 342. This aircraft spent 15 months assigned to Det 4 from late 1985 until early in 1987.

The SR-71 had obtained significant intelligence data during its 25 years of operations, enabling key military planners to advise policymakers accordingly. Many senior politicians with the appropriate security clearances were privy to the material obtained, and used it to guide their decision-making for national and international policy. There were

> *The **SR-71** had obtained significant **intelligence data** during its **25 years** of **operations**, enabling key military planners to **advise policymakers** accordingly.*

frequent calls for the SR-71s to be reactivated for Operation *Desert Shield* in 1990, but these requests were denied. However, continued instability in the Middle East, combined with ethnic violence in the Balkans, provided an impetus for the pro-SR-71 lobby to become increasingly vocal. During the spring of 1994, a deterioration of relations between the USA and North Korea was, to many, the final straw. The SR-71 was needed to monitor the situation in these regions, with many senators and congressmen joining the call for the programme to be reinstated.

Despite the SR-71 no longer being operated by the USAF, the National Aeronautics & Space Administration (NASA) at Edwards AFB in California continued to operate one SR-71A and one SR-71B on high-altitude test missions, with another SR-71A held as a spare. The Administration's usage was well placed, as Congress appropriated $100m in the FY 1995 defence budget to reactivate all three in USAF service. A programme office was established at Wright-Patterson AFB, Ohio, to oversee the reactivation, with the aircraft being assigned to a detachment of the 9th Reconnaissance Wing. Despite the Wing's headquarters being located at Beale under Air Combat Command, the SR-71 operation was to remain at Edwards AFB as the newly-formed Detachment 2.

On April 15, 1996, Deputy Defense Secretary John White directed the USAF to ground the SR-71. This was just one of many hurdles which the SR-71 cruised over on its rocky path back to operational status, although the number of airframes to be reactivated was dropped to just the two SR-71As.

Lockheed Martin was contracted to prepare the two aircraft for operational duty, while the two erstwhile overseas operating locations, Kadena and Mildenhall, began to prepare for possible deployments by the SR-71 on an occasional basis. The Balkans, embroiled in civil war, was one of the most likely areas of interest, as were hostile Middle Eastern nations. Both of these "hot spots" could be covered from Mildenhall.

On January 1, 1997, Det 2 at Edwards was declared mission-ready. The two SR-71As, 61-7967 and 61-7971, adopted the dark-red fin band of the 9th RW containing the familiar four Maltese crosses and the tailcode "BB." It seems logical to assume that the USAF would not devote so much funding to the programme just to have the aircraft flying training missions over the high desert around Edwards AFB. Thus the return of SR-71 operations to Mildenhall seemed a certainty.

NOT SO FAST...

The *Senior Crown* programme had few friends at top level within the USAF, however, and Chief of Staff Gen Ronald Fogleman was against its reactivation from the outset. Despite considerable political will to see the programme reactivated, the primary operator's negative stance presented a massive hurdle. It was to be one which even the fastest operational aircraft in history could not overcome. Less than a year after

ABOVE: With a nod to one of the local pastimes, the sign beside Det 4's hangar at Mildenhall depicted a Blackbird and a U-2 superimposed on a dartboard with a dart firmly embedded in the bullseye. The motif was only ever applied to the fins of one aircraft, 61-7980, in 1990, but was quickly replaced with NASA logos. *Bob Archer*

BELOW: Leaving a heat haze in its wake, 61-7958 taxies out from the barns to the end of the runway at Mildenhall on June 2, 1984. The total weight of the aircraft for a mission was usually more than 50 tons (50,800kg), of which almost 40 per cent was low-volatile JP7 fuel. Note the numerous support vehicles accompanying the Blackbird. *Bob Archer*

ABOVE: With vortices streaming from the aircraft's fuselage and engine nacelles, 61-7980's starboard J58 coughs out a tail of flame during a particularly spirited display at the Mildenhall Air Fête in May 1986. The result of a temporary flame-out, unburned fuel ignited in the hot jet efflux, throwing out a fireball. The aircraft landed safely. *Bob Archer*

the Blackbird was declared operational again, all funding for SR-71 operations in FY 1998 was withdrawn. On October 15, 1997, President Bill Clinton imposed a Line Item Veto on SR-71 funding, effectively killing off the programme. Two weeks later HQ USAF directed the termination of all SR-71 operations, and ordered a swift disposal of the fleet. The veto prevented any further opportunity by politicians to rekindle SR-71 operations at a future date. The revitalised programme did not perform any overseas deployments, and the preparations at Mildenhall for a possible return were quietly abandoned.

The final movement by an SR-71 in the UK was not by air, but was completed at a far more sedate pace, with 61-7962 being dismantled and taken by road from Palmdale to board a ship bound for England. The final part of the journey was again by road, to the Imperial War Museum at Duxford, Cambridgeshire, to become one of the star exhibits at the new American Air Museum. The Blackbird arrived on April 11, 2001, and, following reassembly, was formally handed over

by Gen Joseph Ralston, Supreme Allied Commander Europe, at a ceremony held on June 14 the same year.

To some, the static exhibit lacks the intensity associated with the Blackbird's daily operations. The stillness arguably obscures the dangers which the aircraft and its crews faced every time they flew operationally, close to the borders of hostile nations. Blackbird missions were hazardous; more than 1,000 surface-to-air missiles were launched at the type during its operational career, most by North Vietnamese air-defence sites. None reached their targets – a testimony to an extraordinary and unsurpassed aircraft.

The SR-71 operated from Mildenhall over a period of some 16 years, 11 of which comprised regular operations, the remainder being largely ad hoc missions. Limited documentation has been released concerning SR-71 operations in Europe, but we know that more than 1,000 missions were flown, most of which were operational. Decades later, military and political figures still talk of the contribution the aircraft is capable of whenever the USA is embroiled in foreign military adventures. During the Kosovo campaign and the second Gulf War, there were calls for the reinstatement of SR-71 operations, owing to a lack of time-sensitive reconnaissance. The final death knell for the SR-71 was the advent of small, highly capable unmanned aerial vehicles (UAVs), cheap to operate and able to loiter for longer periods to obtain data. While not providing the same quantity of intelligence, they are as flexible, and are considered "disposable" owing to the lack of an onboard crew. No SR-71 advocate can argue against such advantages.

The emblem of Det 4 was a large SR-71 super-imposed on a dartboard, reinforcing the cultural link between the two nations. The emblem was never displayed on the fin of an aircraft while at Mildenhall,

> The **SR-71** operated from **Mildenhall** over a period of some **16 years,** 11 of which comprised **regular operations,** the remainder being **largely ad hoc missions.**

BELOW: Trailing its distinctive "tiger tails", 61-7964 blasts off from Mildenhall for the last time, on January 18, 1990. On taking off from Mildenhall, SR-71 pilots would bank slightly to starboard, offering spectators a thrilling view of the diamond-pattern shockwaves. *Bob Archer*

124 AVIATION CLASSICS: AMERICAN COLD WAR STORIES

instead being exhibited only on the sign outside the unit's hangar and within the small office complex. Each aircraft was only with the Det on a temporary duty basis, and remained the property of the parent Wing throughout its overseas deployment, hence the lack of individual unit insignia. However, Blackbird 61-7980 had the Det 4 emblem applied to its fins in February 1990 for its delivery flight from Palmdale to nearby Edwards for service with NASA. The emblem was soon replaced with a NASA symbol.

Within the Det 4 offices at Mildenhall were several murals devoted to the SR-71 and its support units. Among these was a handwritten poem celebrating the 25th anniversary of the SR-71, based on a popular Pepsi-Cola television advertisement of the time. It read:

"Kelly-inspirin Rich-thinkin Skunk-workin recon-seein two-seatin intelligence-gatherin J58-drivin JP7-burnin missile-avoidin MiG-loosin [sic] high-flyin record-settin Mach-bustin... BLACKBIRD!"

The anniversary celebrated the type's quarter-century of operational service, from December 22, 1964, to December 22, 1989. Despite the intervening three decades since the SR-71 ceased operations in Europe, the type is remembered with much fondness by those who experienced a Blackbird take-off. Legendary designer Kelly Johnson and his assistant Ben Rich have both since died, taking with them the slide-rule technology that created the SR-71 and later the F-117A. It is unlikely such technological masterpieces will again be produced using the creative genius of men of vision, computers having largely replaced the "man in the loop". They and their products may be consigned to history, but their contribution to the defence of the USA and its Nato allies is almost immeasurable. ●

LOCKHEED SR-71 VISITS TO THE UK, 1974–1990

Some 36 visits to the UK were made by 14 individual Blackbirds (including one under a false identity) for stays of varying duration between September 1974 and January 1990, when the last example left the UK. The visits by the individual aircraft are listed here in chronological order.

Date	Aircraft
September 1–13, 1974	61-7972
April 20–30, 1976	61-7972
September 6–18, 1976	61-7962
January 7–17, 1977	61-7958
May 16–31, 1977	61-7958
October 24–November 16, 1977	61-7976
April 24–May 12, 1978	61-7964
October 16–November 2, 1978	61-7964
March 12–28, 1979	61-7972
April 17–May 2, 1979	61-7979
October 18–November 13, 1979	61-7976
April 9–May 9, 1980	61-7976
September 13–November 2, 1980	61-7972
December 12, 1980–March 7, 1981	61-7964
March 6–May 5, 1981	61-7972
16 August 16, 1981–November 6, 1981	61-7964
(Arrived from Bodø; diverted on flight from Beale AFB on August 13)	
December 16–21, 1981	61-7958
January 5–April 27, 1982	61-7980
April 30–December 13, 1982 (at Bodø May 7–9)	61-7974
December 19, 1982–July 6, 1983	61-7972
December 23, 1982–February 2, 1983	61-7971
March 7–September 6, 1983	61-7980
July 9–30, 1983	"61-7962" (actually 61-7955)
August 2, 1983–July (unknown) 1984	61-7974
September 9, 1983–June 12, 1984	61-7958
June 14, 1984–mid-July 1985	61-7979
July–October 16, 1984	61-7975
October 19, 1984–mid-October 1985	61-7962
July 19, 1985–October 29, 1986	61-7980
October 29, 1985–January 29, 1987	61-7960
November 1, 1986–July 22, 1987 (for repairs)	61-7973
February 5, 1987–mid-March 1988	61-7964
July 27, 1987–October 3, 1988 (from RAF Lakenheath)	61-7980
March 13, 1988–February 28, 1989	61-7971
October 5, 1988–January 18, 1990 (to RAF Lakenheath)	61-7964
March 2, 1989–January 19, 1990	61-7967

BELOW: Blackbird 61-7974 is firmly anchored to the ground for static engine runs at Mildenhall in May 1982. The distinctive chined forward fuselage provided useful additional lift at supersonic speeds. The Blackbird's innovative air inlet control system (AICS) featured movable spikes that travelled some 26in (66cm) fore and aft to regulate airflow to the engines. *Bob Archer*

...BLAAAAM!
Six dramatic minutes over Angola

August 1988: a Botswanan defence force British aerospace 125 carrying the president to a vital meeting in the Angolan capital strays unwittingly into hostile airspace; within minutes a Cuban-manned MiG-23 has been scrambled and has the target "LOCKED ON". TOM COOPER puts us in the pilot's seats of both aircraft...

There have been many instances of commercial airliners being intercepted by combat aircraft. Most of the time such incidents are caused by accident rather than by design and end peacefully. However, sometimes things go wrong – and when they do, they usually end with catastrophic results. Incidents such as the shooting-down of a Korean Airlines Boeing 747 by a Soviet Sukhoi Su-15 near Sakhalin in September 1983, the loss of an IranAir Airbus A300 from a missile launched from the US Navy cruiser USS *Vincennes* (CG-49) in June 1988, or, more recently, the Malaysian Airlines Boeing 777 shot down by SA-17 surface-to-air missiles (SAMs) operated by pro-Russian separatists in the Ukraine in July 2014, have provoked well-known international scandals.

Many other cases remain less well-known. Here we take a look at a little-known accident that occurred over a "forgotten" corner of the world at a time when attention was very much focused elsewhere. The incident ultimately ended well too, largely thanks to the outstanding airmanship of a British pilot.

THE ANGOLAN WAR
In 1988 the civil war that had blighted Angola since 1975, and which had seen the involvement of several major international powers, appeared to be nearing its end. Following negotiations supervised by the United Nations (UN), the governments of the Soviet Union, Cuba and South Africa reached an agreement for a phased withdrawal of all foreign troops from the country, and this was soon in full swing. However, the insurgency led by the *União Naçional para a Independência Total de Angola* (National Union for the Total Independence of Angola – UNITA) against the government in the Angolan capital, Luanda, continued, with the rebels still receiving clandestine support from South Africa and the USA.

The Angolan government continued to acquire arms from Moscow, despite the latter's efforts to establish commercial relations with South Africa. Indeed, in August 1988, one of two *Força Aérea Popular de Angola/Defesa Aérea e Antiaérea* (Angolan People's Air Force/Air Defence Force – FAPA/DAA) units equipped with Mikoyan-Gurevich MiG-23ML *Flogger-G* interceptors was still manned by Cubans, who flew not only combat air patrols (CAPs), but also ground-attack sorties against UNITA forces. Furthermore, owing to flights made by unidentified transport aircraft which often violated Angolan airspace to bring in supplies for the insurgents, the FAPA/DAA's ground-based air defences were still on high alert.

It was under these tense circumstances that the President of Botswana planned to visit Luanda, as recalled by the British pilot who was to fly him there, Arthur Ricketts: "I had been employed on the test and demonstration programme for the British Aerospace 125 series of aircraft for the previous eight years. One of these [125-800B c/n 258112, coded OK1] was operated by the Botswana Defence Air Force Air Wing, and I was tasked to fly His Excellency Quett Masire, President of Botswana and eight other government officials from the capital of Botswana, Gaborone, to Luanda. The aircraft was crewed by Col Albert Scheffers, CO of the Air Wing, and me, employed as a transport and training captain with British Aerospace. Scheffers had completed his type conversion in the UK and I was continuing his line training in Botswana."

INTO THE COMBAT ZONE
On August 7, 1988, the 125 entered Angolan airspace while flying at 35,000ft (10,700m) along a commercial corridor which connected Mavinga in Angola's Cuando Cubango province and the capital. The flight was announced to Luanda air traffic control (ATC), which had also received a note from the FAPA/DAA about the closing of this commercial corridor to all traffic, owing to combat operations in the Kuito Bié province.

Teniente Coronel Eduardo Gonzalez, Operations Commander of the Cuban MiG-23 squadron assigned to the FAPA/DAA (the unit in question had no official designation) based at Menonque AB in Cuando Cubango, was serving his second combat tour in Angola: "It was during Operation *Second Congress* in 1985 that we asked ATC in Luanda to close this corridor to all commercial traffic because it overflew a combat zone. We repeated such requests on a number of occasions, and documents on the matter were signed, but to no avail. Airlines continued to fly over what everybody in the area should have known was a war zone. Even today I do not understand how any responsible airline could ever accept a flightplan that overflies a combat zone."

Concerned about the likelihood of causing a major embarrassment and diplomatic incident, Gonzalez ordered his pilots to take precautions before opening fire: "As the world's 'black sheep', we [Cubans] could not afford a similar mistake to those experienced by the Soviets and Americans before. I instructed my pilots that before launching their missiles at any such target in daylight, they must visually identify it. Despite all the calls to ATC in Luanda, twice a month in broad daylight I intercepted a DC-10 from Mozambique under way somewhere over Mavinga heading in the direction of Luanda."

By night, the situation was entirely different. The Angolan authorities were eager to intercept regular intruders which had been delivering supplies to UNITA for years. However, because of the size of the country and its relatively poor radar coverage, this proved difficult. Indeed, Gonzalez was the only pilot, Angolan or Cuban, ever to have managed to intercept a South African Air Force Lockheed C-130 Hercules over Angola, which he did on April 4, 1986: "My radar

BELOW: On August 7, 1988, Angolan Mikoyan-Gurevich MiG-23ML Flogger-G C479, flown by Cuban pilot Capt Albert Olivares Horta, fired a pair of air-to-air missiles at Botswana Defence Force BAe 125 serial OK1 after an Angolan air traffic control oversight put the latter in proscribed airspace. *Ian Bott / www.ianbottillustration.co.uk*

AVIATION CLASSICS: AMERICAN COLD WAR STORIES 127

ABOVE: Continuing the line that began in the early 1960s with the de Havilland D.H.125 Jet Dragon, the British Aerospace 125-800 made its maiden flight on May 26, 1983, incorporating state-of-the-art avionics and a pair of Garrett turbofans. The Botswana Defence Force acquired OK1 in 1988, when it joined Z1 Transport Squadron. *TAH Archive*

ABOVE: His Excellency Quett Masire, President of Botswana.

picked up two South African C-130s, and I fired two R-24 [Nato reporting name *Apex*] missiles at one of them. Neither scored a hit. One passed at supersonic speed so close to the port wing of one of the transports that the crew felt the thud from the shockwave."

THE INEVITABLE INCIDENT

The FAPA/DAA continued scrambling its *Flogger-Gs* for further interceptions, including at night, even though it was clear that the pilots would have next to no ability to identify intruders visually before having to open fire – or run out of fuel. As the violations of Angolan airspace continued on an almost daily basis, the situation was set to lead to an inevitable incident, much to Gonzalez's concern: "I was terrified that if a passenger aircraft entered the zone by night, we would not be able to establish a visual ID. I was sure an incident involving a civilian airliner was going to happen sooner or later."

By early August 1988 the stage was set for just such an incident. After Luanda ATC failed to warn the Botswanans about sending OK1 over the combat zone, and furthermore failed to warn the FAPA/DAA that a VIP transport was about to pass overhead, Gonzalez's fears turned into reality, as he explains: "The aircraft in question first came under fire from an Angolan SAM site near Cuito Cuanavale. The site was on full readiness and attempted to identify the 'bogey'. There was no friendly IFF [identification friend or foe] response and a 'clear to fire' order was issued. Four missiles were fired but all missed; they were out of sync with the fire-control radar."

The small business jet was still not outside the danger zone. Headquarters FAPA/DAA then scrambled MiG-23ML serial C479, flown by a Cuban pilot, Capt Albert Olivares Horta, from Menonque. Horta recalls: "I accelerated to Mach 1·9 to catch the intruder but never established a visual ID before opening fire. I fired two missiles; the first was an R-24T from port wing station No 3, launched from a range of 20km [12½ miles]. This scored a hit, and that was when I sighted my target for the first time. Then I fired an R-24R from starboard wing station No 4. Luckily for the crew and passengers, this missile went astray. With the first missile scoring a hit and the MiG running out of fuel, I then disengaged."

BELOW: In one of the more unusual Cold War anomalies, it is thought that up to three MiG-23 units of the FAPA/DAA (Força Aérea Naçional de Angola since the mid-2000s) were staffed entirely by Cuban personnel during 1985–89. Two-seat MiG-23UB trainers, including I21 seen here, were shared between the Cubans and Angolans. *via Mark Lepko*

> *I fired **two** missiles; the **first** was an **R-24T** from port wing station No 3, launched from a range of **20km [12½ miles]**. This **scored a hit**, and that was when I sighted my target for the **first time**.*

128 AVIATION CLASSICS: AMERICAN COLD WAR STORIES

Map annotations:

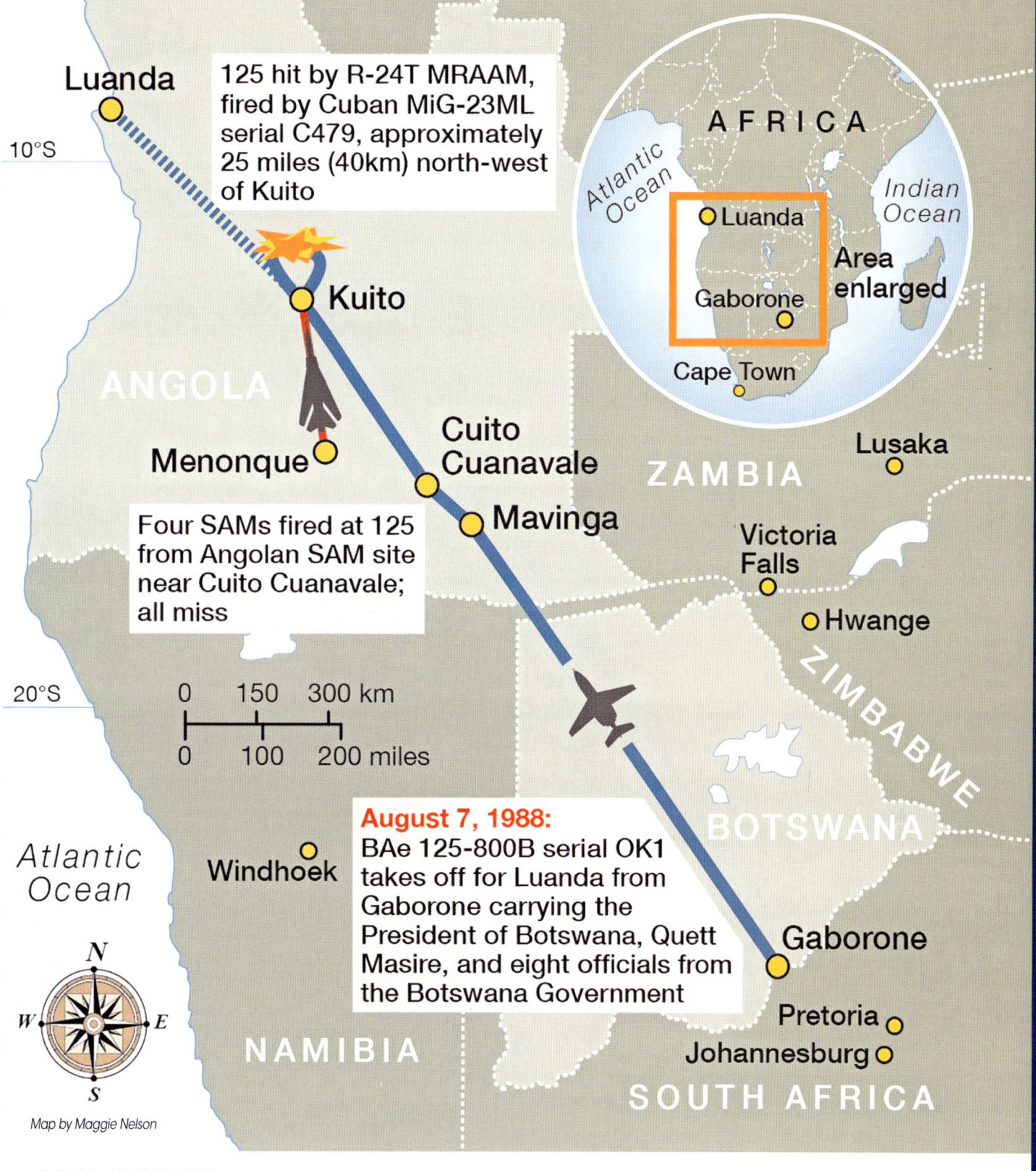

- 125 hit by R-24T MRAAM, fired by Cuban MiG-23ML serial C479, approximately 25 miles (40km) north-west of Kuito
- Four SAMs fired at 125 from Angolan SAM site near Cuito Cuanavale; all miss
- **August 7, 1988:** BAe 125-800B serial OK1 takes off for Luanda from Gaborone carrying the President of Botswana, Quett Masire, and eight officials from the Botswana Government

Map by Maggie Nelson

COOL, CALM AND COLLECTED

The impact of the first missile blew the 125's starboard engine clean off. Arthur Ricketts recalls the drama that then unfolded aboard the badly damaged business jet: "At the point of impact Col Scheffers was rendered incapacitated by the instantaneous application of approximately 33g [calculated by BAe stress engineers later, based on damage to the fuselage frames], which threw him hard against the port cockpit wall, and he played no further part in the recovery of the aircraft. Also at this time the engineer travelling with us was thrown into the cockpit from the cabin. The aircraft sustained damage to the pressure cabin which resulted in explosive decompression.

"At least one window was shattered by shrapnel from the engine, approximately a ton and a half of fuel was lost from the damaged starboard wing tanks, all radio navigation systems failed and the cabin oxygen masks failed to deploy automatically.

"My first instinct was to regain control of the aircraft by rolling it away from the vertical and establishing a stable descent, which I achieved by the time we reached FL 280 [28,000ft/8,500m]. Initially we were descending at about 6,000ft/min [1,800m/min], which gave me about six minutes to sort everything out before arriving very hard in Africa. In that six minutes I managed to transmit two *Mayday* calls; one to Luanda, which was apparently not received or understood, and the other on HF [high-frequency] radio which was picked up and acted on by Santa Maria in the Azores.

ABOVE: Mikoyan-Gurevich MiG-23ML Flogger-G serial C479 as marked during the shootdown of OK1 on August 7, 1988. Note the Vympel R-24T infra-red homing missile (NATO reporting name AA-7 Apex) mounted on the port wing. Angola's Floggers are still very much in service and operational. *Artwork by TOM COOPER*

"I had substantial previous experience of flying in Africa and assessed that there was probably an airstrip of sorts at Kuito, some 25 miles [40km] behind the point at which we were hit. During the descent I had assessed the aircraft systems remaining and had made the decision to leave extending the flaps and undercarriage until shortly before landing, not expecting them to work. However, when the engine departed the airframe, the quick-release couplings on the hydraulic pump, starter/generator and alternator did their job and I had the use of flaps, undercarriage and brakes – certainly necessary as the damage demanded a landing speed of some 150–160kt."

Considering the severity of the damage to the aircraft, it was a miracle that OK1 remained intact, enabling Ricketts to land at Kuito safely. Subsequent investigation of the aircraft revealed that the entire cabin of the aircraft was knocked out of its fasteners and inclined at an angle of 15° to the fuselage. A number of passengers suffered serious injuries, as Ricketts recalls: "Injured passengers were attended to at the hospital in Kuito, before we were eventually uplifted to Luanda. President Masire was injured by a fan blade that penetrated the cabin and hit the back of his seat. He was subsequently flown to England by the RAF for treatment."

Arthur Ricketts was awarded the Diploma of Outstanding Airmanship in 1989 by the *Fédération Aéronautique Internationale* – an honour awarded only once a year, and richly deserved in this case. Arthur still holds a valid Air Transport Pilot's Licence (ATPL) well into his seventies. ●

BELOW RIGHT: The starter/generator and alternator hang at the end of wiring looms and cables at Kuito. Although the airframe sustained severe damage, the sturdy bizjet was rebuilt by BAe and sold to a new owner in Brazil as PT-OBT. It survives today and is regularly operated by a company in Georgia, USA, as N812GJ. *Arthur Ricketts*

BELOW: With just the skeletal remains of the starboard engine mounting still attached, OK1 is the subject of much discussion at Kuito in the aftermath of the incident. Although the aircraft looks relatively unscathed, it was heavily damaged. *Arthur Ricketts*

ABOVE: British Aerospace 125-800 demonstration and display pilot Arthur Ricketts had a wealth of experience of flying in Africa, having previously flown Vickers VC10s for East African Airways. When the pilot of OK1, Albert Scheffers, one of Botswana's pioneer pilots, was incapacitated, it fell to copilot Ricketts to act quickly and decisively.

TOM COOPER is the co-author, along with Peter Weinert, Fabian Hinz and Mark Lepko, of the indispensable African MiGs series published by Harpia Publishing, which details the little-known activities of MiGs and Sukhois of the various air forces of Sub-Saharan Africa. Volume 1 (ISBN 978-0-982553-95-4) covers Angola to Ivory Coast; Volume 2 (ISBN 978-0-982553-98-5) looks at Madagascar to Zimbabwe. For full details of Harpia's extensive book catalogue visit the website at www.harpiapublishing.com.

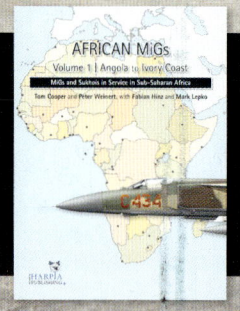

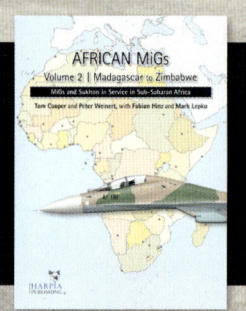